Trivialization and Public Opinion

"Taking a transdisciplinary view, this innovative title serves both as an important addition and a challenge to the existing research in communications and in social sciences more generally. Trivialization offers a useful perspective on public discourse and a sensible entry-point to the often hidden universe of mostly unquestioned assumptions, all requiring a thorough debate. I highly recommend this book to all readers seeking a more complete picture of change, so needed in our increasingly complex society."
—D. R. F. Taylor, *Distinguished Research Professor, Carleton University, Canada, and 2014 Killam Prize recipient*

"This is an important book that should be read by anyone concerned about the current state of political discourse in the industrialized democracies. Further, it adds significantly to the scholarly debates in its field. Readers will no doubt tend to ask themselves what we can learn from history, whether we can modify academic approaches to critical thinking to handle complexity and contingency and avoid 'incredible certitude.' We should all learn to listen and to ask: 'how do you know?'"
—Fred Fletcher, *Professor Emeritus of Communication Studies and Political Science, York University, Canada*

Oldrich Bubak · Henry Jacek

Trivialization
and Public Opinion

Slogans, Substance, and Styles of Thought
in the Age of Complexity

palgrave
macmillan

Oldrich Bubak
Department of Political Science
McMaster University
Hamilton, ON, Canada

Henry Jacek
Department of Political Science
McMaster University
Hamilton, ON, Canada

ISBN 978-3-030-17924-3   ISBN 978-3-030-17925-0   (eBook)
https://doi.org/10.1007/978-3-030-17925-0

This Palgrave Macmillan imprint is published by the registered company Springer Nature Switzerland AG
The registered company address is: Gewerbestrasse 11, 6330 Cham, Switzerland

Sapere aude!

PREFACE

It has been nearly three decades since John Brockman published his essay giving a new meaning to Lord Snow's concept of third culture. For Snow, a third culture was a reconciliation among literary humanists and scientists, two rival cultures seen as major sources of social and political influence. For a time, literary humanists dominated the public intellectual space, with mass press neglecting the contemporaneous scientists and their publicly oriented writings. Third culture was to be a settlement between the two groups, opening a dialog and allowing scientific ideas to reach the public through the customary journalistic channels. Instead, as Brockman observed, scientists began to communicate their findings in an engaging and accessible manner directly to the general public, capturing their interest and giving rise to a different third culture. To Brockman, this was a triumph, an entrance into the public discussion of a new generation of thinkers, open-minded empirical scholars "defining the interesting and important questions of our times."

Much has happened since the publication of the essay and the book that soon followed. We have entered the information age giving most people the capacity to access an unprecedented volume and variety of digital content growing at an unimaginable rate; to find, create, monitor, and share information with others at an instant; or to become commentators, entertainers, or broadcasters gaining their own following, large or small. Finding an expression in *Edge.org*, the expanded third culture movement is now competing for attention not only with other well-developed websites on philosophy and science but also with a range of other more or less reliable online outlets. In the end, the dream is fulfilled, it seems, as people have the freedom to choose what they want to read or whom to listen.

In parallel, we have been witnessing a growing skepticism toward the elite, those who identify problems, recommend options, make the decisions, or tell us about it. Many are not surprised given the still vivid memory of the recent financial crises and the incongruous policy action in their aftermath. There too are the rising inequalities, challenges with outcomes in health and education, the increasingly evident problems stemming from the runaway application of technology, and other issues—hard to accept in what appears an age of scientist intellectual. And people are responding to these realities in a variety of ways, including with their decisions at the ballot boxes. How can we understand this landscape?

First, we observe that not only the two groups of intellectuals described above avoid conversation, but that many scientists do not talk with each other either, as hinted by the voices of third culture. Unfortunately, there is little need or possibility for a dialogue outside of these circles as well. Why is this? If we begin by taking note of public discourse and listen to ourselves more attentively, we observe a lapse, a common obstacle to a reasoned discussion we identify as *trivialization*. We argue that getting to an inclusive conversation requires us to understand trivialization and deal with its causes. We thus set out to explore what it is, what sustains it, what its implications are, and if possible, what it may take to liberate ourselves from its clutches.

As we open this book, what at first may seem rare and uncommon quickly becomes familiar. We start to recognize not only how pervasive trivialization is, but that most of us, whether directly or indirectly, are helping to perpetuate it. Our quest takes us into our cultural history and realities more recent, into our imagination, and closer to an understanding of the limits and potentials of the human mind. We identify a set of fundamental issues rooted in culture, a single, evolving culture we are all a part.

Perhaps in line with the ostensible (sub)cultural divisions outlined above, critics often place the blame for our condition at the feet of either the elite, or the incapable, disinterested public. Yet, while the intellectuals claim to talk *to* the public as they share their ideas, define agendas, and shape opinions, they are also responding to the audience's signals, catering to their tastes and biases. Everyone is involved. Change must thus evolve from within, through tools of inclusion, mutual learning, and humility. *Developing* understandings more broadly takes priority over the mere provision of information, particularly when faced with limited resources. This, we believe, is especially important in the age of misinformation and rising irrationality.

Some say our technologies—and the socio-technical systems of which they are a part—are advancing so rapidly we can neither understand their implications nor handle them. While there is surely a point, we, as a society, know and possess the capacity to do much more than what the mainstream thought holds. We have coherent analyses, answers to difficult questions, and solutions to problems generally presented as intractable thanks to the foresight and the will of the people going against the convention and daring to think differently. Their findings, many of which we drew upon in this volume, give us optimism about the road ahead.

Hence, we would first like to acknowledge these scholars and practitioners and express our appreciation for their efforts. We are also grateful to those who have set aside time to discuss, offer valuable comments, or otherwise help our project: Katherine Boothe, Peter Graefe, Mark Holliday, Stephen McBride, Torsten Müller, Dani Rodrik, and Andrew Sayer. Also, we appreciate the expertise and support of our editor, Mary Al-Sayed, and the team at Palgrave Macmillan all of whom were integral in making this volume a reality. Finally, we would like to recognize our institution, McMaster University, an inspiring environment.

Hamilton, ON, Canada
January 2019

Oldrich Bubak
Henry Jacek

CONTENTS

ACRONYMS

ACA	Patient Protection and Affordable Care Act
ACO	Accountable Care Organization
ACP	American College of Physicians
BC	British Columbia
BCE	Before the Common Era
CA	Citizens' Assembly
CAS	Complex Adaptive Systems
CBO	Congressional Budget Office
CDC	Centers for Disease Control and Prevention
CDS	Credit Default Swap
CMA	Canadian Medical Association
DNA	Deoxyribonucleic Acid
EBM	Equation-Based Modeling
EEA	European Environment Agency
EHB	Essential Health Benefits
EU	European Union
FCIC	Financial Crisis Inquiry Commission
HM	His/Her Majesty
IAD	Institutional Analysis and Development Framework
IDA	Institute for Defense Analyses
IMF	International Monetary Fund
IPE	International Political Economy
IQ	Intelligence Quotient
IR	International Relations
MAS	Multi-Agent Systems
MIT	Massachusetts Institute of Technology

MMP	Mixed Member Proportional Representation
NES	National Election Studies
NHS	National Health Service
NIC	National Issues Convention
NIH	National Institutes of Health
NORC	National Opinion Research Center
OECD	Organisation for Economic Co-operation and Development
ON	Ontario
PP	Precautionary Principle
PUC	Public Utility Commission of Texas
SCC	Social Cost of Carbon
SMP	Single-Member Plurality Electoral System
STV	Single Transferable Vote
TFEU	Treaty on the Functioning of the European Union
TTIP	Transatlantic Trade and Investment Partnership
UK	United Kingdom
UKIP	UK Independence Party
US	United States of America

LIST OF TABLES

LIST OF BOXES

PART I

On Trivialization

CHAPTER 1

Introduction

[T]his last establishment will probably be within a mile of Charlottesville, and four from Monticello, if the system should be adopted at all by our legislature who meet within a week from this time, my hopes however are kept in check by the ordinary character of our state legislatures, the members of which do not generally possess information enough to percieve the important truths, that knolege is power, that knolege is safety, and that knolege is happiness.

—Thomas Jefferson (1817)

A founding father of the American republic, a respected statesman, and a polymath, Thomas Jefferson has left a lasting legacy of lucid, prescient views on democracy, the state, and governance. One can only imagine his interest and marvel at the world of two centuries ahead of his own, a world of media, mass education, consumer culture, or global production. Perhaps his greatest awe would be the access to information and knowledge,[1] unimaginable to his contemporaries, yet taken for granted by the modern-day multitudes. Without a doubt, he would have many a question about its impacts on society and its implications for democracy. And there is no shortage of contemporary developments that would lead him not just to answers but also to a disturbed re-examination of some of his seemingly ageless pronouncements. A curious headline, "The British are frantically Googling what the E.U. is, hours *after* voting to leave it" (Fung 2016, emphasis added), hints to one such a scenario.

© The Author(s) 2019
O. Bubak and H. Jacek, *Trivialization and Public Opinion*,
https://doi.org/10.1007/978-3-030-17925-0_1

3

The headline, of course, refers to the June 23, 2016 decision made by the voters in the UK on their membership in the European Union (EU). The referendum was the second opportunity in the last four decades for the people to weigh in on whether to stay in the largest trading block in the world. This time the decision was different: a vehement out.

There exist many analyses of the reasons behind the so-called Brexit. While both the proximate triggers, including the salient EU immigration and the global and regional economic challenges, and the ultimate causes, including the unique British geography and history (Cooper 2016; Dennison and Carl 2016), have merit in explaining the outcomes, the referendum can be seen as a product of a miscalculated political choice. Conservative leader David Cameron promised a vote to placate his political base, to help deprive various Eurosceptic parties including the UK Independence Party (UKIP) of votes, and thus to secure his party's victory (Calamur et al. 2016). The voters were *let* to the polls on the assumption they appreciated the benefits of remaining or the drawbacks of leaving the EU, and with the anticipation of a result in line with the 2014 Scottish vote to stay a part of the UK. Ultimately, political careers on both sides of the argument came to an end, and the country is left in the state of ambiguity and trepidation.

Instructive across many dimensions, this case is especially revealing of the sociocultural dynamics in the UK and beyond. First, it is the way the question was posed. "Should the United Kingdom remain a member of the European Union?" suggests a solution that can be distilled to a menu-like option—yes or no, remain or leave. The choice not only forces the voter to select the less undesirable; it also obscures the nature and gravity of the problem framed as coming squarely from the membership in the economic union.

Only when the voters woke up the next day to find their currency at 30-year lows, the markets in disarray (BBC 2016), and were exposed to the many alarmed international commentaries, they began their anxious search for answers referenced in the above headline. The remorse set in (Curtice 2016). Yet, this should not have been a surprise as many sobering analyses have been just a click away.[2] The doubt alone brings dramatic material and social implications. As one observer aptly noted:

> [it is the uncertainty] about the new arrangements, which will lead to less investment, slower growth, lower pay and higher unemployment. In the long run, we will not have the same access to the European single market, which will mean lower exports, less foreign investments. It will mean that we are all poorer. (John Van Reenen as quoted in Urquhart 2016)

Going beyond economics, there are also the geopolitical consequences. Breaking from the European Union project, a successful antithesis to the continent historically fragmented and bellicose, will mean diminished British influence in Europe and globally. Now, with the British government triggering the Article 50 of the Lisbon Treaty and entering the formal secession process, Scotland is likely to push for a new independence vote that could end with the disintegration of the UK itself.

While the decision seems surprising in the age of universal literacy, instant access to virtually endless information, and the 24-hour news cycle, a closer examination of the general discourse reveals an environment conducive to these (mis)steps. Difficult, dangerous, turbulent, and out-of-control are terms deployed with frequency when framing the problems of the day. We also hear the society stands at a precipice, inflection point, or crossroads. Such statements are usually followed by simple and confident prescriptions about what we must do, how to change, or whom to tap to correct the course. And this is just one among the many streams of trivializations borne of the environment that, by design and desire, induces us to distill multifaceted dilemmas to binary choices, neglect the big picture, gloss over alternatives, or filter reality through a lens of convenience.

It is this setting that enabled the Brexit vote and molded its outcomes and the same environment that played a role in another case unfolding an ocean away. California, once a paragon of social and fiscal responsibility, is now a state with perennial deficits, runaway education costs, and a plethora of social challenges. In a series of referenda starting with Proposition 13 in 1978, the people consistently opted for increased government spending while limiting the state's ability to draw a stable income (*The Economist* 2011). Would informed citizens privy to the flaws of democratic pluralism and its short-term, interest-pleasing decisions, and inoculated to the messaging torrents of highly organized factions vote differently? Would they countenance this line of initiatives at the outset? Research shows that even with nominal guidance, citizens make different choices (Jacobs and Matthews 2012; Chapter 6).

Simplicity is comforting and appealing as it seems natural to explain, classify, organize, or navigate the world with effortless intuition and common sense. Thus, perhaps unsurprisingly, the deceptively plain choices offered to consumers, members of communities, or citizens with confidence are received with gusto and are often difficult to contest. The problem is, however, that the consequences of the above are progressively more costly. Whereas in the not-so-distant past, our decisions would have limited effect and could be reversed without much impair, today they are amplified through the various connections and dependencies among jurisdictions and carry global ramifications. Returning to the above example, the Brexit *decision* has caused trillion dollar market losses and led to the International Monetary Fund's (IMF) downgrade of the global economic growth outlook for 2016 and 2017 (IMF 2016). Accordingly, this intricate sociopolitical environment where trivialization reigns requires our close attention.

INFORMATION ASYMMETRIES AND SOCIAL CHANGE

As hinted above, there exist many more or less apt generalizations of the world today. Without engaging in a distracting debate, it can be said this era is very *different* from any other time in the past. One can confidently point to technology driving advances in communications and transportation, in turn opening unparalleled opportunities at a global scale. But there is another, less obvious but equally important distinction between the times past and present. The difference lies in the asymmetric developments in the public use and treatment of information—and by extension knowledge—on the one hand, and the increasing importance of knowledge in all aspects of the social order on the other. A short trip through history is needed to explain this central idea.

Since the Middle Ages, we can identify four cumulative events that put information with increasing volume, speed, and accuracy in the hands of more people. Each opened new possibilities for social and institutional transformations. The first was the invention and the spread of the printing press in the fifteenth and sixteenth centuries, respectively. It is no accident that the Reformation, a movement to realign the contemporary practices of the Catholic Church with the expectations of the masses, took place on the heels of this invention. Of importance here are not the mechanics behind the Reformation itself, but the fact the printing press enabled the first mass media campaign in history (Edwards 2005), answering the desire of the people for alternate views and interpretations and channeling change. Such a transformation was made possible with the word in print; the continent and the history was, at last, never to be the same again.

The second event was the introduction of the telegraph in the early nineteenth century. Now the information could be relayed across distance with speed and made available on a mass scale with the convenience of a newspaper, itself revolutionized with the introduction of an upgraded, steam-powered rotary press. Kearns Goodwin notes the amazement of a perceptive European tourist at the popular consumption of information in the mid-nineteenth-century America: "You meet newspaper readers everywhere; and in the evening the whole city knows what lay twenty-four hours ago on newswriters' desks.... The few who cannot read can hear news discussed or read aloud in ale-and-oyster houses." Newspapers were thus crucial in the nascent, predominantly rural, nation where the participation of the citizens in the civic life was higher than in any subsequent period.[3] The social stability based on, as one author observes, information asymmetry was not to last (Dudley 2008). Newspapers, whose effectiveness and appeal were amplified by the telegraph, peeled back the curtain on the cleavages in the American society and eroded this imbalance. Civil and political turmoil and irreversible social change were to follow. Similarly, in Europe, newspaper and telegraph became a critical layer in the substrata nourishing the Revolutions of 1848.[4]

Occurring a century later, the third event was tightly coupled to the drastic upheavals during and following the Second World War. The times witnessed not only the intensification of print and communications (now through telephony) but also the deployment of radio and television on a mass scale. Applebaum (2014) tells of a less known, yet consequential, wartime experiment of the American publishers. In the depression and post-depression era, books were very expensive and difficult to obtain throughout the country. Quality literature, customarily bound in a costly hardcover format, was generally unaffordable. Some progress has been made in the late 1930s as the usual selection of books sold at newsstands was expanded with paperback editions of select literary pieces. The real shift, however, came through an unprecedented wartime decision to make a variety of more or less prestigious titles available en masse and in a disposable format to the troops overseas. W. W. Norton, a major publisher at the time, reasoned: "[t]he very fact that millions of men will have the opportunity to learn what a book is and what it can mean is likely now and in postwar years to exert a tremendous influence on the postwar course of the industry" (Applebaum 2014). More than 120 million books were printed and distributed to the soldiers during the war, shattering preconceptions about books and reading in the process. The ensuing demand for books across formats and genres confirmed the success of the experiment; reading was democratized.[5]

Radio and television, however, began to compete for the attention of the consumer of information. Television, in short order, became the dominant mass medium, central to life in the postwar liberal democracies, and namely in America. Edgerton comments on this extraordinary rise:

> No technology before TV ever integrated faster into American life. Television took only ten years to reach a penetration of thirty-five million house holds, while the telephone required eighty years, the automobile took fifty, and even radio needed twenty-five. By 1983, moreover, the representative U.S. house hold was then keeping the TV set turned on for more than seven hours a day on average; two decades later, this mean was up to eight hours a day and counting. (2007, xi)

Indeed, due to its key features—convenience, accessibility, and effortlessness—television has quickly become *the* educator, entertainer, advertiser, platform for shaping public opinion, and a medium for construction and amplification of popular and consumer culture. Television has become so deeply embedded into the social fabric that its effects have been rendered invisible (McLuhan and Fiore 1968). And thus while it is not possible to draw direct links between television and the upheavals of the 1960s, the shifts of the 1970s, or the revolutions of the 1980s, there is little doubt television had an integral and transformative role[6] in these events.

Finally, it was the series of technological breakthroughs that lead to packet-switched networking, the underpinning of the global information revolution. Supplanting the inefficient point-to-point circuit switching, this paradigmatic change in technology transformed communications and, within a couple of decades, enabled ubiquitous access to information. Several hardware and software ecosystems now compete to satisfy the eclectic popular preferences enabling the consumers to create, find, transform, relay, or share information instantly, across the globe, and at low cost.

The unprecedented connectivity has brought many challenges including the oft-deflected concern over privacy versus security, as well as opportunities such as the ability to perform big data analyses or to conduct mass notifications. To be sure, technology and namely the highly popular social media-driven tools have helped various prototypical, yet expectations-defying movements including *los Indignados* in Spain, surprising in their reach, their exclusion of the usual institutional structures such as the unions or political organizations, and the positive response they garnered in the media; the *Put People First* campaign, a movement diverse, transnational, and highly visible in the media; or the *Wutbürgers* in Germany, a network of apolitical citizens with a focus on their local concerns (Berggruen and Gardels 2013, 80; Bennett and Segerberg 2012, 740–741). What is more, social media played an outsized role in the responses to various disasters including the 2011 East Japan earthquake and tsunami or Hurricane Irene (Peary et al. 2012).[7]

Yet, any major social and political shifts we would expect as students of history have not materialized.[8] Consider the events of the Arab Spring of 2011, where social media played an integral role (Howard et al. 2011) in triggering, but not effecting, transformation. Berggruen and Gardels, authors and experts in governance issues, argue that "[w]hile the participatory power of social networks, as we have seen in Egypt and Tunisia, can tear down authority by mobilizing diasporas of the disaffected, we have *yet to find* through them the means of consensus-building that can establish the enduring legitimacy of governing authority…. You can't tweet a constitution" (2013, 84, emphasis added). As apparent from the above examples, the access to technology and information is not a panacea as the value and purpose of information has shifted. And thus we picture Jefferson revisiting his statement in view of this great social experiment. It is not knowledge itself that is power and happiness. The power lies in its proper treatment and its fitting utilization.

The four milestones presented above could certainly be contested, hinting at the complexity inherent to the study of transformative events within social systems. Nevertheless, it is evident that emerging disruptive technologies interact with ideas (or, more generally, with goals) over-time, create various feedback effects—including the generation of new, previously absent demand—and give rise to change,[9] in turn affecting future developments. The goal here was to use the four momentous stages in the advancement of information to show that the society has historically been *ahead* of information. That is, the demand for information in various forms outstripped its availability. We also noted that change to the distribution of information triggered and enabled social change.

Now, for the first time, however, information is ahead of society. People can now access the same information once available to the select few or not available at all. They can find analyses, data, critiques, guides, reviews, and many other artifacts and, importantly, share them with others. What can we expect? Consider, for example, the most frequently tweeted UK news site stories in 2014 (Box 1.1), the year of the Scottish referendum, Ebola outbreak, and multiple geopolitical crises. "Perhaps fittingly for a nation of dog-lovers a *Daily Mail* article about a YouTube TV show which teaches dog-owners how to prepare homemade meals for their pets, took the top position," comments Searchmetrics (2015). Not to forget, this ranking is especially revealing as the users must invest additional time and effort in sharing the story with others.

Box 1.1 Most frequently tweeted stories from UK newspaper web sites in 2014

1. *Daily Mail*, Paw-fect recipes for your pet's plate: The cooking show that teaches dog owners how to prepare homemade treats for their four-legged friends.
2. *Daily Mail*, WORLD EXCLUSIVE: Jack the Ripper unmasked: How amateur sleuth used DNA breakthrough to identify Britain's most notorious criminal 126 years after string of terrible murders.
3. *The Daily Telegraph*, Revealed: the Palestinian children killed by Israeli forces.
4. *The Mirror*, Devoted dad makes best Halloween costume ever for his disabled son.
5. *The Guardian*, Turkish women defy deputy PM with laughter.
6. *The Independent*, Tamir Rice: 12-year-old boy playing with fake gun dies after shot by Ohio police.
7. *The Independent*, Girl, 7, gets Tesco to remove 'stupid' sign suggesting superheroes are 'for boys'.
8. *Daily Mail*, 36 now feared dead in Japanese volcano disaster.
9. *The Mirror*, Fury as Tory party donors are handed NHS contracts worth £1.5BILLION under health reforms.
9. *The Sun*, Heaven 'n Ell. Revealed: The stunner in Heyman's corner.

Source Searchmetrics (2015)

It is thus not difficult to recognize that despite the unprecedented *access* to information, the way information is employed and knowledge is built within society at large has not kept pace with the modern age need for reasoned individual and collective decision making in areas ranging from the civic to the financial. This environment is dominated by outmoded lines of thinking and perpetuates systemic lapses, which in turn directly or indirectly reproduce a variety of problems plaguing governance, education, application of technology, and many other domains.

Intrigued by this mismatch, *Trivialization and Public Opinion* sets out to explore the contemporary condition through the lens of one such a lapse, *trivialization*, seen both as a reason for and a symptom of compound failures to keep up with the demands of the modern, fast-moving times. We hope to demonstrate that coping with the wide range of issues faced today cannot rely on shallow discourses glossing over assumptions, methods, uncertainties, and other essential information. We make the case that making inroads into the intricate issues borne of the progressively interdependent modern world that is both enabled and constrained by technology requires a society comfortable with ambiguity and complexity, and one in which multicausal relationships are appreciated, options debated, and where uncertainty is not a reason to avoid action. This requires a broad shift in our thinking at multiple levels, an advancement of understandings, and new cognitive tools. Such a shift is partly enabled by the way we learn to perceive and talk of the world around us.

THE ROADBLOCKS

Recall trivialization pushes its adherents away from cognitive engagement and reflection, from asking difficult questions and going beyond the comfortable, if superficial, world of ideas as expressed by sound bites, myths, or stereotypes. It steers the discourse away from reality, or even attempts to redefine reality itself, avoiding a substantive debate and undermining the argument for deliberation. On one level, many a crucial sociopolitical failure could be traced to trivialization, here represented by the two cases outlined above, surely attesting to its gravity. Yet, a more comprehensive engagement with this phenomenon has been largely dormant. This could be broadly attributed to three reasons.

First, a productive effort in this area requires transdisciplinary approaches. As apparent from this Introduction, merely locating trivialization and explaining some of its problematics draws on history, sociology, political studies, and, to an extent, philosophy. But bringing experts from different fields together is not an easy task, not the least given the legacy institutional arrangements, which preclude cooperation and integrative research. Cutting-edge research across domains that takes place at the Santa Fe Institute, a unique research organization that has been conducting pioneering transdisciplinary inquiry, shows this is not only possible but necessary, if we are to find answers to questions including on the roots of financial crises or evolution of social systems such as markets and various organizations.

Second, despite the numerous strides made in the recent decades in sciences in general and social sciences in particular, new perspectives needed not only to understand but also to tackle modern-day issues and address the repeated failures have not yet been embraced sufficiently broadly so as to have an impact. Namely, the recognition that economies, bureaucracies, and other social arrangements are systems—complex networks of actors, interacting, interpreting information, and responding to stimuli based on their histories and evolving schemas—of whose special properties we are increasingly aware forces us to revisit assumptions about equilibriums, perfect rationalities, or independence of actors within them (Chapter 9). They also open new avenues to question our collective discourse, significantly influenced by traditional philosophies and views (Chapter 3).

Third, there are political implications constraining progress in this area. Deceptively simple and no less influential arguments, many conveniently aligned with the prevailing political winds of the day, are finding their way from within or without the academe. The arguments, however, sit atop of glossed over or obscured assumptions (Chapter 7), which too become victims of trivialization. Bring the assumption to the daylight and the argument—embedded in policies, rules, or regulations or developed in books and articles—collapses. To no surprise, these products are among the most fiercely defended.

A familiar example is the infamous supply-side economics, built on the assumption that tax reduction primarily on capital results in a broader economic growth. Although mostly abandoned by its early proponents, it is still invoked with verve by politicians promoting their minimalist fiscal policies. Bruce Bartlett, an adviser and treasury official in Ronald

Reagan and George H. W. Bush's administrations, pushes back at these tired claims: "[t]his is a simplification of what supply-side economics was all about, and it threatens to undermine the enormous gains that have been made in economic theory and policy over the last 30 years" (Bartlett 2007). How is this possible?

Another example comes through a less known but revealing exchange between two public intellectuals with a breadth of expertise, Sam Harris and Noam Chomsky.[10] Harris challenges Chomsky's use of moral equivalence and his neglect to consider the ethical aspects of intent in his critiques of the United States' interventions abroad. Due to brevity, we will not conduct an analysis of the authors' at first glance compelling narratives. Rather, we point out their very different assumptions, or precepts, onto which they build their arguments. Chomsky, claiming that professed intentions "carry no information," suppresses the ethical dimension to intent. Harris disagrees and claims that despite our lack of a systematic understanding of ethics, we can and must consider intent— bringing us to different conclusions than Chomsky's. The trouble is, however, we can never know the true intent; we can only *infer* it. And while we seek a robust and agreeable means of inference, the opportunity for discourses based on trivialized premises will be aplenty.

THEMES IN LITERATURE

In spite of the barriers outlined in the previous section, there is an increasing number of discerning authors identifying the symptoms, critiquing the consequences, or promoting one or more solutions—mostly from the points of view of their corresponding discipline, however. Broadly, the existing literature can be classified into three categories.[11] We briefly describe each group and introduce some prominent authors notable for the *public* exposure of their work, especially important given our focus on developments in the society at large.

The works in the first category point out the various forms of trivialization directly. Physicist Leonard Mlodinow is among the authors privy to the general trivialization of science and its progress. Specifically, alarmed by the popular misconception of great breakthroughs as products of sudden flashes of genius, the author writes "the oversimplification of discovery makes science appear far less rich and complex than it really is" (Mlodinow 2015). In reality, scientific theories are formulated over years of painstaking work. Assuming otherwise means removing an entire layer of understanding of human struggle, progress, and change. The implications, less obvious but no less alarming, include a misplaced sense of agency as manifested, for example, by the confidence in technology to solve the outstanding issues of the day (such as the climate change or issues in education).

The academe, for the reasons presented earlier, is both actively and passively furthering the trends to trivialize the consequential. Economists are among the most visible offenders due to the centrality of their discipline to everyday life and the resulting exposure their views receive. Scholars of various skill, moral compass, and political ideology opine publicly on trade, financial regulation, reform, environmental policy, integration, international affairs, and others. A notable exception is Dani Rodrik, an economist without reservations to lift the curtain on the alarming realities behind the scenes of economic research and promotion, namely on economic globalization. "In public, economists can always be counted upon" to praise free trade, but their arguments, he observes, are weak and disconnected from rigorous theoretical justification (Rodrik 2012, 64). The public is thus conditioned by the unqualified and easy to absorb input instead of a disinterested analysis of competing options. Consider the case of the Transatlantic Trade and Investment Partnership (TTIP) representative of the central theme here. TTIP is one in a series of recent free-trade agreements under negotiation that aims to facilitate transatlantic commerce by removing trade barriers and encouraging investment. While objective analyses of economic research on TTIP based on a range of assumptions and producing competing results are freely available (Rodrik 2015), they are absent from the mainstream discourse mostly centered on incomplete and very simplified commentaries.[12] A sensible deliberation in the public forum, or elsewhere to be sure, cannot take place without this integral element.

The focus of the second category is on complexity in social systems. Authors, including Brian Arthur, Dirk Helbing, and Kieron O'Hara, offer their readers a set of complementary perspectives sharing a common theme: the need for a new mindset. Arthur and Helbing assert that traditional ways of disciplinary thinking about market equilibriums, market efficiency, and self-regulation, as well as rational behavior of its actors, are inadequate (Arthur 2014; Helbing 2015). Consequently, the policies and regulations based on the assumptions such as normality in forecasting or primacy of liquidity over stability have proven to be behind bubbles, crashes, and various imbalances. Arthur notes that the twentieth century's mathematical macroeconomics

> led to a stiffness in thinking, to a righteousness in what was permitted as economic theory and what was not, and to a closedness to other ideas. Shut out were the effects on the economy of politics, of power, of class, of society, of fundamental uncertainty, and of formation and creation and development. In the end it could be argued that the program—at least the extreme hyper-rational version of it—failed. (Arthur 2014, xx)

Indeed, it failed through a series of pops, the various financial crises in South America and Asia of the 1990s, and a bang, the global financial crisis of 2008 and 2009 (Chapter 8).

In a complementary view, political philosopher Kieron O'Hara conveys the need to be mindful of complexity inherent to social and natural systems and presents two guiding precepts. The first is the *knowledge principle* stating that, due to the dynamic and complex nature of social systems, we cannot make any conclusions about them with certainty. The second is the *change principle* which holds that we must be risk averse in the face of change and ensure rigor and caution in its implementation, given the prospect of unintended consequences (O'Hara 2011).[13] The two principles are embracing of change, tradition, and responsibility to the society and the environment, yet they are the basis of O'Hara's definition of true, small "c" *conservatism*.

The third and predictably the richest category in our classification is centered on people or groups and their cognitive limitations or intellectual shortcomings. It clusters around two themes. The first sees an updated governance as the answer to the individual challenges borne of the modern-day disruptions and complexities brought by, among others, new technologies and economic integration. Richard Thaler and Cass Sunstein, for example, draw on findings in behavioral economics and offer ideas on optimized rules and regulations and advocate light interventions, so-called nudges, to steer unaware citizens toward more self-preserving behaviors (Thaler and Sunstein 2008; Sunstein 2013). Taking a broader view, Berggruen and Gardels (2013) recognize the traditional forms of governance are insufficient in the age of megacities, increasing diversity, and the rise of "dumb mobs" enabled by social media technologies, and propose a new, more responsive and robust system of governance. Intelligent governance, they argue, must *involve* and *devolve*. Specifically, it must allow for more popular decision making at the community level—where citizens possess the most information as well as shared interest—while leaving the distant, long-term matters at the state level in the hands of accountable and competent institutions insulated from the short-term preferences of the impulsive public (Chapter 4).

The second theme in this group is descriptive, often critical account of the human state of mind (mostly in America). The influential book of Richard Hofstadter dealing with the American character was among the first major treatises on the rise and the vigor of anti-intellectualism and its ramifications (Hofstadter 1963). More recently, Susan Jacoby (2008) supplied her analysis of the cultural and intellectual collapse within American society. In her view, the decline of the fragile middlebrow culture, borne of the postwar democratization[14] of learning, allowed the resurgence of the dormant anti-intellectualism, now in full force in the media, education, and politics.

On a similar note, Mark Bauerlein provides a sobering exposition of the Internet generation's intellectual underperformance: "No cohort in human history has opened such a fissure between its material conditions and its intellectual attainments. None has experienced so many technological enhancements and yielded so *little mental progress*" (2008, emphasis added). Bauerlein goes on to identify the (mis)use of technology as the chief reason behind this expectations-defying situation, a development similar to the cultural shifts following the popularization of television. Indeed, considering Jacoby and Bauerlein's work together paints a gloomy image of the future of American society, with its democracy having only tenuous prospects for remediation.

We have identified a diverse body of literature sharing a common concern: the need for action to address the deficiencies of the existing beliefs, structures, and institutions in dealing with increasing social and technical complexity. Perhaps unsurprisingly, the authors' primary locus of study is the United States, a country filled with contradictions borne of the struggles of its fast-changing, increasingly diverse society to find a way forward in a progressively interdependent world. While all cases are individually instructive and inspiring, we here look past the American anti-intellectualism or the culture of its youth. Our focus is on an issue that we understand as fundamental and one that goes beyond a single jurisdiction—trivialization. Rather than critique, our goal is to describe, understand, motivate the reader to learn more, and inspire action.

As seen through the works above, recipes for improvements are wide ranging. Some assign blame to social media and related technologies distracting individuals from learning and engagement, to the shortcomings in our systems of education, or to the consumer culture. Others see fault in the elites who have effected yet failed to manage change driven by opening markets and increasing interdependence, and by rapidly evolving technology. Nevertheless important, the arguments are mostly concentrated on their authors' domains of interest.

A more comprehensive view, which we hope to advance, reveals the contemporary state of affairs not as a product of one dominant, but rather a set of related issues. Namely, neither the culture, capacities, or choices of ordinary citizens nor the failures of the elite can be advanced separately as *the* cause. While much work on cognitive, cultural, and social dimensions of discourse remains to be done across and beyond social and behavioral sciences, we can identify some fundamental lapses and begin to understand their roots (Chapters 3 and 7). In the process, we find that in conducive settings people are capable of making good collective decisions (Chapter 5), we recognize we can learn to cope with our cognitive limitations and make better choices individually (Chapter 6), and we have a better grasp of how public reasons (Chapters 5 and 6), motivating us to consider constructively the opinions of the public rather than to trivialize them. Learning from history, we know what meanings we must develop more broadly to advance our culture (Chapter 10), possess coherent philosophies on how to do this (Chapter 11), and have a proven know-how in delivering systemic change (Fullan 2010). And while we understand social systems are not amenable to control, our aims can be achieved from the bottom-up in an empowering environment, a policy application that is, after all, already in practice (Chapter 9). These findings are a source of optimism we can do better.

The Blueprints

As hinted, engaging systemic issues such as trivialization opens a number of questions, whose answers naturally lead to other equally deserving questions. Hence, we start from the basics asking what is this lapse and how is it sustained, what can discourse and public opinion reveal about our collective and individual state of mind, and, importantly, what are our limits, can we cope with them, and how? Corresponding with this chain of investigation, the chapters in this book have been organized into four related modules: On Trivialization, Opinions and Their Public, Approaching Complexity, and Shifting Cultures. We thus begin with trivialization, continue with an exploration of public views and their formation, discuss a new frame of reference and its promises, and finally take a trip into the history of our social and cultural development. As customary, this section provides a high-level blueprint of the book while highlighting the main questions posed in each chapter. Readers seeking a detailed review of the volume complemented with an analysis may turn to the final chapter (11).

No doubt trivialization has a number of conceptions, some channeling intent, other unawareness, or even focus on the content. Nevertheless, shall we agree it is a problem warranting our understanding, we must seek a useful definition. In Chapter 2, we thus ask *How can we best define trivialization?* and, with this in mind, *What does trivialization look like in action?* In our definition, we capture the fundamentals of trivialized discourse and hope to reduce the subjectivity at times at play in identifying trivialization. The two salient examples that follow are designed to provide a window on trivialization, its extent, and implications. The first is the discourse around free trade, a complex matter often treated in the most reductive manner, including by those trusted to know better. The other example involves US health care, in particular the contentious, yet virtually substance-free conversation surrounding its recent reforms.

Our examples show that trivialization's roots reach deeper than political ideology or polarization. In Chapter 3, we ask *What are some intrinsic enablers of trivialized discourse?* We make the case there exist three broadly embraced assumptions or philosophies impacting the way we approach, interpret, and talk about the world around us. We identify essentialism, a drive to organize our environment into natural categories, each with some essential, causal set of characteristics; reductionism, an assumption that all phenomena can be explained in terms of their basic elements; and relativism, an idea that there is no independent reality, and all knowledge can be assessed only with respect to a particular context. We offer a number of illustrative examples of the implications each of these problematic views has on our discourse. We conclude the chapter with a lesson from history motivating a closer attention to the current condition.

We thus establish a relationship between some deeply held assumptions and our discourse. Both are reflected in public opinion, whose study, we believe, is indispensable shall we want to understand and improve our conversations, integral in taking on effectively the issues with contemporary governance. The overarching intent of the ensuing three chapters is to probe what people think and why, and obtain an insight into opinion formation and individual reasoning, all with hopes to understand better trivialization and its potential correctives. We explore people's views and the realities and logic behind these views; consider the relationship between a new model of governance, the tools of democratic renewal, and public discourse; and show that we can gain the capacity to make good decisions, both collectively and individually.

Chapter 4 begins with a discussion of some alarming trends observed over the last few decades in the opinions of the public: increasing levels of skepticism toward the government, distrust of the media, or cynicism toward politics. According to some, these are due to the rise of critical citizens, politically active individuals questioning current institutions and advocating for reforms, augmenting the ranks of those historically mistrustful of government yet cognizant of the legitimacy of democratic governance. Yet, as others observe, there has been a notable erosion in people's trust in liberal democracy and an associated increase in preferences for authoritarian leadership. A closer look at political and policy outcomes as well as the failures of various institutional reforms to revitalize democratic engagement only reinforce these findings. *What is behind these developments? What might it take to create a legitimate and effective governance for the new age?* are the central questions. An examination of developments over the past several decades reveals that democracies are growing increasingly dysfunctional. They are unable to consistently deliver results in public interest, maintain their legitimacy, and improve our social and economic conditions inclusively—especially in the face of increasing interdependence, diversity, and technology-driven shifts in the distribution of power (Berggruen and Gardels 2013). This means we must look to new modes of governance, changing decision-making structures as well as roles and expectations for leaders and citizens alike.

If such a redesign is possible depends partly on whether a large portion of society can comprehend and have a discussion on the underlying issues. Exploring these matters is the goal of Chapter 5, where we learn what people look for in assessing governance, what is their understanding of politics, and what is their vision of an ideal system of government. *What is the logic behind people's views on governance?* We find much insight in the work of Hibbing and Theiss-Morse (2004), who have questioned the traditional views of citizens clamoring for more say in government, of policy outcomes as the primary concern of most voters, and of greater political engagement as the key to civic satisfaction. The authors argue that people's attitudes toward politics build on a misperception of political consensus, a trivialized perspective that informs their understanding of governance. As a result, most people reason that since the key policy questions are settled, governance is predominantly a technical matter. This view thus sees political conflict as a product of ineliminable special interests, and election a disciplinary tool rather than an instrument of governance. *How can we cope with such a trivialization contributing to dissatisfaction, stagnation, and decay?* We find a manifold promise in managed deliberation. We show that with adequate opportunity, people can not only make good collective choices, but also learn, and improve their sense of civic worth. In these environments, citizens start to recognize the diversity of views, the depth of issues, and thus begin to appreciate politics and their role in it.

While the preceding chapters have engaged the bigger picture, the reasoning, ideas, and choices at the macro-level, the purpose of Chapter 6 is to focus mainly on the individual. We begin the chapter with a look at select public opinion research with an interest to understand the process of opinion formation. Our main questions are: *What are the limits to individual reasoning? Can we overcome them?* We engage two complementary bodies of work revealing a more complex picture of how people come to their opinions than the conventional "stances as dances" view (Hibbing and Theiss-Morse 2004, 30), where individuals take what is on top of their mind to satisfy the hurried pollster. While the research findings suggest an array of factors influencing public opinion,[15] we argue that dominant is our cognitive engagement with information flows—in which ideas or slogans prevail. Discourses reflect how most people think as well as what they are willing to sanction within a broader politico-cultural environment. We continue with a discussion of select cognitive limitations playing a role not only in opinion formation but also in our problem solving and decision making. We highlight research suggesting we can overcome these barriers with proactive measures and training.

Many popular science authors have been tempted by certitude—a confident conclusion glossing over assumptions, evidentiary limits, and balance—in propping up their argument and satisfying their audience uncomfortable with uncertainty. Indeed, this form of trivialization is ubiquitous in public discourse, yet remains underappreciated despite its ramifications in policy making and regulation and its impact on the public's trust in government, and in the social elite more broadly. *Why is this lapse so widespread?* we set out to learn in Chapter 7, our transition to the next part of the volume. We reach to Manski (2011, 2013) whose analysis of practices leading to, in his words, incredible certitude suggests answers. We continue with an illustrative case study of certitudes, upon a closer look far from credible yet with deep consequence to all of us. Here, public agencies, the media, and the research community all play a role in communicating a message which is not exactly reliable. *What can be done about this?* There is an important counterweight to scientific certitude, gaining salience not the least due to the lessons of history, with the potential to effect change beyond policy making.

In Chapter 7, we have alluded to a range of failures in policy making and regulation, which can be traced to, as we noted, our misplaced sense of confidence—not only about matters we have not yet been able to validate but also about issues inherently unknowable. Underpinned by an inadequate worldview, such attitudes permeate our discourse and lead to repeated crises. In Chapter 8, we start with the global financial system and its recent crises helping us highlight issues with the traditional perspectives used to study both the physical and the social world. Due to advances in mathematics and simulation technology which have over the past decades stimulated interest in complexity science, scholars beyond biology have become increasingly aware of the necessity to consider previously neglected properties of social and natural systems. We thus discern a gradual embrace of elements of a new paradigm, one very different from the reductionist frame of reference dominating science since its rise. *What is this paradigm? How does it help advance the study of social systems?* are among the questions we investigate in this chapter.

Whether complexity is a new paradigm and whether we are amidst of a complexity shift is subject to debates, not the least due to the varied conceptions of what constitutes a paradigm and its change. Nevertheless, if considered at a meta-theoretical level, embracing the new worldview becomes a significant departure from the established assumptions on how to study and represent the world. And it offers much promise to transform not only the way we do science or make policy but also our discourse. In Chapter 9, we thus explore the various dimensions of the new paradigm and its potential implications. *How can we understand such a shift? What are its promises?*

A recurrent theme in the volume is thinking, reasoning, or cognitive engagement, surely more important than merely getting informed in this age of virtually unlimited information flows of varying credibility. Television networks and online spaces for the "tribes of the likeminded" (Berggruen and Gardels 2013, 31), various fake news outlets, and even the content of television programming indicate that people do not think alike and have varied capacity to tell truth from fiction. On the other hand, most people do not believe in magical characters as they did in the past, a sign of our cultural and cognitive progress. This is also the focus of Chapter 10 in which we first examine the cognitive development at an individual level and review our social evolution in preparation for a discussion of the cultural evolution in our cognition. *How does thought evolve? How may we understand our cognitive condition and our prospects for the future?* We find Barnes's (2000) Piaget-inspired analysis valuable in the study of the developments of styles of thought across time.

Chapter 11 brings all the arguments and findings of the volume together, adding further insights and discussion. After such a winding voyage, we may ask what is next. *How can we get ahead?* Perhaps the expected answer is education. Indeed, but it will be a new education, a system departing from its traditional philosophies which have reached their limits. The approach (Egan 1997), familiar to readers of the previous chapter, involves the development in students of a range of understandings of increasing difficulty and the associated cognitive tools. Learning how to *think* is the prerogative.

NOTES

1. Information can be defined as processed, organized, and contextualized data. Knowledge is the understanding or interpretation of this contextualized information. We assume here knowledge can be both transferred, for example by digital means, or developed individually through learning and discovery.
2. Giles's (2016) article is among many.
3. For more about the role of telegraph and newspaper in high politics of mid-nineteenth century United States, and specifically in the time leading up to and the presidency of Abraham Lincoln, see Kearns Goodwin (2005).
4. And not just for their informational roles. The situation where "for every one Parisian who had the right to vote in parliamentary elections prior to 1848, there were twenty who subscribed to a newspaper" (McKeever and Rapport 2013), was unsustainable.

5. This case, demonstrating both the push and pull of information, is very important and will be revisited later.

6. See, for example, Edgerton (2007) and Dudley (2008).

7. The authors comment on the 2011 earthquake in Virginia: "Twitter users in New York City and other locations saw tweets about the earthquake, which originated in Virginia state, up to 30 seconds before it was felt, showing that information moves faster through networks than the earthquakes themselves" (Peary et al. 2012).

8. And here we merely refer to transformations that are local or regional, rather than global as described by, for example, McLuhan's "global village" imagery (1962). There, aside from the variety of institutional constraints, including the copious filters, screens, or regulations preventing the global from entering the local, language remains one of the barriers to the integration of digital cultures. A study sponsored by the European Commission finds that 61% of Europeans do not understand a foreign language well enough to be able to communicate online (EC 2012). This statistic alone is suggestive of a digital society that is not only less communicative, but also one, contrary to McLuhan's vision, less aware of what lies beyond the boundaries and borders.

9. To find out about the small events in history which had large implications to the society-information nexus (as one may expect in a complex system), see Dudley (2008).

10. This debate, an uncommon opportunity to peek behind the scenes and witness erudite friction, is centered on ethics in politics, namely in international relations. See Harris and Chomsky (2015).

11. Although some works straddle the boundaries between two or more categories.

12. See, among others, Spence (2016) and Walker (2015).

13. As we will explore (Chapter 7), this is one class of reframing necessary in coping with trivialization in politics.

14. To which we have alluded in an earlier section, Information Asymmetries and Social Change.

15. Here, additional research promises to further our understanding of public discourse.

REFERENCES

Applebaum, Yoni. 2014. "Publishers gave away 122,951,031 books during World War II." *The Atlantic*, September 10. http://www.theatlantic.com/.

Arthur, Brian W. 2014. *Complexity and the economy*. Oxford: Oxford University Press.

Barnes, Michael Horace. 2000. *Stages of thought: The co-evolution of religious thought and science.* New York: Oxford University Press.

Bartlett, Bruce. 2007. "How supply-side economics trickled down." *The New York Times,* April 6. https://www.nytimes.com/2007/04/06/opinion/06bartlett.html.

Bauerlein, Mark. 2008. *The dumbest generation: How the digital age stupefies young Americans and jeopardizes our future.* New York: Penguin Books.

BBC Business. 2016. "Pound plunges after Leave vote." *BBC Business,* June 24. http://www.bbc.com/news/business-36611512.

Bennett, Lance W., and Alexandra Segerberg. 2012. "The logic of connective action." *Information, Communication & Society* 15 (5): 739–768.

Berggruen, Nicolas, and Nathan Gardels. 2013. *Intelligent governance for the 21st century: A middle way between west and east.* Cambridge, UK: Polity Press.

Calamur, Krishnadev, Matt Ford, and Kathy Gilsinan. 2016. "Britain, post-Brexit." *The Atlantic,* July 22. https://www.theatlantic.com/news/archive/2016/07/brexit-results/488561/.

Cooper, Andrew. 2016. "The Brexit vote is history. A closed or open Britain is the defining battle now." *The Guardian,* July 4. https://www.theguardian.com/commentisfree/2016/jul/04/post-referendum-politics-eu-vote.

Curtice, John. 2016. "Brexit buyers' remorse? There's more evidence of abstainers' regret." *LSE Analyses: British Politics and Policy.* http://blogs.lse.ac.uk/politicsandpolicy/.

Dennison, James, and Noah Carl. 2016. "The ultimate causes of Brexit: History, culture, and geography." *LSE Analyses: British Politics and Policy.* http://blogs.lse.ac.uk/politicsandpolicy/.

Dudley, Leonard. 2008. *Information revolutions in the history of the West,* 174. Cheltenham: Edward Elgar.

EC (European Commission). 2012. "Special Eurobarometer 386: Europeans and their languages." Directorate-General for Education and Culture. http://ec.europa.eu/commfrontoffice/publicopinion/archives/ebs/ebs_386_en.pdf.

The Economist. 2011. "The perils of extreme democracy." *The Economist,* April 20. https://www.economist.com/leaders/2011/04/20/the-perils-of-extreme-democracy.

Edgerton, Gary R. 2007. *The Columbia history of American television.* New York: Columbia University Press.

Edwards, Mark U. 2005. *Printing, propaganda, and Martin Luther.* Minneapolis: Fortress Press.

Egan, Kieran. 1997. *The educated mind: How cognitive tools shape our understanding.* Chicago: University of Chicago Press.

Fullan, Michael. 2010. *All systems go: The change imperative for whole system reform*. Thousand Oaks, CA: Corwin Press.

Fung, Brian. 2016. "The British are frantically Googling what the E.U. is, hours after voting to leave it." *The Washington Post*, June 24. https://www.washingtonpost.com/news/the-switch/wp/2016/06/24/the-british-are-frantically-googling-what-the-eu-is-hours-after-voting-to-leave-it/.

Giles, Chris. 2016. "What are the economic consequences of Brexit?" *Financial Times*, February 22. https://www.ft.com/content/70d0bfd8-d1b3-11e5-831d-09f7778e7377.

Harris, Sam, and Noam Chomsky. 2015. "The limits of discourse." Unpublished correspondence. https://www.samharris.org/blog/item/the-limits-of-discourse.

Helbing, Dirk. 2015. "How and why our conventional economic thinking causes global crises." *Thinking ahead, essays on big data, digital revolution, and participatory market society*, 39–52. Cham: Springer.

Hibbing, John R., and Elizabeth Theiss-Morse. 2004. *Stealth democracy: Americans' beliefs about how government should work*. Cambridge, UK: Cambridge University Press.

Hofstadter, Richard. 1963. *Anti-intellectualism in American life*. New York: Knopf.

Howard, Philip N., Aiden Duffy, Deen Freelon, Muzammil M. Hussain, Will Mari, and Marwa Maziad. 2011. "Opening closed regimes: What was the role of social media during the Arab Spring?" SSRN: http://ssrn.com/abstract=2595096.

IMF. 2016. "IMF cuts global growth forecasts on Brexit, warns of risks to outlook." *The International Monetary Fund News*, July 19. https://www.imf.org/en/News/.

Jacobs, Alan M., and J. Scott Matthews. 2012. "Why do citizens discount the future? Public opinion and the timing of policy consequences." *British Journal of Political Science* 42 (4): 903–935.

Jacoby, Susan. 2008. *The age of American unreason*. New York: Pantheon Books.

Jefferson, Thomas. 1817. "A letter to George Ticknor, November 25." Thomas Jefferson Foundation. https://www.monticello.org/.

Kearns Goodwin, Doris. 2005. *Team of rivals: The political genius of Abraham Lincoln*. New York: Simon and Schuster.

Manski, Charles F. 2013. *Public policy in an uncertain world: Analysis and decisions*. Cambridge, MA: Harvard University Press.

Manski, Charles F. 2011. "Policy analysis with incredible certitude." *The Economic Journal* 121 (554): F261–F289.

McKeever, David, and Mike Rapport. 2013. "Technology and the revolutions of 1848 and 2011." Konrad Adenauer Stiftung. https://www.kas.de/web/guest/einzeltitel/-/content/technology-and-the-revolutions-of-1848-and-20111.

McLuhan, Marshall. 1962. *The Gutenberg Galaxy: The making of typographic man*. Toronto: University of Toronto Press.

McLuhan, Marshall, and Quentin Fiore. 1968. *War and peace in the global village*. New York: Bantam.

Mlodinow, Leonard. 2015. "It is, in fact, rocket science." *The New York Times*, May 16. https://www.nytimes.com/2015/05/16/opinion/it-is-in-fact-rocket-science.html.

O'Hara, Kieron. 2011. *Conservatism*. London: Reaktion Books.

Peary, Brett, Rajib Shaw, and Yukiko Takeuchi. 2012. "Utilization of social media in the east Japan earthquake and tsunami and its effectiveness." *Journal of Natural Disaster Science* 34 (1): 3–18.

Rodrik, Dani. 2012. *The Globalization Paradox: Democracy and the future of the world economy*, 62–65. New York: W. W. Norton.

Rodrik, Dani. 2015. "The war of trade models." http://rodrik.typepad.com/.

Searchmetrics. 2015. "The Guardian tops list of most popular UK newspaper sites on Twitter, finds new study," January 20. London: Searchmetrics. https://www.searchmetrics.com/news-and-events/most-popular-uk-newspaper-sites-on-twitter/.

Spence, Peter. 2016. "What is TTIP and how is it supposed to make us better off?" https://www.telegraph.co.uk/business/2016/05/05/what-is-ttip-and-how-is-it-supposed-to-make-us-better-off/.

Sunstein, Cass. 2013. *Simpler: The future of government*. New York: Simon and Schuster.

Thaler, Richard, and Cass Sunstein. 2008. *Nudge: Improving decisions about health, wealth, and happiness*. New Haven: Yale University Press.

Urquhart, Conal. 2016. "The worst of the Brexit fallout is still to hit the U.K." *Time*, July 1. https://www.yahoo.com/news/worst-brexit-fallout-still-hit-163844661.html.

Walker, Andrew. 2015. "TTIP: Why the EU-US trade deal matters." *BBC World Service Economics*. https://www.bbc.com/news/business-32691589.

CHAPTER 2

Trivialization

Truth can be found through observation and testing. More democracy is better. One should not work on Sundays. Tax cuts create jobs. Elementary particles gain mass through their interaction with the Higgs field. People on welfare do not want to work. Species evolve over time through the processes of natural selection. Markets best operate without government interference. Science and religion can coexist without conflict. A democracy can only exist until the voters discover that they can vote themselves money. Onion skins very thin, mild winter coming in; onion skins thick and tough, coming winter cold and rough. God does not play dice with the universe. These few familiar statements belong to the flows of ideas we may hear, internalize, adapt, or relay every day. Appearing plain and easy, some are formulated to evoke emotion, recast problems, compel, or distract. Some are rooted in years of scientific inquiry, while others are based on useful assumptions made to fit a given agenda. Some have proven their value, others have repeatedly disappointed. Based on conjecture or myths, many lack a substantive backing altogether. Frequently, however, this does not seem to matter—a condition that points to the roots of trivialization.

Oxford dictionary defines the verb *trivialize* as to "treat as unimportant, minimize, play down, underplay, make light of, treat lightly, think little of, dismiss, underestimate, undervalue, devalue." Capturing both intent and ignorance, trivialization can thus be seen as an individual or collective miscalculation of severity of issues, inattention to detail and complexity, or an outright dismissiveness of alternatives. While the lexical definition gives us the terms to describe it, it does not say much about the

O. Bubak and H. Jacek, *Trivialization and Public Opinion*,
https://doi.org/10.1007/978-3-030-17925-0_2

discursive process. What happens in this process? Is there an observable pattern we can generalize? To obtain an analytical conception of trivialization, we build on the discussion we have presented so far. Before doing so, however, we will need to briefly explore the world of information.

IDEAS AND INFORMATION

Whether a part of the "ideas, interests, and institutions" framework (Hall 1997) used to explain policy outcomes, or as a key to understanding social change more generally, working with *ideas* has become increasingly popular in social and political sciences. Scholars have realized that reaching to groups, power relations, or rationality of actors is insufficient in explaining fully the outcomes in politics, and thus began to bring ideas into their analyses. There has hence been interest in *explaining* ideas (e.g., Berman 2010) as well as in explaining *with* ideas (Stone 1989; Kingdon 1995; Béland 2005; Béland and Cox 2010; Bleich 2002, among others).

"Ideas" is an encompassing term, often suffering from a lack of an adequate definition. Some see ideas as "casual beliefs," products of human cognition capturing our connection to the material world through interpretations and guiding our action (Béland and Cox 2010). Aucoin sees ideas "as 'paradigms' for the simple reason that they combine both intellectual and ideological dimensions... They are models which have appeal because they *appear* to describe reality, they offer an explanation for the same, and they prescribe ways to change in desired directions" (1990, 116, emphasis added). Similarly, Parsons views ideas as "the subset of institutions (practices, symbols, norms, grammars, models, identities) through which people interpret their world" (2007, 100).

Apparent in these views or definitions is that ideas are found at various levels of abstraction, from those capturing a particular solution to broadly shared subjectivities including philosophies and worldviews. Mehta (2010) maps ideas as *policy solutions, problem definitions,* and *public philosophies* (or zeitgeist), useful in the studies of policy process and beyond. Policy solutions are specific roadmaps to address a set of problems in line with broader social objectives. For example, a carbon tax becomes a solution to reducing greenhouse emissions. Problems too are ideas. Problems are constructed, or created based on a level of shared understanding of reality. As Stone (1989) notes, difficult conditions can turn into problems only once the society has a means (and thus a choice) to do something about them. Having new, alternate sources of energy, for instance, means that it becomes possible to talk of the elimination of fossil fuels, which have a visibly negative impact on the environment. Finally, public philosophies—"a disparate set of cultural, social, or economic assumptions that are overwhelmingly dominant in public discourse at a given moment in time" (Mehta 2010, 40)—are important variables in determining the way the society views and prioritizes the problems and their solutions. Here, the idea of health care as a right versus a product serves as an apt example.

This typology is rooted in research on ideas, where scholars have asked *questions* about the mechanics of which problem formulation becomes salient, which policy solutions get selected, and how we can explain change in public philosophies (Mehta 2010). With regard to the mechanics of problem definition, a number of factors determining the *success of problem formulation* have been identified. These include how the issues as portrayed (Stone 1989), which solutions are available (Hall 1993), or what is the fit between problems definition and the environment, among others. For the latter, for example, asking why the US welfare state in more limited in the United States than in Europe, Alesina, and Glaeser (2004), find ideas—general attitudes toward the poor, views on effort versus luck in success, and perceptions of social mobility—rather than economics to be behind the persistent differences between the welfare states of the US and Europe. The authors add that institutions, such as the prevalent proportional representation and parliamentarism, which have shaped ideas in Europe, have not developed in the United States. And importantly, the authors observe reinforcing feedback effects between ideas and the system of redistribution. The second question emanating from the discussed typology is *which public solutions get adopted and how?* Here, Kingdon (1995), Hall (1989, 1993), and Oliver and Pemberton (2004), for instance, offer insights into conditions and actions needed for new ideas to take hold.

And importantly, we can also discern change in public philosophies. An outstanding example is Inglehart's (1997) observation of a broad social reorientation toward postmaterialist values, which became apparent in the 1970s. Inglehart studied party platforms and noted their shift away from consumerism and social conservatism toward inclusiveness, equality, and environmental consciousness. This change in public philosophy, according to Inglehart, was rooted in the existential security achieved by the postwar generation. In turn, the recent appeal of nationalism and populism is explained as a "cultural backlash" by those affected by economic dislocations (Inglehart and Norris 2016). Some thus argue that changes in public philosophies are cyclical in nature, but, as we will discuss, such systemic phenomena can be understood only in hindsight.

Above all, and this is often less appreciated, a complete analysis must consider these classes of ideas together, as they not only interact, they may remake each other (Mehta 2010). For example, proven or successful problem solutions may become public philosophies, as was the case with Keynesianism.

Thus far, we engaged ideational scholarship distinguishing between different types of ideas based on their level of generality. We noted the increasing popularity of bringing *ideas* into the study of the social world. This is not the least as ideas are on the whole readily identifiable, easier to trace through time and connect to other ideas, and certainly ubiquitous. Yet, such thrusts also reflect a deeper issue in public discourse— the peculiar dominance of bits of information "presented in terms that are simple and easy to digest...which do not presuppose that either politicians or bureaucrats will have to read the original sources of these ideas" (Aucoin 1990, 116). While speaking in the context of politics and public administration, Aucoin captured a deeper reality of culture and society more broadly. The author noted ideas, on the whole, are easily relayed and understood and tend to be uncoupled from their sources. Indeed then, using a common analogy, an idea *may* be the tip of a large iceberg—a body of numerous assumptions, years of extensive scientific inquiry, or logical reasoning, a majority of which is submerged, out of sight and mostly out of mind. It may just be a snow cone—made up of appetizing hunches, guesses, or superstitions, without much substance behind it at all. Or it may lie somewhere in between these two extremes. Importantly, differences among them are often not at all apparent.

As ideas are information, often sitting atop or connected to other information, it is essential for our purposes to draw a distinction between different informational types. We thus present information typology based on its various abstractions (Table 2.1). There are the three types of ideas—problem formulations, solutions, and public philosophies—along with their examples, as discussed above. We add another category—ideas communicating philosophies of science, which include various ontological and epistemological assumptions. These meta-theories provide the ultimate framework for how we interpret, define, or talk about the world around us and thus delimit ideas, their usability and meaning. These are primarily the views on causality and the nature of reality and knowledge.

Table 2.1 Types of information: ideas and knowledge

Abstraction	Example
Problem formulations	Global warming
Solutions	Carbon tax, emission standards
Public philosophies, worldviews	Keynesianism, postmaterialism
Assumptions/philosophies	Reductionism, holism
Folklore	Myths, tales, contrived news items
Information bases, substantive knowledge	Simulations and models, analyses, contextualized data

There are also what we call information bases, or substantive knowledge, consisting of bodies of research, philosophical thought, outputs from simulations and experiments, analyses, and other coherent interpretations of contextualized information (data). These cannot be relayed in a sentence; rather, their engagement requires more time and sustained attention. Finally, there is folklore, a term here employed more broadly to encompass a variety of tales, conspiracies, fake news headlines, superstitions, or myths. Some are traditional, surviving generations, others are more recent, crafted and amplified through modern information channels capable of reaching mass audiences at an instant.

About Trivialization

We observed the general discourse to be dominated by ideas, ranging from public philosophies to folklore, while turning away from substantive information. This pervasive and consequential dismissiveness of the big picture, the whole story, or the context, especially acute in the age of information, thus deserves to be recognized and classified. We thus conceptualize it as trivialization and define it *as an inclination to conflate ideas with substance, treat them as qualitatively the same, or dismiss the need to go beyond ideas and engage with their grounding altogether.* It leads to a distillation of public and private discourses into clichés accepted as true by some and false by others, obfuscating most nuances and complexities, thus eliminating the avenues or even a need for dialog.

We must emphasize in this context substantive information or knowledge is not restricted to a singular description of the world, broadly accepted as true. Instead, we refer to a reasoned, coherent, and intelligible set of claims to be *contrastable* with others. Hence, we view trivialization as a lapse in the parameters, rather than in the content of discourse as others may suggest. Robinson, for example, begins her critique with a call to revisit the assumptions of modernist scientism which "trivialize and discredit" the human mind (2010, xviii). On this account, trivialization ultimately stems from a reliance on scientific logic in understanding the world, a limiting enterprise in its attempts to "explain away...the experience and testimony of the individual mind" (22). To us, however, trivialization is not *what* is conveyed, but how it is done. Our judgment on trivialization thus limits subjectivity in locating trivialization.

For illustration, let us consider here a vivid case of trivialization as manifested through one of the key issues of our time—free trade. *Does economic globalization make countries better off?* has been a frequent question, namely during the recent election cycles. Setting aside for the moment its inherently trivialized formulation, Rodrik (2011) engages two answers from those thought to have credence on this matter—economists. The first is the prevalent "Yes," a confident recommendation communicated to the public in an easily digestible phrase. The second is a less common, complicated response ridden with caveats, mostly reserved for university classrooms: "...in most of our models free trade makes some groups better off and others worse off... under certain conditions, and assuming we can tax the beneficiaries and compensate the losers, freer trade has the *potential* to increase everyone's well-being" (Rodrik 2011, 61, emphasis original). The answer makes vivid at once the non-trivial nature of this topic and the body of knowledge, including assumptions, a list of specific conditions (Box 2.1) and economic models, that exists to support it.

Box 2.1 Preconditions to a sensible free trade

The import liberalization must be complete, covering all goods and trade partners, or else the reduction in import restrictions must take into account the potentially quite complicated structure of substitutability and complementarity across restricted commodities. (So in fact a preferential trade agreement with one or a few trade partners is unlikely to satisfy the requirement.) There must be no microeconomic market imperfections other than the trade restrictions in question, or if there are some, the second-best interactions that are entailed must not be too adverse. The home economy must be "small" in world markets, or else the liberalization must not put the economy on the wrong side of the "optimum tariff." The economy must be in reasonably full employment, or if not, the monetary and fiscal authorities must have effective tools of demand management at their disposal. The income redistributive effects of the liberalization should not be judged undesirable by society at large, or if they are, there must be compensatory tax-transfer schemes with low enough excess burden. There must be no adverse effects on the fiscal balance, or if there are, there must be alternative and expedient ways of making up for the lost fiscal revenues. The liberalization must be politically sustainable and hence credible so that economic agents do not fear or anticipate a reversal.

Source Rodrik (2011, 62)

Unsurprisingly, the public, conditioned by images of closed factories, experiences with unemployment or underemployment, financial crises, as well as protectionist messaging, is confused about free trade. Note that polls reveal a reversal in views on free trade along party lines. Respondents identifying as Republicans were more likely than Democrats to think such trade was beneficial to the American economy, consumers, and US standards of living in 2004 and 2006 polls. Yet, a significant shift of this opinion was observed in 2016 polls, with more Democrats now viewing trade more positively. The lowest proportions of positive responses are on trade and jobs (in 2016), with 30 and 41% of Republicans and Democrats, respectively, thinking that trade is good for jobs security and 34 and 47% for job creation (Smeltz et al. 2016). And the above question, posed in a leading manner and obscuring the efforts invested into research in trade economics and policy, only reinforces these orientations. Instead, we get a simple yes from one group or no from the other, pushing out of focus the informed answers, available and waiting to be brought into a substantive conversation.

Some might note this is just a reality of an elite discourse, much of it designed and used to support a particular point of view and agenda and to shape the highly pliable public opinion. This discourse, we should realize, is by its very nature partial and not necessarily based in reality, they might add. As Zaller explains:

…much of the information carried in elite discourse is neither neutral nor strictly factual. A news report implying that the Pentagon is awash in scandal and mismanagement, or a presidential remark to the effect that most unemployed persons could get jobs if they tried hard enough, constitute factual information in that they *may contain some simple facts*, and that they convey sincerely held beliefs about factual states of affairs. Yet they are not neutral, since they have been framed for partisan purposes and can be reasonably disputed by fairminded people. (2005, 22, emphasis added)

Zaller provides some examples of basic issues to which the public may be exposed in the media. While some are myths entirely, others may indeed contain some element of truth and can be challenged. Yet, there are much more complex and consequential issues, also trivialized in this manner, engagement of which is an order of magnitude more difficult. We may hear similar statements on the state and the causes of the changing climate, on the safety or dangers of genetically modified organisms, or on the binary options in trade policy. Here, fair-mindedness is not sufficient in contesting a public discourse on highly complex topics which has been stripped of substance. How else to react, question, build a robust opinion, and have a joint dialogue that does not elude public interest? To further these points, we will take a closer look at the recent health care reforms in the US, where trivialization and its effects were on full display.

TRIVIALIZATION IN ACTION: REFORMING HEALTH CARE

"Together we're going to deliver real change that once again puts Americans first. That begins with immediately repealing and replacing the disaster known as Obamacare … You're going to have such great health care, at a tiny fraction of the cost—and it's going to be so easy," proclaimed Donald Trump, then a US presidential contender at his 2016 campaign rally in Florida. Less than five months later, speaking at the Whitehouse as the president, Trump admitted "[i]t's an unbelievably complex subject. Nobody knew that health care could be so complicated" (Politico 2017). Trump was speaking of the ill-functioning US health care system, which saw a historical attempt at its overhaul in the Patient Protection and Affordable Care Act of 2010. As a signature accomplishment of his predecessor, the Affordable Care Act (ACA) has also been known as Obamacare. The discussions and events preceding and following the enactment of the ACA have shone the light not only on the state of the US health care system, the country's politics and discourse, but also on prospects of a deeper reform.

The United States is the only high-income industrialized country without a universal health care system. Understanding the development of the US health care system is equally challenging as mapping the "disjointed amalgam" (Faguet 2013) it has become, and outside of scope here.[1] Nevertheless, it must be noted that at its core sits a highly entrenched and corporate interest dominated private insurance market, a product of a series of choices made at key points in time including on the "[m]assive subsidies for medical technology and infrastructure, tax and labor policies promoting employment-based insurance, and a framework of government health insurance that removed from the market the most vulnerable and difficult to insure segments of society" (Hacker 1998, 107). The US health care system hence developed private and public segments, the latter of which consist of Medicare (for the elderly), Medicaid (for the poor), the Military Health System (for active military and their families), Veterans Health (retired military), and programs for Native Americans. Evolving together, the private and public sectors consumed about 53 and 47% respectively of the total health spending in 2010 (Faguet 2013).

While the US health *care* is generally considered to be the best in the world, its health *system* is deficient. "For most Americans, high-quality care generally is readily accessible without long waits but at high cost. However, the uninsured and, increasingly, the underinsured, the poor, and members of underserved minorities often have poor access to health care and poor health outcomes—in some cases worse than that of residents of developing countries," explains American College of Physicians (ACP 2007). To place these statements in perspective, in 2009, 50.5 million people (16.7% of the population) were without health insurance, while 95 million (31%) were covered by government insurance; 7.3 million or 9.8% of children under 18 were uninsured (UCB 2010). The "gaps in health insurance coverage and proper primary care, poorer health-related behaviours and poor living conditions for a significant proportion of the U.S. population," are lowering life expectancy (OECD 2014) and overall health outcomes. In 2011, life expectancy in the US was 1.5 years lower than the average for the Organisation for Economic Co-operation and Development (OECD) member countries, and lower still among its leading countries (OECD 2014).

Importantly, these outcomes are despite the enormous per capita health outlays. The US spends 2.5 times the OECD average, 25% more than the next highest spending country, Switzerland,[2] 80% more than Germany, and nearly twice as much as Canada, France, or Japan (OECD 2017). More specifically, in 2016, the US health spending reached $3.3 trillion (17.9% of the country's Gross Domestic Product). This is a 4.3% growth over the prior year, reaching over $10,000 per person (CMS 2018). This certainly invites the critical, yet often suppressed, question on the reasons behind these extraordinary costs. Most apparently, we may claim it is technology that is behind such high prices, as the medical industry is the only sector of the economy where the use of technology increased, rather than lowered prices.

But there exists a host of deeper reasons. In his book on the ACA, Faguet (2013) paints an alarming account of waste, abuse, and misalignment of values that became to permeate the industry.[3] First, a series of historical moves in the delivery of health care meant that health providers gained autonomy and pricing power, insurance companies (which in some markets hold a virtual monopoly) were exempt from anti-trust legislation, and government options in negotiating drug prices were limited. The employer-provided health insurance, the defining feature of the US health care system, means that insurance is seen as an employment benefit to be used to its fullest, encouraging consumption and leading to the overutilization of health products. Consumers demand and are indulged with often unnecessary diagnostics and procedures, medicines, and specialist care. Furthermore, the lifestyles and unhealthy behaviors of the consumers are behind preventable ailments, dramatically increasing demand for medical treatment. Note that the medical costs of obesity alone have been estimated at $147 billion a year (Finkelstein et al. 2009). The commercialization of medicine brought with it great advances in the field, yet it also altered behavior of medical providers, equipment and drug manufacturers, and also the choices of medical students and physicians. The resulting search to maximize profits (leading to alarming cases of fraud, shortages in the lower paying primary care positions, and increases in medically unnecessary procedures, among others) is frequently against the best interest of the patients and has broad social implications. Finally, there is also the system of medical liability, which encourages what are often frivolous lawsuits and requires costly malpractice insurance. These costs are ultimately borne by the patient (or their insurance provider). Moreover, as physicians choose to limit risky procedures lowering their exposure to potential lawsuits, the patients' options are limited. The medical malpractice and defensive medicine are estimated to cost between $50 and $200 billion annually (Faguet 2013). These are some of the reasons why the US medical system as a whole delivers lower value at skyrocketing costs.

Cognizant of the runaway health care costs, the barriers faced by people in small group and individual insurance markets in obtaining reasonable and affordable coverage, as well as the past challenges in passing health care reforms, the ACA designers crafted a legislation to be acceptable to the industry[4] as well as to (many) voters. At the high level, the ACA set out to meet three key goals (Rawal 2016). The first was to expand the coverage of the uninsured individuals, a steadily growing group that numbered nearly 50 million people by 2010. The second goal was to steer the health care system toward paying for value rather than volume. As well, the legislation was to be financially sustainable. Among the key strategies to temper the increasing costs were to bring more individuals to the insured pool thus reducing the uncompensated care costs, and to reform payment and delivery (Rawal 2016), hence making these goals complementary.

The central design of the ACA was inspired by a solution adopted in Massachusetts in 2006. The legislation became known as Romneycare, for the state's conservative governor, Mitt Romney, who had supported it and signed it into law. This design was partly informed by the work of an MIT economist Jonathan Gruber, who, working within the politico-industrial realities (Brill 2015), developed a "three-legged stool" model (Gruber 2010) of health insurance reform. New regulations, called "guaranteed issue," prohibit insurance providers from denying coverage based on a client's preexisting conditions or gender, form one of the tripod's legs. The premiums are to be determined solely based on one's age and tobacco use, so they will be the same price for people in these categories. However, while this appears to be a fair approach, it is not a complete solution. If consumers can purchase insurance at any time, especially in time of need, they may opt not to buy insurance. These "free riders" then drive the system to ever higher prices. The second leg, a mandate for everyone to buy insurance, thus aims to distribute risk among the more and less healthy and provide community-rated pricing to the client pool. Finally, not the least for the skewed US health care costs, the community-rated pricing may not be affordable to all individuals aiming to buy insurance. Hence, the third leg of the stool is insurance subsidies by the government.

All three of the above components are essential to a working solution. "Pulling out any of the legs while leaving one or two intact will critically undercut gains from reform," explains the designer (Gruber 2010, 3). Gruber felt like it was crucial to reiterate this logical proposition, given the guaranteed issue and subsidies were welcome while the individual mandate received repeated political pushback (until it was finally repealed in 2017). Without such a mandate, experience showed, the nongroup markets saw extreme increases in premiums. Moreover, Gruber estimated that removing the mandate would reduce the legislation's gains from coverage by 75% while reducing spending by only 25%. It is not difficult to appreciate that allowing the healthy to opt out of the markets while subsidizing those that need the insurance undermines the system.

The ACA's 400,000 words, and the post-enactment regulations exceeding 30 times this number (Starr 2013), suggest the scale of the undertaking. The result is a complete rebuilding of individual insurance markets which were serving about 13 million people in 2012, the largest expansion of Medicaid since its 1963 establishment, along with a number of other innovations.[5] The ACA has created health exchanges, or regulated insurance marketplaces, where individuals can select from and purchase standardized plans. These and all other plans offered by private and public providers must meet the Essential Health Benefits (EHB) requirements, giving everyone the same level of expectations and access to basic services. Further, the plans cannot have limits on annual or lifetime benefits. Both requirements meant that most of the so-called catastrophic plans were non-compliant and had to updated or canceled. In terms of employer requirements, large firms are "subject to new reporting requirements, waiting period requirements for new employees, new taxes on high-cost plans, maintaining young adults on their parents' policies until 26 years of age, requiring coverage with no cost-sharing for approved preventive services, and contributing to the Patient-Centered Outcomes Research Institute" (Rawal 2016). To aid businesses with 100 employees or less, the ACA established health exchanges for small businesses while offering tax credits to reduce their coverage costs (Rawal 2016).

In order to try and control the rising costs, nearly all the Act's interventions are targeted at the Medicare program on account of its political feasibility and strategic value, aiming to reduce or eliminate unnecessary items and services, and prevent fraudulent claims (Kinney 2015). Specifically, this established programs including the Accountable Care Organizations (ACOs), Hospital Readmissions Reductions Program, or Value-Based Purchasing for hospitals (Rawal 2016). As well the ACA focused on "encouraging the implementation of patient centered medical homes (PCMHs), temporarily increasing Medicaid payments to primary care providers, workforce training and loan repayment programs aimed at increasing the number of primary care providers, and additional funding for Federally Qualified Health Centers" (Rawal 2016), aiming to prop up primary care, the decline of which was seen as a contributing factor to quality and cost issues.

The Act's reforms have made coverage possible for many who could not previously obtain insurance due to costs or preexisting conditions. These changes were accompanied by much uncertainty for the insurers in terms of the numbers and types of potential clients and hence in calculating costs and premiums. To mitigate the insurers' initial uncertainty, the ACA has thus provided two temporary mechanisms, risk corridors and reinsurance, placing limits on insurers' gains and losses and subsidizing insurers' expenses on costly consumers, respectively. It has also provided risk adjustment, a permanent mechanism designed to transfer payments from insurers with a lower-risk pools to others with riskier subscribers. Finally, to make the legislation budget neutral, the designers included a series of revenue-generating measures effective over time, including tax increases on various medical sector businesses and (mainly high income) individuals, reduced payments to Medicare providers, and established penalties against employers with 50 or more employees who do not provide health care. Uninsured individuals who opted not to purchase insurance were also subject to a penalty, which was designed to be an incentive rather than a way to increase revenue.

On Full Display

The ACA passed narrowly and without bipartisan support, perhaps foretelling of its difficult future. Following its enactment, the ACA survived multiple attempts at its repeal as well as two Supreme Court challenges, one (in 2012) on the constitutionality of the individual mandate, the other (in 2015) on the legality of its subsidies. The individual mandate—a failed policy experiment for some, a vital component of a sustainable solution for others—was repealed at last in 2017 (Scott and Kliff 2017). As well, the ACA outreach and advertising were cut by 90%, enrollment support reduced by 40%, and cost-sharing reductions, or payments to insurers to reduce low-income subscribers' out of pocket expenses, were eliminated (Scott 2018). The uncertainty that has lead up to these changes together with the structural problems of the marketplace (both of which are ongoing) have caused some insurers to pull out of certain locales, while others have withdrawn from individual health insurance markets altogether (Beasley 2017).

While split relatively evenly between support and opposition when measured shortly after the enactment as well as in 2016, the public opinion on the ACA has been relatively volatile in between these pollings (Swift 2016). On the whole, the left-leaning supporters (mostly Democrats) have hoped for a more equitable, accessible, and sustainable health care, ultimately leading to better health outcomes of the population. The conservatives (mostly supporters of the Republican Party), on the other hand, have supported keeping the government away from interfering in pricing, management, and innovation in health care, and thus have been disinterested in government involvement in extending health care to everyone (Rawal 2016). Yet, there are other undercurrents to reforming health care, one of the most sensitive issues in America. As Brill (2015) notes, given health care is the biggest sector of the economy and the largest expense faced by an average American family, it is about money. As well, it is about interests, whether of unions protecting the prerogatives of their members, health providers and manufacturers maximizing their profits, or individual politicians striving to bring benefits to their jurisdictions. But, as Brill reminds, it is also about the fear of sickness which comes with the desire to prevent it and, if needed, cure it effectively. It is hence about emotion too (2015).

Such a contentious policy area and a complex legislation should have made the public conversation on the ACA diligent, extensive, and technical. This is especially the case considering the alarming trends in costs and outcomes described at the outset. However—and this is why we have chosen to use it an example—the discourse became the opposite, rather trivialized. In general, confident claims had been advanced on how the ACA would alter access to care, reduce the number of jobs, limit consumer choices, affect those with employer-provided coverage, provide disincentives for people to work, increase taxes, as well as on its financial sustainability. In fact, many of these were statements based on obscure assumptions, distractions neglecting the key issues altogether, or myths disconnected from reality.

Let us return to Gruber for a moment who admitted during the design discussions that while Romneycare was successful in expanding coverage, there were budget overruns (Brill 2015). This is one of the reasons some saw prudence in a four-legged stool design that adds a *public option*, or the ability for consumers in individual markets to purchase a Medicare-type government plan. Without it, some argued, "the other parties that comprise America's nonsystem of health care—private insurers, doctors, hospitals, drug companies, and medical suppliers—have little or no incentive to supply high-quality care at a lower cost than they do now" (Reich 2009). More specifically, given its economies of scale, this publicly run insurance plan would not only increase competition in the insurance markets, it could also use "its bargaining power to push back against drug makers, medical device manufacturers, hospital systems and other health care providers that have become increasingly consolidated" (Hacker 2016). Moreover, as a public service, the public option was seen to improve accountability, and to provide a not-for-profit alternative to consumers now subject to individual mandate (Halpin and Harbage 2010). Finally, it would help to improve coverage of the underserved markets.

While a consensus around the basic public option model had developed among the supporters, it began to break during the design debates that centered on "how much to pay physicians and hospitals; whether there should be a single, federal purchaser or a number of smaller state or regional purchasers; and how to determine eligibility for purchasing in the exchange" (Halpin and Harbage 2010, 1120). Ultimately, "[b]oth sides of the debate suffered from a lack of data to make their points, with ideology often trumping analysis and opinion offered in lieu of evidence," comment Halpin and Harbage (2010, 1120). This was indeed the quintessence of the greater ACA debate, one in which the benefits and drawbacks of the major elements of the solution "could be condensed into sound bites about 'taking on big insurance companies' or 'a government takeover of health care' in a way that the complex issues of health care financing could not," observe Halpin and Harbage (2010, 1120). It was a debate with which the public had seemed to go along very well. At last, despite its inclusion in the House of Representatives' version of the health care bill and some last-minute maneuvering in the Senate (Halpin and Harbage 2010), the public option did not make it into the final legislation, changing with it the depth and the direction the reform has taken.

The "government takeover of health care" frame was not unique to the aforementioned debate. Indeed, it was the most popular argument throughout the legislative process. The credit for this idea is due to a Republican strategist Frank Luntz, who had authored a memo titled "The Language of Health Care 2009" (Luntz 2009), offering what ended up to be widely used talking points against the planned reforms. Acknowledging the crisis and the need for reforms but reframing both as a bureaucratic problem, the memo channels some familiar messages (also exemplified by Fig. 2.1):

> "Time" is the government health care killer...Nothing else turns people against the government takeover of health care than the realistic expectation that it will result in delayed and potentially even denied treatment, procedures and/or medications...Delayed care is denied care...You'll notice we recommend the phrase "government takeover" rather than "government run" or "government controlled" [sic] It's because too many politician say "we don't want a government run healthcare system like Canada or Great Britain" without explaining those consequences. There is a better approach. "In countries with government run health care, politicians make YOUR health care decisions. THEY decide if you'll get the procedure you need, or if you are disqualified because the treatment is too expensive or because you are too old. We can't have that in America". (Luntz 2009)

To be sure, as outlined above, while the ACA reorganized individual insurance markets, added requirements for insurance plans, reformed further the Medicare program, and added a number of medical industry regulations, it was no takeover. Ironically, "it was a classic Republican/business lobbyists' solution that was exactly the opposite: The government was fortifying the private market by subsidizing millions of new paying customers for the still-private health care system," notes Brill (2018). What made this discourse particularly striking was the fact that "[a]t no time did the Republicans offer an alternative to Obamacare, no doubt because Obamacare had always been *their* alternative," adds Brill (2018, emphasis original) recalling Romneycare. In the end, the government takeover sound bite became so ubiquitous that a major fact-checking website, Politifact, designated it as the "Lie of the Year" (Adair and Holan 2010).

Aside from the dominant talk of takeovers, there were a number of other trivialized claims made on both sides of the argument, including the ongoing debates on cost. Each camp has used different assumptions

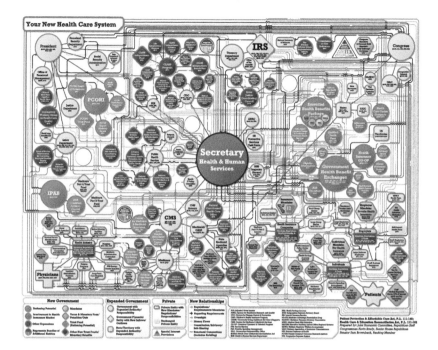

Fig. 2.1 "Your New Health Care System" [6]

and timeframes while drawing selectively on the Congressional Budget Office (CBO) estimates and other sources:

> Republican estimates of the cost of the law took later years into account or asserted that the cost of the law is rising because of the flaws in the law itself—not because of the general underlying cost trends in health care. Meanwhile, Democrats have focused not on the cost of the coverage expansion itself, which is significant, but on the fact that the cost is paid for in the law and does not add to the deficit,

notes Rawal (2016). So "the primary reason for disagreement on the cost of the ACA is that opponents and supporters of the law are comparing apples and oranges," adds the author (2016). While CBO provided some baseline as per its mandate, it must be added that in these complex politico-economic systems even "minor deviations from initial assumptions can lead to massively different long-term outcomes" (Faguet 2013, 3), rendering long-term forecasts highly unreliable. Consider, for example, that "not expecting major fiscal policy changes and American involvement in two wars that reversed balanced budgets achieved during President Clinton's second term in office, CBO projected continuous budget surpluses after 2001, reaching \$5.6 trillion by 2011" (Faguet 2013, 3), rather than a deficit several fold this number.

There are many other implications of the ACA that cannot yet be known, including on its overall effects on health outcomes, the ACOs' quality improvements and cost reductions, the efficacy of helping small businesses to insure their employees, or its impact on the rising health care costs, especially in light of the recent legislative changes. The lack of any meaningful evidence has not stopped the proponents and opponents in making claims for or against these with vehemence as in the examples provided.[7] We do not intend to engage these further, as we believe the above discussion was sufficient in meeting its aims.

Conclusion

A prominent author once noted: "If you're going to tell the truth about something as complicated as health care and health care reform, you probably need at least four sentences," adding "[y]ou can't do it in four words."[8] While this comment was made in the context of the "government takeover of health care" frame, it nevertheless shows another, deeper issue in contemporary thinking. A *few* sentences will neither get us to the truth nor bring us to a reasoned dialogue on contemporary matters. Indeed, the chapter's case study can serve as an illustration on this point. We began with the main characteristics of the US health care system, supplied relevant data, and presented its chief challenges, before engaging the key parts of a complex and contested legislation aiming to cope with some of these issues. Mindful of space, we still took up several pages to establish a minimum foundation to begin to discuss the limitations of the legislation and the political discourse around it. We hoped to highlight that any discussion of the reform must be privy to these fundamentals. Only then we can show that despite the criticisms, the reform maintains the system's reliance on the markets in the delivery of coverage and services. As well, it has not altered the industry-wide pricing power (Faguet 2013) and thus did not address the fundamental issue of spiraling costs. A closer look at some of the lapses in the discourse surrounding its enactment then invites the question on the outcomes of an informed, substantive political dialogue—one that avoids trivialization, one prioritizing public interest.[9]

Through our examples above, we have seen phrases and slogans dominate the public discourse. At the same time, we witnessed virtually a complete lack of substance. Thus, the frequently mentioned ideology and polarization cannot be the only barriers to a dialogue and to rebuilding public culture. There must be other factors which enable, and in turn are reinforced by, this condition. These factors hold us back from a broad appreciation of a world filled with nuances and complexities, and from recognizing the importance of working with more than just ideas. Such factors must be deeper, rooted in the way we think. In the next chapter, we identify the key ones and show how they enable trivialization.

NOTES

1. More in Hacker (1998).
2. When adjusted for purchasing power.
3. Also in Mahar (2006) and in a high-profile exposé by Brill (2013).
4. The medical industry was the main obstacle of the Clinton health reform of 1993–1994 (Rawal 2016).
5. Unless otherwise noted, the ACA discussion in the rest of this section draws on Rawal (2016).
6. This chart was produced by the Joint Economic Committee of the US Congress (JEC 2010). Its then chair, Rep. Kevin Brady, and his Republican colleagues used it to support the position the ACA "reform morphed into a monstrosity of new bureaucracies, mandates, taxes and rationing that will drive up health care costs, hurt seniors and force our most intimate health care choices into the hands of Washington bureaucrats" (JEC 2010). The brief document accompanying the chart comes short of substantiating such a statement, however.
7. The reader may find more on the facts and fiction in the ACA debate in Rawal (2016).
8. Attributed to author Maggie Mahar (in Adair and Holan 2010).
9. What might such a solution look like? Faguet (2013), an accomplished physician and author, offers his blueprint for a systemic reform.

REFERENCES

ACP (American College of Physicians). 2007. *Achieving a high performance health care system with universal access: What the United States can learn from other countries.* Philadelphia: American College of Physicians. https://www.acponline.org/system/files/documents/advocacy/where_we_stand/assets/highperf_hc_universal_access_2007.pdf.

Adair, Bill, and Angie Drobnic Holan. 2010. "Politifact's Lie of the Year: 'A government takeover of health care.'" *Politifact.com*, December 16. http://www.politifact.com/truth-o-meter/article/2010/dec/16/lie-year-government-takeover-health-care/.

Alesina, Alberto, and Edward Ludwig Glaeser. 2004. *Fighting poverty in the US and Europe: A world of difference.* New York: Oxford University Press.

Aucoin, Peter. 1990. "Administrative reform in public management: Paradigms, principles, paradoxes and pendulums." *Governance* 3 (2): 115–137.

Beasly, Deena. 2017. "Aetna fully exits Obamacare exchanges with pull-out in two states." *Reuters*, May 10. https://www.reuters.com/article/us-aetna-obamacare/aetna-fully-exits-obamacare-exchanges-with-pull-out-in-two-states-idUSKBN1862XK.

Béland, Daniel. 2005. "Ideas and social policy: An institutionalist perspective." *Social Policy & Administration* 39 (1): 1–18.

Béland, Daniel, and Robert Henry Cox, eds. 2010. *Ideas and politics in social science research.* Oxford: Oxford University Press.

Berman, Sheri. 2010. "Ideology, history, and politics." In *Ideas and politics in social science research*, edited by Daniel Béland and Robert Henry Cox. Oxford: Oxford University Press.

Bleich, Erik. 2002. "Integrating ideas into policy-making analysis: Frames and race politics in Britain and France." *Comparative Political Studies* 35 (9): 1054–1076.

Brill, Steven. 2013. "Bitter pill: Why medical bills are killing us." *Time*, March 4.

Brill, Steven. 2015. *America's bitter pill: Money, politics, backroom deals, and the fight to fix our broken healthcare system.* New York: Random House.

Brill, Steven. 2018. *Tailspin: The people and forces behind America's fifty-year fall—And those fighting to reverse it.* New York: Knopf.

CMS (Centers for Medicare and Medicaid Services). 2018. "National Health Expenditure Data." https://www.cms.gov/Research-Statistics-Data-and-Systems/Statistics-Trends-and-Reports/NationalHealthExpendData/NationalHealthAccountsHistorical.html.

Faguet, Guy. B. 2013. *The Affordable Care Act: A missed opportunity, A better way forward.* New York: Algora Publishing.

Finkelstein, Eric A., Justin G. Trogdon, Joel W. Cohen, and William Dietz. (2009). "Annual medical spending attributable to obesity: Payer-and service-specific estimates." *Health Affairs* 28 (5). https://doi.org/10.1377/hlthaff.28.5.w822.

Gruber, Jonathan. 2010. *Health care reform is a "three-legged stool": The cost of partially repealing the Affordable Care Act.* Center for American Progress Action Fund.

Hacker, Jacob. 1998. "The historical logic of national health insurance: Structure and sequence in the development of British, Canadian, and U.S. medical policy." *Studies in American Political Development* 12 (1): 57.

Hacker, Jacob. 2016. "A public option would greatly improve Obamacare." *The New York Times*, August 24. https://www.nytimes.com/roomfordebate/2016/08/24/is-obamacare-sustainable/a-public-option-would-greatly-improve-obamacare.

Hall, Peter A, ed. 1989. *The political power of economic ideas: Keynesianism across nations.* Princeton, NJ: Princeton University Press.

Hall, Peter A. 1993. "Policy paradigms, social learning, and the state: The case of economic policymaking in Britain." *Comparative Politics* 25 (4): 275–296.

Hall, Peter A. 1997. "The role of interests, institutions, and ideas in the comparative political economy of the industrialized nations." In *Comparative politics: Rationality, culture, and structure*, edited by Mark I. Lichbach and Alan S. Zuckerman, 174–207. Cambridge, UK: Cambridge University Press.

Halpin, Helen A., and Peter Harbage. 2010. "The origins and demise of the public option." *Health Affairs* 29 (6): 1117–1124.

Inglehart, Ronald. 1997. *Modernization and postmodernization: Cultural, economic, and political change in 43 societies.* Princeton: Princeton University Press.

Inglehart, Ronald, and Pippa Norris. 2016. "Trump, Brexit, and the rise of populism: Economic have-nots and cultural backlash." HKS Faculty Research Working Paper Series (RWP16–026).

JEC (Joint Economic Committee). 2010. "Health Care Chart." https://www.jec.senate.gov/public/index.cfm/republicans/committeenews?ID=bb302d88-3d0d-4424-8e33-3c5d2578c2b0.

Kingdon, John W. 1995. *Agendas, alternatives and public policies.* 3rd ed. New York: Longman.

Kinney, Eleanor D. 2015. *The affordable care act and medicare in comparative context.* Cambridge, UK: Cambridge University Press.

Luntz, Frank. 2009. "The language of health care 2009: The 10 rules for stopping the 'Washington takeover' of health care." https://www.politico.com/pdf/PPM116_luntz.pdf. As cited in Rawal (2016).

Mahar, Maggie. 2006. *Money driven medicine: The real reason health care costs so much.* New York: HarperCollins.

Mehta, Jal. 2010. "The varied roles of ideas in politics: From 'whether' to 'how'." In *Ideas and politics in social science research*, edited by Daniel Béland and Robert Henry Cox. Oxford: Oxford University Press.

OECD. 2014. "OECD health statistics 2014: How does the United States compare?" http://www.oecd.org/unitedstates/Briefing-Note-UNITEDSTATES-2014.pdf.

OECD. 2017. "Health expenditure per capita." In *Health at a glance 2017: OECD indicators.* Paris: OECD Publishing. https://www.oecd-ilibrary.org/social-issues-migration-health/health-at-a-glance_19991312.

Oliver, Michael J., and Hugh Pemberton. 2004. "Learning and change in 20th century British economic policy." *Governance* 17 (3): 415–441.

Parsons, Craig. 2007. *How to map arguments in political science*. Oxford: Oxford University Press.

Politico. 2017. "18 confusing things Donald Trump has said about health care." https://www.politico.com/magazine/story/2017/07/20/18-confusing-contradictory-and-just-plain-kooky-things-donald-trump-has-said-about-health-care-215402.

Rawal, Purva H. 2016. *The Affordable Care Act: Examining the facts*. Santa Barbara: ABC-CLIO.

Reich, Robert. 2009. "Why we need a public health-care plan." *The Wall Street Journal*, June 24. https://www.wsj.com/articles/SB124580516633344953.

Robinson, Marilynne. 2010. *Absence of mind: The dispelling of inwardness from the modern myth of the self*. New Haven: Yale University Press.

Rodrik, Dani. 2011. *The globalization paradox: Democracy and the future of the world economy*. New York: W. W. Norton.

Scott, Dylan. 2018. "After one year of Trump, Obamacare is actually doing fine." *Vox*, April 5. https://www.vox.com/policy-and-politics/2018/4/5/17198362/obamacare-enrollment-2018-trump-sabotaging.

Scott, Dylan, and Sarah Kliff. 2017. "Republicans have finally repealed a crucial piece of Obamacare." *Vox*, December 20. https://www.vox.com/policy-and-politics/2017/11/14/16651698/obamacare-individual-mandate-republican-tax-bill.

Smeltz, Dina, Craig Kafura, and Lily Wojtowicz. 2016. "Actually, Americans like free trade." *The Chicago Council on Global Affairs*, September 7. https://www.thechicagocouncil.org/publication/actually-americans-free-trade.

Starr, Penny. 2013. "11,588,500 words: Obamacare regs 30x as long as law." *CNSNews*, October 14. http://cnsnews.com/.

Stone, Deborah A. 1989. "Causal stories and the formation of policy agendas." *Political Science Quarterly* 104 (2), 281–300.

Swift, Art. 2016. "Americans slowly embracing Affordable Care Act more." Gallup, Inc. http://www.gallup.com/.

UCB (U.S. Census Bureau). 2010. "Income, poverty, and health insurance coverage in the United States: 2009." https://www.census.gov/library/publications/2010/demo/p60-238.html.

Zaller, John R. 2005 (1992). *The nature and origins of mass opinion*. New York: Cambridge University Press.

CHAPTER 3

The Uneasy World of "Isms"

Why does trivialization occur, and, moreover, how do we allow it? For one, as Eno suggests, "[i]f we don't know the sources of the attitudes we hold, we can avoid taking responsibility for them and leave ourselves plenty of ways of saying we weren't really wrong—or that the thing that has turned out to be wrong wasn't what we meant anyway" (in Brockman 2009). This false peace of mind found in the surrendering of our responsibility to think is among the reasons. And, if history is of any indication, it carries potentially deep consequences, as we will discuss. But as apparent from the preceding chapter, trivialization may also be a product of more or less deliberate behaviors enabled by a number of cultural features and legacies. Here, we argue there are several underlying, related, and broadly committed failings in the way we describe and understand the world which shape our discourses and sustain trivialization. These are the persistence of essentialism, the drive toward reductionism, and the appeal of relativism, as discussed in turn.

Essentialism

A part of the drive to interpret and understand our environment is a propensity to organize it, map its elements into natural categories based on various properties, and trace causes to these categories. Such groupings—including political economies, languages, people, or histories—are intuitively taken to have intrinsic, defining properties, an *essence*. The essence, in turn, explains the similarities among the categories' elements. Moreover,

O. Bubak and H. Jacek, *Trivialization and Public Opinion*,
https://doi.org/10.1007/978-3-030-17925-0_3

words referring to these natural or social categories are presumed to map directly onto them (Gelman 2003). While this thinking, legitimated most famously by Plato, works well in some categories such as geometry and can be useful as an analytical guide, its generalization has proven to be a barrier to scientific work as well as to our perceptions and designs of social and political domains. To illustrate, consider a set of essentialist propositions in Box 3.1.

Box 3.1 Key assumptions of essentialism

1. The category of "birds" is not an artificial grouping invented simply for the convenience of humans. Rather, birds belong together in some natural sense. We discovered the category of birds.
2. There are many nonobvious properties that birds have in common with one another, including properties that people haven't yet discovered but will discover in the future.
3. There is some underlying property (maybe genetic code? maybe evolutionary history?) that causes birds to be alike.
4. Many commonalities that birds share are biologically determined.
5. Throughout its existence, an entity that is once a bird is always a bird—it cannot be turned into some other kind of thing.
6. Something either is or is not a bird—it can't be kind of a bird or "partly" a bird.

Source Gelman (2003, 23)

While at first glance intuitive, it is not difficult to see the distracting potential of this thinking, especially when dealing with the continuous, adaptive, and interrelated character of natural and social *systems* whose constituents evolve gradually, over extended periods of time. In the context of biology, for instance, given the efforts that have gone into taxonomies bringing into salience the labels for various ancestors in the phylogenetic tree, it may be tempting to conclude that there was an essential individual, the first in line of a new species. But it was the rejection of these notions that lead Darwin to refocus from the traditional study of variation with respect to a model individual toward the study of population-wide variation and its transmission. Hence possible was the formulation of his theory of evolution by natural selection.

Nevertheless even as this new perspective gained purchase, "essentialism held fast, as biologists declared that genes are the essence of all living things, fully accounting for Darwin's variation" (Barrett 2015). The ensuing research thus tried to connect various outcomes with particular genes, reflecting thinking there was a clear causal mapping between, for example, an ailment and a gene. This essentialist thinking, Barrett points out, led to apparently plausible and easy to understand conclusions, such as: "Gene X causes cancer." As biologists learned the crucial role environmental factors—such as diet, temperature, air, or water quality—play in the expression of genes, they have pushed their field into a new paradigm. An updated conclusion, channeling the recognition that most natural phenomena have multiple causes, was thus formulated: "A given individual in a given situation, who interprets that situation as stressful, may experience a change in his sympathetic nervous system that encourages certain genes to be expressed, making him vulnerable to cancer" (Barrett 2015). This was great progress, but scientists in general have not fully rejected essentialism, instead finding causes in more elaborate, reclassified types. "This technique of creating ever finer categories, each with its own biological essence (rather than abandoning essentialism, as Darwin and Einstein did) is considered scientific progress," notes Barrett (2015). Intense debates hence continue, fueled by tendencies to separate and classify.

Even more visible have been the persistent nature versus nurture arguments across psychology, linguistics, or cognitive sciences. "Human-nature thinking leads to the conclusion that causes of behavior can be divided into nature and nurture," comments Richerson (2015). Looking for causes in either nature or nurture and arguing for dominance of one over the other distracts from the possibility that they are mutually constitutive. Indeed, there is mounting evidence these are inseparable.

> The elaboration of technology over the last 2 million years has roughly paralleled the evolution of larger brains and other anatomical changes. We have clear examples of cultural changes driving genetic evolution, such as the evolution of dairying driving the evolution of adult lactase persistence. Socially learned technology could have been doing similar things all throughout the last 2 million years,

adds Richerson (2015). As we examine the progress of knowledge, we are increasingly privy to the pitfalls of essentialism in sciences, and see partial successes in freeing inquiry from its grip. Encompassing change, however, will require a new worldview, a new way of asking questions. This, as we will discuss, may be on the horizon (Chapter 9).

Essentialism, as hinted, is not restricted to sciences. Indeed, this has been one of the pitfalls of general discourse. Reinforced by what some call *state simplifications* (Kohli et al. 1995), we encounter much of it daily. Given their prerogatives to make policies and deliver services, among other functions, governments standardize. They group, label, count, measure, and codify while emphasizing simplification, regularity, and uniformity. People, for example, are classified by their age, income, education, race, employment status, or employment type, among others, in forms, statistics, legal documents, or reports. "All auto workers, if we are classifying by industry, are the same. All Catholics, if we are classifying by religious faith, are the same," observes Scott (Kohli et al. 1995). Unfortunately, these broad strokes condition us to judgments not unlike those of essentializing science. Consider Dawkins (2015) as he discusses some of the manifestations of what he calls "the tyranny of the discontinuous mind:"

> We define a poverty "line": You are either "above" or "below" it. But poverty is a continuum. Why not say, in dollar-equivalents, how poor you actually are? The preposterous Electoral College system in U.S. presidential elections is another, and especially grievous, manifestation of essentialist thinking. Florida must go either wholly Republican or wholly Democrat—all twenty- nine Electoral College votes—even though the popular vote is a dead heat. But states should not be seen as essentially red or blue: They're mixtures in various proportions.

Tyranny may be a strong word, nevertheless, it is apparent from Dawkins's comments that essentialism narrows horizons even in critique. Speaking of a poverty line focuses attention on income and hints to solutions that involve a type of monetary intervention, such as redistributive or minimum wage policies. This construct may have been apt in the growing, industrial economies of yesteryear. But what if poverty is redefined as the inability of individuals to reach their full potential? Here, questions of education and underemployment, especially acute in today's polarized economies, come to the fore. Likewise, speaking of reds and blues or the Electoral Colleges distracts from a problem of the increasingly deficient majoritarian, two party system. This design may have helped in solving the governance challenges of a young nation, but becomes a significant obstacle to modern-day demands for representation of an increasingly diverse population.

It too must be noted that not all implications of essentialist reasoning are negative. As it admits the presence of unobservable properties, it also recognizes that "observable surface features cannot be privileged, simpler, or more basic" (Gelman 2003, 13), helping us to obtain a more comprehensive mapping of the world around us. At the same time, Alberts can advance essentialism as a way to "describe a class of empirical and analytic approaches in which variables are titrated, distilled, inserted, and/or modeled in an effort to reveal the essential elements necessary and sufficient for the expression of complexity" (2002, 379). Unfortunately as discussed above, essentialist thinking can be problematic. Recall Gelman's propositions from Box 3.1 and, in an exercise of essentializing, consider replacing the word "bird" with an identification for some group of people. It is easy to see how such thinking feeds stereotyping as peoples come to be "treated as distinct in deep, nonobvious ways, and social group differences are assumed to be innately determined and fixed" (Gelman 2003, 13). This at best misinforms causes and leads to inappropriate solutions and at worst leads to groupism and social division.

REDUCTIONISM

What factors determine the creation and consolidation of democratic regimes? is a perennial question of social sciences. Acemoglu and Robinson's *Economic Origins of Dictatorship and Democracy* (2005) is among the more visible attempts to answer it. Aware of the extent of this task, the authors' use Occam's razor, an idea that "entities must not be multiplied beyond necessity,"[1] a favorite of an English friar-philosopher William of Ockham.

> Given the complexity of the issues with which we are dealing, we frequently make use of this principle in this book not only to simplify the answers to complex questions but, perhaps even more daringly, to also simplify the questions. In fact, in an attempt to focus our basic questions, we use Occam's razor rather brutally and heroically. We abstract from

> many interesting details and also leave some equally important questions
> out of our investigation,

explain Acemoglu and Robinson with candor (2005, 16). The authors thus embark on their study informed by a non-scientific principle which has been applied for centuries across disciplines in guiding theoretical choices. Occam's razor has been used to simplify the object of study, as did Acemoglu and Robinson. It has also been invoked to adjudicate among several theoretically grounded explanations of a given phenomenon. The most parsimonious explanation is to be preferred over one which appears complex or superfluous.

Overarching here has been a philosophy that all sciences can be *reduced* to physics, that is, we can understand all complex phenomena in terms of the properties and interactions of their constituent elements. Impressed by the successes of reductionism in natural sciences, whose fundamental laws elegantly describe physical realities, scholars across sciences have thus been driven in the same direction. Acemoglu and Robinson are then welcome to condense a set of complex social interactions—which unfold over time within different institutional contexts among numerous factions with varied interests and worldviews—into a parsimonious model capturing a contest between two economically motivated groups, the citizens and the elites. Ultimately, the argument made is that factors leading to democracy, including the level of inequality, economic stability, or the ability to organize, are predictable. But can political, economic, sociocultural, and other complex systems be reduced into a few elements and their outcomes reliably predicted?

> The social sciences are hard because human beings differ fundamentally
> from inanimate objects. People insist on making or finding meaning in
> things. They do it collectively, creating baroque cultural landscapes that
> can't be explained parsimoniously, and they do it individually, creating
> their own unique symbolic worlds nested within their broader cultures. As
> the anthropologist Clifford Geertz put it, "Man is an animal suspended in
> webs of significance he himself has spun." This is why it's so hard to predict what any individual will do,

comments Haidt (2015), hinting to an answer to the above question. Indeed, it is not just social sciences, but other domains—dealing with types of systems whose elements interact with each other and their environment—that pose similar challenges. This is because these interactions often produce emergent phenomena, higher-order properties that cannot be understood solely from the study of the individual units. These phenomena are thus inherently unpredictable, even in cases with relatively few units. For instance, consider a flock of birds in the typical V formation. There is no leader or central coordinator, as each bird responds only based on the positions of the adjacent birds. The V shape of the flock thus emerges based on a set of pair-interaction rules (Sawyer 2005). Similarly, a litter of Norway rats, animals known for their huddling behavior, exhibits characteristics which are different from its individual pups. These huddles display an emergent, energy-conserving property, whereby the exposed surface of the huddle is dynamically adjusted with respect to the temperature of the surrounding environment (Alberts 2002).

In these examples from the natural world, the signals used in interactions among the units are relatively basic, making them easier to study. So, especially challenging is the study of social systems, including economies, nations, or markets whose human constituents interact with symbols and languages that undergo a continuous (re)interpretation. Any reductive attempts at understanding these systems or at making predictions about their outcomes are at best partial, and, as we will discuss, can be deeply consequential.

We have touched on reductionism in social sciences, which, as we will discuss (Chapters 8 and 9), is at last being challenged with research made possible by novel methods and technologies. Unfortunately, just as its cousin essentialism, reductionism permeates the social discourse—influencing the way we treat causes, see problems, and accept solutions—with broad implications. Among the most significant are individualistic explanations where the social is distilled to the individual (Sayer 2010). In this view, personal outcomes such as education, social stratum, and income are wholly determined by individual actions. In the contrary view, the influence is reduced upwards, from the individual to society. Here, individuals have little control over their fortunes which are seen as products of cultural, material, or social forces and their combinations. Such a thinking in turn informs a number of fundamental positions on equality, fairness, mobility, and any associated preferences and solutions. For instance, accepting that individual effort and ability, rather than factors such as luck or connections, determine one's success, leads to (and justifies) other ideas, such as economic meritocracy. In this system, economic resources are distributed based on individual merit, rather than class or heritage. As economic outcomes are connected to one's effort, inequalities in these outcomes are accepted as normal. Consequently, leveling the playing field and providing equality of opportunity become the key social concerns; and education is expected to provide the solutions.[2]

A look behind the curtain reveals that these are mere ideas, appealing reductions disconnected from evidence. In their earlier mentioned study, Alesina and Glaeser (2004) note the disparities in the perceptions of social mobility in the United States and Europe. The authors point out that about 60% of US respondents believe that their land of opportunity provides an upward mobility to those willing to work hard. In Europe, the same proportion believes just the opposite. Yet, while measuring income mobility has some limits, multiple studies have shown its levels in the US and Europe to be comparable, or even worse for low-income Americans. "Differences in popular beliefs about income mobility are shaped by politics and indoctrination, not by reality," conclude the authors (2004, 185). And it is reductionism that serves as the enabler of these politics and the policies that follow.

Indeed, due to its natural appeal in explaining economic declines, political and economic doctrines, crises, conflicts, pathologies, accidents, and other phenomena—issues embedded in systems with many layers, dimensions, and relations—in terms of their parts or themes, reductionism can easily lead to misattribution of causality (Sayer 2000). This also means, as hinted above, reduction, whether upwards to structures or downwards to individuals, allows useful *manipulations* of causality toward political, economic, or legal ends. Apt here is Stone's work on causal theories, "stories that describe harms and difficulties, attribute them to actions of other individuals or organizations, and thereby claim the right to invoke government power to stop the harm" (1989, 282). Stone develops a classification of these stories revealing "a systematic process with fairly clear rules of the game by which political actors struggle to control interpretations and images of difficulties" (1989, 282). Causes are thus divided into four categories based on intent and guidance, yielding mechanical (intended but unguided), accidental (unintended and unguided), intentional (intended and guided), and inadvertent (unintended but guided) positions. Actors, based on their aims, thus try to (re)locate their issue either as accidental or within some type of human control.

For illustration,[3] consider the question of obesity, which can be framed as a result of genetics, beyond individual control, and thus without an immediate solution. More commonly, however, actors may argue obesity to be a product of an intended and guided action, a personal choice to enjoy frequent, high-calorie meals and to shy away from physical activity (right position). Obesity could also be presented as a result of intended and unguided action, an addiction to the increasingly engineered, palatable foods. Finally, obesity could be framed as unintended and guided action, stemming from a lack of knowledge or material resources on proper nutrition and exercise, or from the side effects of medical treatments (left position).

Revealing here is the framing of this condition across actors and polities. The Canadian Medical Association (CMA) reports that "causes of obesity are multifarious and highly complex" (CMA 2015); the UK's National Health Service states that "[o]besity is generally caused by eating too much and moving too little" (NHS 2016); or the US National Institutes of Health informs that "[a] number of factors can play a role in weight gain" (NIH 2016). Indeed, as obesity results from a set of causes, focusing attention on one over the other not only fails to address this serious condition, but may exacerbate it. This is one among the many similar contests over social issues, their origins, and the solution space, all products of causal politics. Contemplating the persistence of this politics, Stone concludes that:

> [w]ithout overarching control, there can be no purpose and no responsibility. Complex causal explanations are not very useful in politics, precisely because they do not offer a single locus of control, a plausible candidate to take responsibility for a problem, or a point of leverage to fix a problem. Hence, one of the biggest tensions between political science and real-world politics. The former tends to see complex causes of social problems, while the latter searches for immediate and simple causes. (1989, 289)

Having just read this section on reductionism, the reader may find much to discuss about this statement, whether on the drivers of political discourse or on the methods and goals in the study of politics. But for us, a deeper question is what allows dispensing with complexity in politics in the first place. What sustains a social environment which welcomes simplifications of causes of and prescriptions to—what with a little effort are found to be—complex matters? We believe the three enablers discussed in this chapter provide a good baseline from which to understand this condition.

Relativism

A hero of the Scientific Revolution, artist, mathematician, and communicator, Galileo Galilei needs little introduction. Galileo is known equally for his magisterial *Sidereal Messenger, Sidereus Nuncius* (1610), a pioneering work in experimental astronomy, as his defiance of the central cultural issues of his time, done in a manner others before him could not (Heilbron 2012). Among the number of Galileo's controversies, the case of the cardinal-inquisitor Bellarmine is considered a model example of the emerging modern science coming to a head "with the entrenched forces of religious bigotry and dogma" (Norris 1995, 10). But not for everyone. In his work, a philosopher of science Feyerabend defended the Church's orders delivered in Bellarmine's presence by Michelangelo Seghizzi, the Commissary General of the Holy Roman and Universal Inquisition. Galileo was "...to abandon completely...the opinion that the sun stands still at the center of the world and the earth moves, and henceforth not to hold, teach, or defend it in any way whatever, either orally or in writing" (Heilbron 2012, 218). Arguing that Galileo changed his observational findings to support his theories while disregarding the Church's reasonable stance (see Norris 1995), Feyerabend thus concluded:

> the judgement of the Church experts was scientifically correct and had the right social intention, viz. to protect people from the machinations of specialists. It wanted to protect people from being corrupted by a narrow ideology that might work in restricted domains but was incapable of sustaining a harmonious life. (Feyerabend 1993, 133)

Feyerabend quickly brushes off the brutality of centuries of Inquisition while claiming that "royal or secular courts often matched those of the Inquisition" (1993, 125). But Feyerabend's mission is not to provide a historical account or decide what is right or wrong, but "to knock away those delusory props of objectivity, truth, method, disinterested (value-free) enquiry ... and thus to restore a sense of the radical contingency – along with the various motivating interests" (Norris 1995, 10). These, in the author's view, are always at play in scientific work.

This section opened with Galileo and Feyerabend, two thinkers working more than three hundred and fifty years apart. One is a harbinger of an era of science, an age of "reason, autonomy and freedom of intellectual conscience" (Norris 1995, 10). The other, writing in 1975, not long after the first manned landing on the moon, the first heart transplant, the invention of the integrated circuit, or the successes of the civil rights movement, yet following the unprecedented atrocities of the total wars, manifest environmental destruction, and various social crises, represents a movement skeptical toward science and knowledge, and critical of the excesses of modernity more broadly. Appealing to a range of intellectuals and artists in and out of academia, this eclectic, if influential, movement has come to be known as postmodernism.

While postmodernism involves an assortment of actors and interests, it can be best understood in the context of the Enlightenment whose philosophical and political assumptions are ultimately being questioned. Based on her reading of major postmodern work, Flax identified a number of key Enlightenment themes and claims, the *contradictory* character of which postmodernists hope to reveal. First, there is the coherent, Enlightenment *self*, able to reason, within knowable limits, not only about its own processes but also about the natural world. The foundation and criteria of discourse are provided by philosophy, ensuring "an objective, reliable, and universalizable 'foundation' for knowledge and for judging all truth claims." Knowledge captures a universal and fixed reality existing *independently* of its producer. Discovering and refining our understanding of reality is the prerogative of *science*, serving as "the paradigm of all true knowledge." Knowledge obtained through scientific reasoning can be neutral, and thus, when applied legitimately, supports freedom and advancement. Furthermore, people are inherently good and require time for "progressive perfection … and the ever more complete realization of their capabilities and projects," seen as the purpose of history. Finally, Enlightenment thinkers assume "a realist or correspondence theory of language in which objects are … merely made present to consciousness by naming or by the right use of language" (1990, 30–31). Objects thus exist independently of language.

At the high-level, postmodernist analyses are deconstructions, aiming "to distance us from and make us skeptical about the ideas concerning truth, knowledge, power, history, self, and language that are often taken for granted within and serve as legitimations for contemporary Western culture" (Flax 1990, 29). The postmodernists hence warn us not to trust sweeping historical narratives, philosophical or political doctrines, and scientific claims (more in Butler 2002), all tools of authority. Instead, they argue, the world can be known through many equally valid conceptual systems, where science is merely one of such systems (Boghossian 2006, 2). Knowledge and truth are then reconceived, as explained below:

> Feminist epistemologists, in common with many other strands of contemporary epistemology, no longer regard knowledge as a neutral transparent reflection of an independently existing reality, with truth and falsity established by transcendent procedures of rational assessment. Rather, most accept that all knowledge is situated knowledge, reflecting the position of the knowledge producer at a certain historical moment in a given material and cultural context. (Lennon 1997, 37)

Thus, departing from the traditional view in which philosophy and science inform the search for truth based on objective observations, for postmodernists "whether a belief is knowledge necessarily depends at least in part on the contingent social and material setting in which that belief is produced" (Boghossian 2006, 6). Knowledge is thus constructed socially, through language and discourse, and truth becomes *relative* to a shared conceptual system.

These ideas, whether in their weak constructivist form, focused on social constructions of linguistic or mental *representations* of social facts, or in its strong constructivist version, concerned with causal and constitutive constructions of these social facts (Pascale 2010), have gained following in academia and inspired discourses beyond it. Focusing our attention on ideational factors, intersubjective beliefs, and their role in constructing actors' interests, such perspectives too have helped to enhance our analyses of politics and international relations (Finnemore and Sikkink 2001). As well, they have facilitated new ways of understanding of culture and tradition. An anthropologist explains:

> Using such "contextual" thinking, I no longer saw a lump of slag found in a 5000 BC female grave in Serbia as chance contaminant, by-product garbage from making copper jewelry. Rather, it was a kind of poetic statement

bearing on the relationship between biological and cultural reproduction. Just as births in the Vinča culture were attended by midwives who also delivered the warm but useless slab of afterbirth, so Vinča-culture ore was heated in a clay furnace that gave birth to metal. From the furnace—known from many ethnographies to have projecting clay breasts and a graphically vulvic stoking opening—the smelters delivered technology's baby. With it came a warm but useless lump of slag. (Taylor 2009, 86)

In this case, taking a relativist perspective helped Taylor to make sense of varying cultural meanings and practices over time. However, relativist thinking of different sorts is now increasingly common outside of academia, affecting discourses in politics and the media, ultimately reshaping individual attitudes toward information in the age of the network. Sayer (2000) identifies two main forms of relativist tendencies. The first includes "attempts to relativize truth as a construction of particular communities or dominant groups" (47). Here, given the belief that knowledge as well as norms and values are situated and context dependent and can be understood solely from within it, "relativism self-consciously divests itself of a series of anthropocentric and anachronistic skins—modern, white, Western, male-focused, individualist, scientific (or 'scientistic')—to say that the recognition of such value-concepts is radically unstable, the "objective" outsider opinion a worthless myth" (Taylor 2009, 86). The concepts such as right, wrong, good, or bad then lose their relevance.

The second form of relativism is *strategic*, as it avoids the question of truth altogether, choosing not to make any conclusions about individual beliefs. Sayer provides examples of this thinking in action:

- "I'm not interested in whether ideas are right or wrong, true or false. I'm interested in where ideas are coming from and what their authors are about. So long as I can work that out I'm satisfied for then I can know how to judge them."
- "I have my values and I just need to know what the various competing ideas are so I can judge them according to my values." (2000, 50)

This strategic relativism offers insight into much of the contemporary discourse, particularly evident in the United States. The 2016 US elections brought into sharp contrast two cultures, the elite, including the academics, journalists, scientists, writers, artists, or lawyers, and the rest. On the whole, the members of the elite are progressive, cosmopolitan, multicultural, exhibiting selective sensitivities. The ordinary people, on the other hand, see themselves as the guardians of traditional values and their customary way of life, now under growing attack from the patronizing elite. The elite's assertion of authority over norms, values, and facts is hence seen as degrading to the people—especially given the elite's intelligence and policy failures leading to wars and crises—bringing an era of "truth as disrespect" (Levinovitz 2017). Facts are thus not evaluated on merit, but relative to their source. The "truth-making mechanisms of academic culture" are to be rejected, creating "uncertainty via indignation and cultural pride" (Levinovitz 2017). Unfortunately, this situation is exacerbated by the elite's own relativism. Levinovitz makes a strong point:

> Often, the very people who cheer journalists calling out Trump's falsehoods are unwilling to do the same when falsehoods are the product of cultures they find more sympathetic or less dangerous. We point out that one culture's science is not another's, that elites wrongly force standards of truth on the less powerful—and then expect people to trust a culture of elites telling us that vaccines are safe, that man-made global warming is real. (2017)

This environment then provides a substrate in which alternate news, conspiracies, and mistrust toward authority bloom. The tools of information, offering a range of substantive views, analyses, and commentaries, are not much of an antidote here. Instead, they are used to reinforce such issues by enabling echo chambers, communication spaces where people seek affirmation of their views from the likeminded.

Writing in 1998, at the opposite end of the science wars of which Feyerabend was an early starter, Trigg reacted to the postmodern conceptions of the world in which reality does not exist apart from human representations:

> The real world is not a dreamworld under my control, a fiction my language has created and can mold to my convenience. Reality is more resistant. At many levels, things are not always as I want them to be, or conceive them to be. Realism has to start with the realization that I or anyone else can be wrong. Fallibility is part of the human condition. Any view which

denigrates reason, and the possibility of truth, and which even doubts our identity, is in fact saying that there is no way in which we can be mistaken, either individually or collectively. Each epoch will have its own views, its fictions and even that view will be a fiction. Even the notion of fiction collapses, since there will be nothing left to contrast it with. If we cannot be right, we cannot be wrong, and if we cannot be wrong, we cannot be right. (Trigg 1998, 159)

There is no objective truth as it is always of our making, and reason is lost. Despite their incoherence, relativist philosophies have been useful to various multicultural and post-colonial movements, loaning their adherents "philosophical resources with which to protect oppressed cultures from the charge of holding false or unjustified views" (Boghossian 2006, 130). Yet, as discussed, these have also been behind an equally insidious development. "Truth exists and we may be wrong, but we, the ordinary people, want neither ideas nor information from them, the elite" is its defining thinking. For the diversity movements, there was no need to listen and engage as everyone had their own truth. The ordinary people, on the other hand, are not about to debate with the insolent ruling class.

LEARNING FROM HISTORY

Above, we have presented a trifecta of enablers of trivialization, a public discourse which strives on slogan, myth, and intuition rather than logic, coherence, and substance. We began with essentialism, a set of deeply ingrained, yet problematic assumptions that continue to alter the way we perceive and approach the organization, properties, and problems of social and natural systems. We also discussed reductionism, a notion that all phenomena, regardless of their domain, can be understood through more basic or fundamental parts. While the social world is replete with emergent phenomena, which cannot be understood solely through the study of their underlying elements, reductionism continues have its hold on social sciences and finds much use in politics, where it facilitates the manipulation of causality and a strategic steering of political agendas. There is an argument to be made that the failures of essentialism and reductionism helped support the rise of postmodern movements as well as the recent resurfacing of various forms of relativism, the idea that truth and knowledge can be judged only relative to a particular situation. The increasingly noticeable relativist postures are becoming obstacles to an effective dialogue in and outside of politics. What do we make of this (re)turn to irrationality?

We can find insights in history which does not get surprised easily, and consider the rise and fall of ancient Greece. With their embrace of method and logic, rationalism, the ancient Greeks have made significant intellectual advancements bringing with these considerable social progress. The classical contribution to mathematics and astronomy was not outdone until the sixteenth century. As well, the great philosophers attempted to make strides in a number of important areas such as botany, zoology, and social institutions (Dodds 1959). Their style of thought in turn began to challenge the existing social structures, opening their society to an unprecedented extent. Speaking of classical Athens, Dodds explains "though the city was there, its walls, as someone has put it, were down: its institutions stood exposed to rational criticism; its traditional ways of life were increasingly penetrated and modified by a cosmopolitan culture. For the first time in Greek history, it mattered little where a man had been born nor what his ancestry was..." (1959, 238). Yet, this was not to last as the Greek civilization entered a period of gradual decline and, in Dodds's words, experienced "the return of the irrational." While scholars debating on the causes of this decline point to wars, economic and political challenges, or intellectual breakdown, among others, Dodds argues the decline began long before these issues. There is evidence of an increasing anxiety, superstition, and the search for relief in the certainties of astrology among the masses, fueled, in the author's view, by people's fear of freedom, "the unconscious flight from the heavy burden of individual choice which an open society lays upon its members" (Dodds 1959, 252). This was reflected

> in the hardening of philosophical speculation into quasi-religious dogma which provided the individual with an unchanging rule of life; in the dread of inconvenient research expressed even by a Cleanthes or an Epicurus; later, and on a more popular level, in the demand for a prophet or a scripture; and more generally, in the pathetic reverence for the written word characteristic of late Roman and medieval times—a readiness, as Nock [1933] puts it, "to accept statements because they were in books, or even because they were said to be in books,"

notes Dodds (1959, 252). It is difficult to avoid drawing a parallel between these observations and the contemporary developments.

Writing in the 1950s, the author observed a similar, yet incomplete, disintegration of the inherited social order with broad implications, "a great age of rationalism, marked by scientific advances beyond anything that earlier times had thought possible, and confronting mankind with the prospect of a society more open than any it has ever known," but also "the unmistakable symptoms of a recoil from that prospect" (1959, 254). Dodds closed his work with some hope that as we understand better the roots of the irrational, we will be able to avoid this lapse.

If writing today, following the social revolutions of the 1960s, the emergence of postmaterialism of the 1970s, the rise of postmodern irrationalism, as well as the current democratic malaise[4] accompanied by a relatively rapid turn inward of societies around the globe, Dodds would likely be less sanguine. Surely, much progress has been made in understanding of our fears and limitations in the past half-century, but this has shown to be insufficient. We lack a cultural engine compelling us to move forward in thinking differently.

CONCLUSION

While we cannot yet make a full sense of all of our progress but know what an irrational society does, we must begin to envisage a different world. Indeed, we can imagine a discourse in which attempts at obtaining political support based on reductionist assignments of responsibility for social and environmental issues and narrow solutions to them are suspect. We can picture a world in which unequivocal endorsements or rejections of free trade, offers of single-handed fixes to troubled systems of health care, claims of the state being external to the economy, demands of an environment where no one can be wrong, and other ideas uncoupled from substance are rejected as uninformed guesses. We can also imagine social sciences which have renounced Occam's razor and began to study societies, economies, and politics in terms of systems rather than isolated parts, inspiring new theories, tools, and ways to engage with the world around us. Indeed, due to their unique position at the intersection of the social and the scientific, social sciences are well positioned to help make this world possible (Chapter 8). At last, we can imagine an attuned populace, encouraged by institutional arrangements to negotiate a new democracy. In what follows we will explore what such a system might look like, starting with a discussion of democracy and alternate systems of government for the new century.

NOTES

1. As translated from the original statement in Latin: *entia non sunt multiplicanda praeter necessitatem.*
2. In a recent speech, for example, British Prime Minister Theresa May calls for meritocracy as the recipe for a people's Britain, one responsive to the needs and interests of ordinary citizens, and hints to economic and social reforms ready to bring it about. "I want Britain to be the world's great meritocracy—a country where everyone has a fair chance to go as far as their talent and their hard work will allow," states May and adds "there is no more important place to start than education" (2016), echoing not only her predecessors but also her counterparts across the Atlantic.
3. Building upon a nutrition example provided by Stone (1989).
4. Only about 30% of US and 45% of the European respondents born in the 1980s think it is "essential" (response of 10 on a 10-point scale) to live in a democracy (Foa and Mounk 2016).

REFERENCES

Acemoglu, Daron, and James A. Robinson. *Economic origins of dictatorship and democracy.* New York: Cambridge University Press, 2005.

Alberts, Jeffrey R. 2002. "Simply complex: Essentialism trumps reductionism." *Current Neurology and Neuroscience Reports* 2 (5): 379–381.

Alesina, Alberto, and Edward Ludwig Glaeser. 2004. *Fighting poverty in the US and Europe: A world of difference.* New York: Oxford University Press.

Barrett, Lisa. 2015. "Essentialist Views of the Mind." In *This idea must die: Scientific theories that are blocking progress,* edited by John Brockman. New York: Harper Perennial.

Boghossian, Paul. 2006. *Fear of knowledge: Against relativism and constructivism.* Oxford: Oxford University Press.

Brockman, John, ed. 2009. *What have you changed your mind about?: Today's leading minds rethink everything.* New York: HarperCollins.

Butler, Christopher. 2002. *Postmodernism: A very short introduction,* vol. 74. Oxford: Oxford University Press.

CMA (Canadian Medical Association). 2015. "Obesity in Canada: Causes, Consequences and the Way Forward." *Submission to the Senate Standing Committee on Social Affairs, Science and Technology.* https://www.sencanada.ca/content/sen/committee/412/SOCI/Briefs/2015-06-10CanadianMedicalAssocWrittenObesityBrief_e.pdf.

Dawkins, Richard. 2015. "Essentialism." In *This idea must die: Scientific theories that are blocking progress,* edited by John Brockman. New York: Harper Perennial.

Dodds, Eric Robertson. 1959. *The Greeks and the irrational*, vol. 25. Berkeley: University of California Press.

Feyerabend, Paul. 1993. *Against method*. London: Verso.

Finnemore, Martha, and Kathryn Sikkink. 2001. "Taking stock: The constructivist research program in international relations and comparative politics." *Annual Review of Political Science* 4 (1): 391–416.

Flax, Jane. 1990. *Thinking fragments: Psychoanalysis, feminism, and postmodernism in the contemporary West*. Berkeley: University of California Press.

Foa, Roberto Stefan, and Yascha Mounk. 2016. "The democratic disconnect." *Journal of Democracy* 27 (3): 5–17.

Gelman, Susan A. 2003. *The essential child: Origins of essentialism in everyday thought*. Oxford: Oxford University Press.

Haidt, Jonathan. 2015. "The pursuit of parsimony." In *This idea must die: Scientific theories that are blocking progress*, edited by John Brockman. New York: Harper Perennial.

Heilbron, John L. 2012. *Galileo*. Oxford: Oxford University Press.

Kohli, Atul, Peter Evans, Peter J. Katzenstein, Adam Przeworski, Susanne Hoeber Rudolph, James C. Scott, and Theda Skocpol. 1995. "The role of theory in comparative politics: A symposium." *World Politics* 48 (1): 1–49.

Lennon, Kathleen. 1997. "Feminist epistemology as local epistemology." *Proceedings of the Aristotelian Society* 71: 37. As cited in Boghossian (2006).

Levinovitz, Alan Jay. 2017. "It's not all relative." *The Chronicle of Higher Education*, March 5. https://www.chronicle.com/article/Its-Not-All-Relative/239356.

May, Theresa. 2016. "Theresa May's speech on grammar schools." *New Statesman*, September 9. www.newstatesman.com/politics/education/2016/09/full-text-theresa-mays-speech-grammar-schools.

NHS (National Health Service). 2016. "Obesity—Causes." https://www.nhs.uk/conditions/obesity/causes/.

NIH (National Institutes of Health). 2016. "What causes obesity & overweight?" https://www.nichd.nih.gov/health/topics/obesity/conditioninfo/cause.

Norris, Christopher. 1995. "Culture, criticism and communal values: On the ethics of enquiry" In *Theorizing culture: An interdisciplinary critique after postmodernism*, edited by Barbara Adam and Stuart Allan. New York: NYU Press.

Pascale, Celine-Marie. 2010. *Cartographies of knowledge: Exploring qualitative epistemologies*. Thousand Oaks, CA: Sage.

Richerson, Peter. 2015. "Human nature." In *This idea must die: Scientific theories that are blocking progress*, edited by John Brockman. New York: Harper Perennial.

Sawyer, R. Keith. 2005. *Social emergence: Societies as complex systems*. Cambridge, UK: Cambridge University Press.

Sayer, Andrew. 2000. *Realism and social science*. London: Sage.
Sayer, Andrew. 2010. "Reductionism in social science." In *Questioning nine-teenth century assumptions about knowledge, II: Reductionism*, edited by Richard E. Lee, 5–39. Albany, NY: State University of New York Press.
Stone, Deborah. 1989. "Causal stories and the formation of policy agendas." *Political Science Quarterly* 104 (2), 281–300.
Taylor, Timothy. 2009. "The trouble with relativism." In *What have you changed your mind about?: Today's leading minds rethink everything*, edited by John Brockman. New York: HarperCollins.
Trigg, Roger. 1998. *Rationality and religion*. Oxford: Blackwell.

PART II

Opinions and Their Public

CHAPTER 4

Democracy (Re)Imagined

Earlier, we have identified some deep lapses in public discourse and alluded to a number of negative political and policy outcomes across the globe. It may thus not be a revelation that the past several decades have seen a disturbing trend apparent in the views and choices of people throughout the democratic world—a declining political confidence and trust in government. These have been observed in European nations, Canada as well as the United States, countries different in their political and social histories (Dalton 2017). Consider some numbers from a recent US poll, the 2016 Survey of American Political Culture. The survey found, for example, that 64% of the American public had little or no confidence in the federal government's capacity to solve problems (up from 60% in 1996), while 56% believed "the government in Washington threatens the freedom of ordinary Americans." About 88% of respondents thought "political events these days seem more like theater or entertainment than like something to be taken seriously" (up from 79% in 1996). As well, 75% of surveyed individuals thought that one cannot "believe much" the mainstream media content (Hunter and Bowman 2016). As in other countries, such numbers, consistent across polls, tell a story much different than responses collected half a century ago.

Some, unsurprised, argue citizens have always had a level of skepticism and mistrust toward their government but appreciated their regime *legitimacy*, a democratic capacity to exercise their will and choose a new government. However, other scholars are arriving at a more pessimistic conclusion: People have begun questioning the very foundations of their

© The Author(s) 2019   71
O. Bubak and H. Jacek, *Trivialization and Public Opinion*,
https://doi.org/10.1007/978-3-030-17925-0_4

systems of government—the legitimacy of liberal democratic regimes. Foa and Mounk, for example, examined responses from three waves of cross-national surveys (1995–2014) focusing on indicators of regime legitimacy: "citizens' express support for the system as a whole; the degree to which they support key institutions of liberal democracy, such as civil rights; their willingness to advance their political causes within the existing political system; and their openness to authoritarian alternatives such as military rule" (2016, 6). They find citizens to be not only progressively critical of their government but also "cynical about the value of democracy as a political system, less hopeful that anything they do might influence public policy, and more willing to express support for authoritarian alternatives" (2016, 7). The authors point out that in 2011, 24% of those born in the 1980s thought democracy[1] was a "bad" system for the US, while 26% of the same cohort believed it is unimportant[2] for people to "choose their leaders in free elections." Also in 2011, 32% of respondents of all ages reported a preference for a "strong leader" who need not "bother with parliament and elections" (up from 24% in 1995). As well, Foa and Mounk (2016) observe a decrease in interest and participation in conventional (including voting and political party membership) and non-conventional political activities (such as participation in protests or social movement).

These responses only beckon more questions, particularly as some scholars believe that "[t]he changing values and skills of Western publics encourage a new type of assertive or engaged citizen who is skeptical about political elites and the institutions of representative democracy" (Dalton 2017, 391). In this and the next chapter, we explore the realities and the logic behind these perspectives. Is the current system working as intended? What can be done to renew the faith in government and citizenship? What can we learn from how public comes to their opinions? We focus primarily on the developments in the United States, providing an extreme case in an evolution of a democratic system and a rationale for revisiting the tenets of governance. We will begin to discern the roots of many of the above stances and see that regaining effectiveness and legitimacy in modern governance demands more than just "more democracy." Governance for the new age is smart, bringing in citizens where they are most capable and engaged. But change will demand a proper understanding of the underlying problems and a collective awareness of the solutions. And getting there requires us to cope with trivialization.

TESTING THE THEORIES OF POLITICS

Let us begin with a look at the key explanations of outcomes in democratic politics of which there is no shortage, particularly in the heavily studied American government. A recent study by Gilens and Page (2014) has caused quite a stir in both the popular and academic press as it not only succeeded to shake the debates on the merits of these long-standing theories but also as it provided empirical evidence on the suspect state of democracy in America. An unprecedented set of data allowed the authors to test the key perspectives explaining the policy outcomes in America against one another. At the same time, the authors were able to suggest the reasons for the persistence of this theoretical multiplicity—revealing of the limits of the state of the art (Chapter 7). This is further relevant in our context, as these limits are frequently beyond any conventional debate on the state of American government.

Before discussing Gilens and Page's conclusions, it is important to introduce the four theoretical traditions used to explain policy outcomes as considered by the authors. These are distinguished by the actors thought to hold the key influence in these outcomes. One sees its system as majoritarian electoral democracy in which the policies are a reflection of the will of the majority of voters. There are several streams of scholarship in this tradition including the rational choice theories of electoral democracy, which connect citizen preferences directly to policy outcomes. Here, for example, the median-voter theorem predicts "two vote-seeking parties will both take the same position, at the center of the distribution of voters' most-preferred positions" (565). While this approach has been criticized on account of its assumptions as well as the neglect of institutional dimensions of a polity, it continues to retain a loyal following.

Elite theories constitute another set of explanations of the US policy outcomes. Broadly, these Economic-Elite Domination theories see the elite as either the main policy makers or steering policy development. The scholarship in this area varies in its definition of "elite," whether the economic elite in control of the wealth, or those holding positions of influence in the political, economic, or administrative spheres. Here, Mills's *The Power Elite* (2000) is an instantly recognizable exemplar of this scholarship.

Interest-group pluralism is another key perspective on American politics. The pluralist theory, at its most basic, posits that political power is held by a dynamic set of competing organized groups interacting and influencing government and its policies. In time, conceptions of pluralism have grown more sophisticated when compared to Madison's original ideas of balance and harmony presented in his *Federalist Paper No. 10.* Smith (1990) identifies classical, reformed, and neopluralist strands, addressing, respectively, the dispersal and competition for power, access, and the advantaged position of business. Gilens and Page choose to distinguish majoritarian pluralism, as understood through the work of David Truman (1971) and Robert Dahl (2006), from biased pluralism, supported by Smith (1990), Lindblom (1977), and more recently by Hacker and Pierson (2010, 2011), who bring to the fore the dominance of the financial sector. Briefly, majoritarian pluralism claims fairness through checks and balances, an even distribution of influence and power in society, and the essential role of groups in governance. Unfortunately, as shown by Olson (2002), if the assumptions here were correct, democracy would function differently, as we will discuss. Biased pluralism, on the other hand, as expressed in neopluralism and reformed pluralism, responds to the shortcomings of the majoritarian view and recognizes an uneven representation and access in favor of business.

There is much quantitative and less qualitative work on the influence of interest groups on public policy outcomes. None, however, is known to have examined the interest group impact while *controlling*[3] for public or elite influences, which is one of Gilens and Page's main contributions. The authors first test separately the effects of the preferences of average citizens, elites, and organized interests on policy outcomes. They find statistically significant support for each of the three theories these variables represent, Majoritarian Electoral Democracy, Economic-Elite Domination, and interest-group pluralism, respectively, attesting to the *continued* application of such theories. But, when these are included *together* in a multivariate model, the authors find the impact of citizens' preferences reduced to nearly zero. This suggests that the predictions of the mainstream Majoritarian Electoral Democracy perspectives can be cast off. "Not only do ordinary citizens not have *uniquely* substantial power over policy decisions; they have little or no independent influence on policy at all," conclude the authors (572, emphasis original). A combination of theories in which interest groups and elites dominate policy making is thus more in line with the contemporary situation in the

US. In sum, in an unprecedented study, Gilens and Page have not only brought into spotlight the concerns some have long had about outcomes produced by systems we have come to call democratic but also added weight to some of the citizen's views on government, often discounted as the stuff of surveys.

THIS HAPPENS IN A DEMOCRACY

While the above conclusions, as most other claims in social sciences, can be challenged on the grounds of methodology, democratic theory, or citizen competence, a look on the ground brings the findings into life. Despite being among the richest countries in the world, the US is also a country with one of the highest poverty rates among the OECD countries. Outcomes in health and compulsory education are equally dismal, even as the US spends the most per capita on schooling and healthcare in the developed world. On the rise since the 1970s, inequality is reaching the extremes of the 1920s. When adjusted for inflation, a median full-time US worker earned less in 2014 than in 1973 (Wessel 2015), entirely decoupled from the growth of the economy (Ford 2015). In 2007, 46% of the US salary income went to the top 10% of earners, with 12% of such income made by only 0.1% earners; and between 1993 and 2010, over half of real income gains accrued to the top 1% (*The Economist* 2012). It would be difficult to make the case that these outcomes are in line with voter preferences.

Aside from the partisan ACA (Chapter 2), the increasingly fragmented US Congress has not enacted any major legislation to address the key social, environmental, or employment issues; it has not even passed a comprehensive budget since 1994 (Brill 2018). To no surprise, with over twenty registered lobbyists per member (Brill 2018), the US Congress has become an epitome of "vetocracy." This dysfunctional system, where powerful lobbies have the capacity to block unfavorable legislation, "prevents governance and produces deficits" (Fukuyama in Berggruen and Gardels 2013, 26) and is unable to function for the long-term good of the public. As, by design, the US political system is dependent on private funds to finance expensive political campaigns, the monied special interests have the upper hand in politics.

Perhaps the most vivid example of this corruption is the complicated and inefficient US tax code. "Special interests pay politicians vast amounts of cash for their campaigns and in return they get favorable exemptions, credits or loopholes in the tax code....Congress is able to funnel vast sums of money in perpetuity to its favored funders through the tax code without anyone realizing it," explains Zakaria (2012). As a result, the tax code is 4 million words long, which is about 10 times longer than its French or German counterpart, diminishing the efficacy of this policy instrument and creating concerns for foreign investors (Zakaria 2016). Aside from the tax code, there is a host of other more or less visible issues including some suspect legal settlements with industry giants (Faguet 2013), the revolving door allowing people to cash in on their connections as they shuttle between the public and private sectors, the political manipulation of electoral district boundaries favoring particular parties, and other challenges to public interest.

A natural question is what happened to the cooperative, problem-solving political environment of a few decades ago? There is no shortage of explanations for the contemporary democratic discontent across the developed world. As we will discuss below, some authors see the answer in the paradigmatic shift in political economy, limiting government options, changing views on the role of the state, and carrying with it various structural changes, ultimately impacting the conditions and the views of the citizens. In an alternate reading, the current malaise can be traced to technological change, not only accelerating economic integration but also deeply changing the employment and socioeconomic landscapes. Still others, trying to explain the unique situation in the US, add to these other factors, more specific to the American polity.

The *political economy* explanations for the troubling social and political conditions across the developed world begin at Bretton Woods at the end of the Second World War, when the representatives of Western democratic powers agreed to establish a system prioritizing full employment and the needs of the nation-state. The goal was to provide social security and stability to help forestall another conflict. Thus emerged a system of "embedded liberalism" (Ruggie 1982, 36), economic liberalism subordinated to domestic needs. In this system, the independent nation-state was able to intervene and protect its industry, people, and markets while benefiting from international trade enabled by the Bretton Woods system. Also, given the financial regulation and capital controls, financial markets were relatively predictable with speculation suppressed. These arrangements have proven to be unsustainable, however. The single-purpose policies prioritizing labor over capital resulted in rising wages and inflation. Ultimately, a confluence of events in the 1970s triggered a "market friendly revolution" (Blyth 2012) beginning the neoliberal era. The priority now was capital, demanding a refocus on deflation and price stability. The governments were thus under pressure to reduce their footprints, balance budgets, privatize, and remove barriers to the flow of capital, driven by the idea that free markets are the answer to economic growth and prosperity. In time, this approach too brought its set of salient problems, such as the more frequent economic crises, stagnant wages, deindustrialization, as well as ones less salient, including the challenges to state sovereignty. This new substrate offers political parties a little choice but to converge on major economic issues, in turn driving the politics of division. As Hardin observed:

> [t]he former left-right antagonism has been reduced to a very short spread from those who prefer more generous welfare programs to those who prefer somewhat less generous programs, and the difference between the two positions represents a very small fraction of national income. Radical reorganization of the economy to achieve some degree of equality or fairness is now virtually off the agenda... For many people, it is a difference that is easily trumped by formerly minor concerns such as items in the social agenda and regional preferences. The odd result is that politics may be noisier and seemingly more intense and even bitter, but it is less important. (Hardin 2000, 43)

In this view, the ultimate reason is the broad agreement on how to organize the political economy—with minimal barriers to the flow of money, goods, and services—affecting too what role people see for the state and its social policy.

The *technology* perspectives trace the postwar economic growth and shared prosperity to innovation and productivity increases across mechanical, chemical, or aerospace engineering sectors, industries which have brought large parts of the population into the middle class. The technological advancements in these sectors reached their limits in the shock-ridden 1970s, a time of high unemployment and falling productivity (Ford 2015). The ensuing innovation was concentrated in information technology—seeing the advancements in computing power, networking, sensors, and software—in turn making possible significant leaps in productivity. It has also deeply altered the overall economic landscape including the labor markets, automating jobs and pushing down the labor's share of income (Ford 2015). Specifically, Ford (2015) identifies several economic trends at play here, including stagnant wages, declines in labor force participation, decreases in labor's share of national income, growing inequality, and market polarization (a labor market where middle-skill jobs are replaced with many low-skill service and a few high-skill technology jobs). While these are often thought to be a product of globalization, financialization, and the failure of politics, the author ultimately traces these problems to the disruptions brought on by the rapidly advancing technology.[4] And so the contemporary discontents are seen as products of the governments' failures to enact policies moderating the dislocations from technological progress. In this light, speaking of the US, Ford notes it "stands alone in terms of the political decisions it has made; rather than simply failing to enact policies that might have slowed the forces driving the country toward higher levels of inequality, America very often has made choices that have effectively put a wind at the back of those forces" (2015, 58). While Ford points to sustained corporate lobbying efforts as the reason for these (in)decisions, there exists a more thorough accounting of the current social and political ills facing the country (Brill 2018).

Similarly to others (such as Hayes 2012), Brill (2018) traces the current condition to the emergent *meritocratic class*, a common theme connecting a number of interrelated developments. The highly competitive and driven members of this new class tapped the American ideals and shaped the features of the system of government to their advantage— while leaving others behind. Brill (2018) thus sees meritocracy, economic liberalism, technological and financial innovations, the Constitution, and democracy itself as the set of mutually reinforcing factors behind the modern-day breakdown of the American democracy.[5]

Brill's explanation begins in the 1960s and the turn toward meritocracy, a system of selection into education and employment elevating skill and competence over status or inheritance. While this helped to supply the brightest and the more ambitious people into the new knowledge economy, it brought with it unintended consequences. The traditional, elite network of inherited privilege gave way to a different class of competitive aristocrats introducing innovations into law, finance, and business, and gaining new opportunities for profits and with it access to power. The world of finance thus saw a plethora of new instruments and schemes, generating income from moving assets around and other speculation, without much concern for economic development and growth in the long term. A new generation of lawyers reconceived what was meant by the rule of law as they flooded regulatory agencies. "In the

hands of thousands of Washington lawyers drawn from the new meritocracy, due process came to mean not just that the government couldn't
take away land or freedom at will, but that an Occupational Health and
Safety Administration rule protecting workers from a deadly chemical
used on the job could be challenged and delayed for more than a decade and end up being hundreds of pages long, filled with clause after
clause after clause whose meaning the lawyers could contest," explains
Brill. Similarly, reinterpreting the American value of free speech embodied in the First Amendment of the Constitution carried significant
consequences. When consumer advocate Ralph Nader fought to give
drugstores the ability to advertise their prices on the grounds of the First
Amendment, he could not have known this would become a harbinger
of a corporate free-speech movement transforming with it the workings
of politics. Ultimately, free speech became a justification for letting thousands of lobbyists engage the government across branches and for allowing unlimited corporate money for political campaigns.

According to Brill, the combination of corporate money in politics,
lobbying efforts, and sophisticated legal resources allowed business interests to dominate those of the middle classes. This was evident, for example, in the businesses' victory in their mostly illegal and coercive anti-union
campaign of the 1970s and 1980s in which the Democrat-controlled
Senate and Congress failed to pass a protective labor reform legislation.
"The result was the virtual end of unions in the private sector, which
extinguished not only the economic power of rank-and-file workers but
also the political muscle that unions had once provided to balance out
business interests," concludes Brill.

The technological advances, enabling powerful data analytics and
new media, have only compounded these issues. Gaining the ability to
conduct data-driven micro-targeting of voters, candidates and their
campaign teams push politics away from the mainstream, further polar-
izing the electorate. The range of cable television programming and now
increasingly greater variety of more or less accurate sources of information online serve only to reinforce the mélange of ideas of the media
consumers. "The days of the country sharing the same set of facts by
watching the news unfold on broadcast television [are] over," adds Brill.
This further encourages polarization and deepens mistrust toward the
media and the system more broadly. In the end, in Brill's view, the win-
ners are the meritocratic elite with a different need for the government
than the ordinary people, who rely on public schools, mass transit, and

hope for employment protections, affordable and accessible health care, and social programs.

Paradoxically, another factor undermining American democracy was efforts to *democratize* US politics and institutions. Among the main shifts was to begin to have voters, rather than party decision makers, pick candidates through primaries and caucuses, furthering the significance of money in politics. "It also produced candidates more likely to appeal to the most committed, and extreme, members of their party, who were most likely to vote in primaries or caucuses," notes the author while identifying this as the root of polarization and impairment (Brill 2018).

Similarly, the Congressional reforms of the 1970s can be seen as contributing to polarization, dismal favorability ratings, and, arguably, an unpredictability of legislative outcomes. These attempts at democratization—which included limiting the powers of committee chairs and changing their selection procedures, increasing the number of sub-committees, opening the committee meetings to the public, or recording votes, among others—designed to make the traditionally opaque Congressional dealings more transparent and responsive to popular forces, carried a number unintended consequences (Zakaria 2007). The choices of the members of Congress were now public and open to scrutiny, especially by powerful interests, and the institutional relations became politicized to the detriment of the legislative process, democratic politics, and the outcomes we have alluded to above (Zakaria 2007).

Other efforts to promote democracy, particularly the California ballot propositions in which the voters get the final say on legislative decisions or propose and approve their own, have also had dismal consequences.

> Many initiatives have either limited taxes or mandated spending, making it even harder to balance the budget. Some are so ill-thought-out that they achieve the opposite of their intent: For all its small-government pretensions, Proposition 13 ended up centralising California's finances, shifting them from local to state government. Rather than being the curb on elites that they were supposed to be, ballot initiatives have become a tool of special interests, with lobbyists and extremists bankrolling laws that are often bewildering in their complexity and obscure in their ramifications,

notes a much-cited article (*The Economist* 2011). Yet, until Proposition 13 in 1978, the century-old system of direct democracy in California functioned reasonably well (*The Economist* 2011), suggesting that institutions have not kept up with the changing environment, just as they have not at the national level.

The contours of modern-day American politics, whether explained by technology, ideas, or ambitious elites shaping the system to their advantage, are thus inviting key questions: Is the status quo sustainable? Are we to expect an eventual crisis? Some place hope in "critical citizens" who are engaged in civic journalism, or pushing for term limits and campaign finance reform in the US, actors who helped to stimulate electoral reforms in Italy, New Zealand, and Japan, or encouraged a set of constitutional initiatives in the United Kingdom, including devolution (Norris 1999). Yet, as we saw from above, rather than *more* democracy, the situation calls for a more fundamental change to governance.

CHALLENGING DEMOCRACY

In his influential work, Olson (2002) challenged the traditionally held assumptions that any group of people will strive to further their interests. Rather, Olson argued, "unless the number of individuals in a group is quite small, or unless there is coercion or some other special device to make individuals act in their common interest, *rational, self-interested individuals will not act to achieve their common or group interests*" (Olson 2002, 2, emphasis original). This logic has direct implications on whose interests get answered and how democracies, in which various factions compete for government's attention, evolve. For example, large groups, such as taxpayers or migrant farm workers without "an independent source of selective incentives," (167) will lack the inclination to organize voluntarily to push forward their common prerogatives. This is as their members realize they cannot make any difference individually and they know they will be automatic beneficiaries of achievements of others. On the other hand, the actions of individuals in small groups sharing a specific set of interests can yield incommensurable benefits, thus offering a powerful motivation for organizing.

Olson builds on this theory in his ensuing work (2008) in which he argues that stable democratic societies see a progressively greater number of special interest organizations, many of which "have little incentive to make their societies more productive, but... powerful incentives to seek a larger share of the national income even when this greatly reduces social output." Such coalitions build up barriers to entry which coupled with "their slowness in making decisions and mutually efficient bargains reduces an economy's dynamism and rate of growth," observed Olson, adding that they "also increase regulation, bureaucracy, and political intervention in markets" (2008). The author provides an example of the United Kingdom, a country that did not experience dictatorships, invasions, revolutions, or other disruptions to its system of government. As a result, "with age British society has acquired so many strong organizations and collusions that it suffers from an institutional sclerosis that slows its adaptation to changing circumstances and technologies" (2008). The economic miracles of Germany and Japan can be attributed to the rebuilt, leaner governance structures with encompassing special interest organizations that emerged following the World War II. Nevertheless, in these countries too, as Olson's theory predicts, the accumulation of distributional coalitions will eventually hinder economic and social progress.

In the US, equally an undisturbed democracy, as we pointed out, lobbying was taken yet to another level on account of two related developments. The first was allowing the unlimited special interest money to enter political campaigns. The second was introducing more *democracy* into the US institutions, giving at once the people and special interests the ability to monitor their politicians. What was formerly a closed system of deliberation and voting could now be scrutinized by motivated cartels threatening to withdraw their financial support. We have also seen that the democratization of candidate selection processes, along with the shifting economic paradigms causing the US political parties to converge on similar economic platforms, refocused politics on extreme issues and fanned polarization. Such a culture, institutions, and economic system are not capable of producing sustainable and effective solutions in public interest (Berggruen and Gardels 2013), resulting in bad governance.

While good governance is essential in tackling the traditional issues with social programs, healthcare, and education, it becomes especially acute as nations face the difficulties brought by a new phase of globalization. Characterized by growing interdependence and diversity, this Globalization 2.0 is, according to Berggruen and Gardels (2013), a source of three key challenges.[6] The first is the spread of social media, carrying the potential to amplify voices, deliver information through its networks at an instant, and disseminate public narratives alternate to those presented in traditional media. They offer the possibility to monitor from below, challenging authority with their capacity to inform and connect their users. Yet, they also enable screening from above, by authorities seeking to control dissent and to create consent. Depending on the provider, social media also allow spreading misinformation with scientific precision, altering opinion where it is needed, possibly without broader notice. Deciding on how to leverage these tools for public good as well as how to regulate such potent, if not well understood, private resources will be a major governance challenge.

The second challenge is the emergence of nation-sized megacities, powerful hubs of globalization, connected by flows of information, people, money, and good and services. These urban areas, often coupled by these flows more extensively to the outside world than to their regions, are different than the cities of the past. Their diverse, connected, and assertive populations face new social, infrastructural, and environmental issues, as well as conflicts between satisfying their short-term consumer wants and long-term sustainability. The rising challenge is thus to find a new "'civic software' that not only fosters the intelligence of connectivity through transparency and participation but also balances empowered individuals and social networks with institutions that filter short term, self-interested choices," explain Berggruen and Gardels (2013, 92).

Finally, there is the dispersion of production across the globe made possible by technology and by the shrinking barriers to the movements of capital and skilled labor. Intended for global consumption, an increasing number of products are no longer designed and made in one place but instead are scattered around a number of interconnected production zones. What is more, in the open global economy companies can quickly respond to more or less favorable conditions and shift their production accordingly at a brisk pace. It is thus not the nation-state but the agile metropolis—closer to the action and able to move quickly to attract or retain capital seeking to optimize their operations, and people seeking to improve their condition—that becomes the driver of economic and social success. For developing localities lower on the value chain, this means staying competitive by offering stability, capable workforce, and economic incentives. No longer able to compete in manufacturing and assembly, the post-industrial zones then require enhancing their capacity to innovate and to produce high-value services. This demands long-term investments into high-tech infrastructure, talent development, and local amenities. Rethinking the role of the public and rebalancing the roles of the city and the state in terms of how economic and political decisions are made then becomes yet another major governance challenge.

A New Constitution

As discussed, the failures of the current systems of government, and the rising challenges and potentials created by the accelerating integration and technological advances, demand a new approach to governance. What might such an approach look like? Before we visit a proposed blue-print, let us set the stage by returning to what is often taken for granted: democracy and its designs. Democracy is commonly defined as a system of government with four essential features: open and fair elections to key positions of political power; universal suffrage; political rights and civil liberties allowing equal opportunity for candidates to be heard; and true authority of those elected to govern (Diamond 2004; Levitsky and Way 2002). This conception alluding to *representation* would be foreign to the democrats of the antique Greece. Indeed, emerging from medieval institutions of government, the idea of representation gained accept-ance in the eighteenth and nineteenth centuries "as solution that elimi-nated the ancient limits on the size of democratic states and transformed democracy from a doctrine suitable only for small and rapidly vanishing city-states to one applicable to the large nation-states of the modern age" (Dahl 1989, 29). However, such a "change in democracy resulting from its union with representation created its own problems. An entirely new and highly complex constellation of political institutions, which we are only beginning to understand, superseded the sovereign assembly that was central to the ancient conception of democracy" (Dahl 1989, 30). Hence emerged political systems dependent on autonomous associa-tions (Dahl 1989) as well as various systems of rules and arrangements to reveal the (first) preferences of (some) citizens for their candidates (Dahl 2006).

Implementing a representative democracy, in the many ways it is pos-sible, is a tall order for constitutional designers, not the least given our limits to understanding the effects of various configurations of institu-tions of government. Here, different forms of government, such as pres-idential and parliamentary regimes, combine with different electoral systems, or rules and regulations governing the selection of representa-tion, such as plurality elections or proportional representation (PR) (Lijphart 1991). These options have inherent trade-offs which must be decided based on the characteristics and the priorities of the polity.

For illustration, consider Norris (1997) who identified four normative criteria for evaluation of electoral systems. The first, government effectiveness, is the ability of government to implement agendas unimpeded by the need to form alliances or coalitions with other parties in order to establish governing majorities. As the majorities are created artificially by amplifying the number of the votes cast for the leading candidate, this system not only leaves out those coming in second but also systematically excludes those unable to produce a plurality of votes. The second criterion is responsive and accountable government, characterized by the trade-off between accountability and power. Of relevance here is the link between the constituent and the local representative, who can be held accountable for the performance of defending the constituents' prerogatives, particularly evident in single-member districts. Similarly, in a two-party system, a party with a majority has the capacity to implement its agendas easily, but if underperforming, a relatively small number of votes can remove it from power during the next election. Another criterion is fairness to minor parties, where inclusiveness is elevated over the effectiveness and stability of governance. In this system, even minor parties have a voice, but majorities generally require forming of coalitions; stalemates are common and so are snap elections. Finally, social representation describes the overall composition of representative bodies as balanced by gender, race, or class. Here, in the case of ethnicity, for example, there are trade-offs between political inclusiveness and long-term social cohesion, as ethnic reservations tend to reinforce differences between groups (Htun 2004).

Scholars have, of course, studied these designs with the goal of trying to determine which ones have the best social and economic outcomes. While some have focused on electoral systems (Norris 1997) and forms of government (Gerring et al. 2008) separately, others (Lijphart 1991) argued they must be evaluated together as "the type of electoral system is significantly related to the development of a country's party system, its type of executive (one-party vs. coalition cabinets), and the relationship between its executive and legislature" (1991, 72). Lijphart's findings, for example, indicate that parliamentary-PR systems outperform the others in minority representation (gauged by women's representation in national legislative bodies), protection of the interest of minorities (quantified through types and coverage of family policies), participation (gauged by voting turnout), income equality (captured as the percentage of total income earned by the top 20% of households), democratic quality (Dahl rating), and the rates of unemployment. Drawing on this as well as his ensuing research, Lijphart developed a set of constitutional recommendations for divided societies. The author argued that power-sharing and group autonomy, enabled by right institutional environment including appropriate constitutional features, are *sine quibus non* to successful governance in polities with cleavages (2004). Lijphart proposed several best practices, favoring parliamentary-PR systems among other arrangements. His findings were met with repeated rejoinders (Lardeyret 1991; Quade 1991), attesting to the challenges in studying these systems, which in the end have missed a larger point toward which we are working in this chapter.

Rather than to enter debates, our brief introduction was aimed to help us make two important points. First, (re)designing a constitutional system is a difficult task, not least as an effective constitution is a balancing act mindful of the unique conditions of *continuously changing* polities. Here, constitutional engineers must ask difficult questions such as:

- *What are the priorities?* There is a trade-off between inclusiveness, responsiveness, and effectiveness.
- *What are the characteristics, or properties of the polity?* What is the social and political geography? Level of development? Historical legacies? Is the society heterogeneous, divided along ethnic or cultural lines, and what is the distribution of preferences? What is the level of political integration with other polities?
- *What is the access to information and the level of education of the electorate?* This was the primary concern of, for example, the founding fathers of the American republic, who have designed into the system institutions and rules including the electoral college, the selection of candidates to the Senate by state legislatures, and the separation of powers to ensure best choices in spite of the informational limits.
- *Who deliberates and who decides?* That is, do citizens share the responsibility with the elite to create and approve proposals and/or policies? If so, how? How should the tools of direct democracy, such as referenda or citizen initiatives, be used?

This is in addition to many other questions, to be sure, including on the criteria on entry into government, how should the government be petitioned, whether voting should be compulsory, who can vote and when, how should authority be allocated among multi-level governments, or how to respond to evolving politico-legal conditions. Some are up to debate, others have been hopefully settled. For example, given what we know now about the eventual outcomes of democratic pluralism—and not just from research (Olson 2002, 2008) but from experience—the traditional recipes to representation and policy making must be reconsidered.

Second, as scholars identify the connections between the forms of government and the quality of governance, they show constitutional designs are linked to political and policy outcomes.[7] As already hinted, there is an agreement that *functioning* democratic systems make good policies, sustainable solutions working in the interest of the public; are seen as legitimate; and help effect an inclusive improvement of the citizens' condition (Hibbing and Theiss-Morse 2004; Berggruen and Gardels 2013). Yet, as shown, the current designs are increasingly incapable of delivering these results. As well, we are privy to the changing power distribution shaped by novel means of civic participation, the demands created by the increasing diversity, and the complexities emerging from the local, national, and global social and economic interdependencies (Berggruen and Gardels 2013), further challenging the traditional constitutions.

Hence, we look to new paradigms. As briefly mentioned in the Introduction, one such a design of new governance has been promoted by Berggruen and Gardels (2013). The authors begin from the observation that democracy tends toward short-term gratification, thus steering away outcomes in public interest, and, like the markets, it is not self-correcting. Inspired by China's modern meritocracy, the authors' solution for a sustainable democratic society is based on a mixed constitution with a combination of elected and appointed institutions of governance, the latter designed to be free to take the long-term view and work in public interest.

Mindful of the declining legitimacy of the current systems of government and the complexities of multi-layer and integrated jurisdictions, the authors advance a new design. The solution lies in combining knowledgeable democracy with accountable meritocracy. Knowledgeable democracy means *devolving* and *involving*, that is, decentralizing decision making and emphasizing an "intelligent electorate," engaging citizens in their communities where they are most knowledgeable and where their input is most appropriate.[8] Distribution of decision making increases the network complexity of the polity, demanding a greater political capacity at the top of the system. This *decision-division* is determined not by politics but by merit. Such a learned meritocracy will thus have "not only the requisite technical expertise, but also the practical wisdom of experience and knowledge of historical precedent," explain Berggruen and Gardels (2013, 104). To eliminate the degenerative pressures of the short-sighted public and special interest, this institution is by design insulated from politics. Yet, as it is an accountable meritocracy, it will be subject to institutional checks by elected representatives and the public.

To demonstrate what such a design might look like, Berggruen and Gardels offer a template of intelligent governance, select features of which we discuss in turn. The authors' model consists of a number of independent institutions, including a bicameral legislature. The lower house is elected indirectly (for a five-year term), while the upper house is appointed (with members serving eight-year terms). A portion of the upper house is selected on merit by the lower house, the executive, and the presidency, while the rest by a scientific sample representing the broader population. A prominent feature of the design is the pyramidal structure of governance aiming to improve the legitimacy by bringing the government closer to the people and letting their voices be heard more effectively. Hence, in this stepped selection system, citizen associations elect delegates (in this design, the base districts have 2000 constituents selecting 10 delegates), who are responsible for choosing qualified deputies. The deputies select representatives, who elect the members of the legislature. "Each higher level of representation is not just a matter of election by the lower levels. Candidates would have to demonstrate capabilities – knowledge and experience – commensurate with the higher level of responsibility," note the authors of the meritocratic elements of their proposal (111). The public administration side also has a pyramidal arrangement, facilitating coordination between the electors and the administrative counselors at their corresponding levels.

Elected by the lower house (or by popular vote on candidates selected by the lower house) for a five-year term, the executive appoints the cabinet and leads the government. As well, the executive nominates candidates to a four-member, collective presidency, to be approved by the lower house for seven-year terms. Transcending politics, the presidency provides a moral anchor and social glue (particularly important in societies with cleavages) and is tasked with appointing a portion of the upper house. It is also responsible for scheduling referenda while ensuring the public is given an informed choice.

Among the institutions with independent authority are the Human Resources Agency (HRA) and the Government Integrity Office (GIO).

The HRA's primary role is to manage civil service personnel, selected based on a qualifying examination. The civil service administrators would be promoted or demoted based on merit, while the citizens would have the capacity to rate their performance online. The administrators are subject to a limit of ten years in any position and to periodic geographical rotations preventing cronyism or capture. The GIO would monitor the performance of elected and appointed members of the legislative, executive, and administrative branches. Crucial here is the integration of this office with active citizenry, engaged in monitoring the government's activities from below. The staff in both agencies cannot be partisan or actively engaged in a business enterprise. As well, cognizant of the issues created by the intensity and volume of information available through innumerable media channels, the authors propose a creation of "an independent media agency that is the benchmark for objective, neutral information – albeit with the necessary safeguards against political control," (108) which the authors see as fundamental to proper deliberation.

To be sure, rather than to provide an authoritative blueprint for adoption, the template is informative, serving to explain the key components and relationships of the proposed system. The challenge for each polity is in deciding the specific parameters of the structures of governance, balancing decision-division, and determining the extent to which to devolve power and involve the citizens. The goal is to address the deficiency of the current systems and operate at a human *scale*, ultimately bringing the citizens into governance, closer to their concerns, while leveraging their knowledge and their potential to join in deliberation.

CONCLUSION

We opened this chapter by highlighting the growing public skepticism toward not only the government's ability to solve problems but also the legitimacy of the very democratic regimes that enable governance. Some, as hinted, see such developments linked to the rise of "critical citizens," politically oriented and assertive individuals who question the adequacy of the current political institutions and the actions of those in power (Dalton 2017). While such scholars would expect a critical citizen to remain committed to liberal democracy, others, examining current surveys, identify an increasing, rather than decreasing affinity to *authoritarianism*, such as military rule or strong leaders unconcerned with elections (Foa and Mounk 2016).[9] With the benefit of time, we have witnessed a number of developments, including the Brexit vote and the outcomes of the 2016 US presidential election, which had cast more doubts on the critical citizen view.[10] We observed a recurrent idea that the familiar democracy is the best system of government, only to be questioned on its democratic deficits (Warren and Pearse 2008) rather than its capacity to resolve its inherent maladies. This is evident even in Olson's comment expecting the society's eventual reckoning:

> May we not then reasonably expect, if special interests are harmful to economic growth, full employment, coherent government, equal opportunity, and social mobility, that students of the matter will become increasingly aware of this as time goes on? And that the awareness eventually will spread to larger and larger proportions of the population? And that this wider awareness will greatly limit the losses from the special interests? That is what I expect, at least when I am searching for a happy ending. (Olson 2008)

The people, Olson hoped, might build a consensus around a corrective and "repeal all special-interest legislation or regulation and at the same time apply rigorous anti-trust laws to every type of cartel or collusion that used its power to obtain prices or wages above competitive levels" (2008). But what if the traditional democratic designs are not self-correcting?

Berggruen and Gardels (2013), as we have explained, argue such an open system is fundamentally incapable of delivering for the long term. A remedy is found in a new design, a restructured governance balancing participatory democracy at the local level with meritocratic, yet accountable, institutions insulated from public pressures at the top of the government. Enabling this system is competition, measured deliberation at all levels of governance, and the monitoring public, scrutinizing the government from within and outside of the new media platforms. And a capable and engaged citizen is central to the legitimacy and the functioning of this intelligent system. Regardless, as we sketched above, a systemic change will demand first a general *understanding* of the situation and the will of both the elite and the public to take on new roles and accede to different decision structures. In the next chapter, we take a timely look at these requisites as we ponder "bringing in the public."

Notes

1. Such a position could stem from the respondents' dissatisfaction with the current system understood to be a democracy. We note even for scholars there is no common ground on the parameters of democracy, and it is often very hard to draw a line between regimes. We invite the reader to consider Schedler's (2002) "chain of democratic choice," a set of conditions for free and fair elections, revealing even the most apparently democratic regimes would have a difficulty meeting his standards for an electoral democracy.
2. "Unimportant" was defined as 1–5 on a 10-point scale of importance.
3. That is accounting for the effects of confounding variables.
4. "To some extent, the question here is one of categorization: If a nation fails to implement policies designed to mitigate the impact of structural changes brought on by advancing technology, should we label that as a problem caused by technology, or politics?," asks Ford (2015, 58).
5. The ensuing four paragraphs are based on Brill (2018).
6. The discussion of the three challenges draws on Berggruen and Gardels (2013).
7. Gerring et al. find parliamentarism to be "a more reliable vehicle for good public policy [given] its capacity to function as a coordination device" (2008, 353), (re)interpreting the role of institutions as facilitators and arbiters of conflict arising from coordination problems.
8. Here we note the authors begin from a premise that the large questions on the rights to healthcare, education, basic economic security, and environment have been decided.
9. The expectations are that the core of the critical citizenry, the postmaterialist cohorts "experienced a relatively high sense of economic and physical security throughout their formative years" (Inglehart 1999, 252), affording them more independence and thus a lesser need for and respect of authority. Yet, scholars are seeing a *reversal* in their attitudes toward authoritarian leadership. It is now more the upper-income (16% in 2011 vs. 5% in 1995) rather than lower-income respondents, who believe a military rule to be a "good" or "very good" idea (Foa and Mounk 2016).
10. Just how many critical citizens are there and what do they want?

REFERENCES

Berggruen, Nicolas, and Nathan Gardels. 2013. *Intelligent governance for the 21st century: A middle way between west and east.* Cambridge, UK: Polity Press.

Blyth, Mark. 2012. *Great transformations: Economic ideas and institutional change in the twentieth century.* Cambridge, UK: Cambridge University Press.

Brill, Steven. 2018. *Tailspin: The people and forces behind America's fifty-year fall—And those fighting to reverse it.* New York: Alfred A. Knopf.

Dahl, Robert. 1989. *Democracy and its critics.* New Haven: Yale University Press. As cited in Powell (2004).

Dahl, Robert. 2006. *A preface to democratic theory.* Expanded ed. Chicago: University of Chicago Press.

Dalton, Russell J. 2017. "Political trust in North America." In *Handbook on political trust,* edited by Sonja Zmerli and Tom W. G. van der Meer. Cheltenham: Edward Elgar Publishing.

Diamond, Larry. 2004. "The state of democratization at the beginning of the 21st century." *The Whitehead Journal of Diplomacy and International Relations* 6 (1): 13–18.

The Economist. 2011. "The perils of extreme democracy." *The Economist,* April 20. https://www.economist.com/leaders/2011/04/20/the-perils-of-extreme-democracy.

The Economist. 2012. "The gap widens, again: No more than a temporary blip from the great recession." *The Economist,* March 10. https://www.economist.com/united-states/2012/03/10/the-gap-widens-again.

Faguet, Guy B. 2013. *The Affordable Care Act: A missed opportunity, A better way forward.* New York: Algora Publishing.

Foa, Roberto Stefan, and Yascha Mounk. 2016. "The democratic disconnect." *Journal of Democracy* 27 (3): 5–17.

Ford, Martin. 2015. *Rise of the robots: Technology and the threat of a jobless future.* New York: Basic Books.

Gerring, John, Strom C. Thacker, and Carola Moreno. 2008. "Are Parliamentary Systems Better?" *Comparative Political Studies* 42 (3): 327–59.

Gilens, Martin, and Benjamin I. Page. 2014. "Testing theories of American politics: Elites, interest groups, and average citizens." *Perspectives on Politics* 12 (3): 564–581.

Hacker, Jacob, and Paul Pierson. 2010. "Winner-take-all politics: Public policy, political organization, and the precipitous rise of top incomes in the United States." *Politics & Society* 38 (2): 152–204.

Hacker, Jacob, and Paul Pierson. 2011. *Winner-take-all politics.* New York: Simon & Schuster.

Hardin, Russell. 2000. "The public trust." In *Disaffected democracies*, edited by Susan J. Pharr and Robert. D. Putnam. Princeton: Princeton University Press.

Hayes, Christopher. 2012. *Twilight of the elites: America after meritocracy*. New York: Crown Publishers.

Hibbing, John R., and Elizabeth Theiss-Morse. 2004. *Stealth democracy: Americans' beliefs about how government should work*. Cambridge, UK: Cambridge University Press.

Htun, Mala. 2004. "Is gender like ethnicity? The political representation of identity groups." *Perspectives on Politics* 2 (3): 439–458.

Hunter, James Davison, and Carl Desportes Bowman. 2016. "The vanishing center of American Democracy." The Institute for Advanced Studies in Culture. http://iasculture.org/research/publications/vanishing-center.

Inglehart, Ronald. 1999. "Postmodernization erodes respect for authority, but increases support for democracy." In *Critical citizens: Global support for democratic government*, edited by Pippa Norris. Oxford: Oxford University Press.

Lardeyret, Guy. 1991. "The problem with PR." *Journal of Democracy* 2 (3): 30–35. https://doi.org/10.1353/jod.1991.0034.

Levitsky, Steven, and Lucan Way. 2002. "Elections without democracy: The rise of competitive authoritarianism." *Journal of Democracy* 13 (2): 51–66.

Lijphart, Arend. 1991. "Constitutional choices for new democracies." *Journal of Democracy* 2 (1): 72–84.

Lijphart, Arend. 2004. "Constitutional design for divided societies." *Journal of Democracy* 15 (2): 96–109.

Lindblom, Charles E. 1977. *Politics and markets*. New York: Basic Books.

McCombs, Maxwell, and Amy Reynolds, eds. 1999. *The poll with a human face: The national issues convention experiment in political communication*. Mahwah: Lawrence Erlbaum Associates.

Mills, C. Wright. 2000. *The power elite*. Vol. 20. Oxford: Oxford University Press.

Norris, Pippa. 1997. "Choosing electoral systems: Proportional, majoritarian and mixed systems." *International Political Science Review* 18 (3): 297–312.

Norris, Pippa, ed. 1999. *Critical citizens: Global support for democratic government*. Oxford: Oxford University Press.

Olson, Mancur. 2002. *The logic of collective action: Public goods and the theory of groups*. Cambridge, MA: Harvard University Press.

Olson, Mancur. 2008. *The rise and decline of nations: Economic growth, stagflation, and social rigidities*. New Haven: Yale University Press.

Powell, G. Bingham, Jr. 2004. "Political representation in comparative politics.' *Annual Review of Political Science* 7: 273–296.

Quade, Quentin L. 1991. "PR and democratic statecraft." *Journal of Democracy* 2 (3): 36–41.

Ruggie, John Gerard. 1982. "International regimes, transactions, and change: Embedded liberalism in the postwar economic order." *International Organization* 2: 36.

Schedler, Andreas. 2002. "The menu of manipulation." *Journal of Democracy* 13 (2): 36–50.

Smith, Martin J. 1990. "Pluralism, reformed pluralism and neopluralism: The role of pressure groups in policy-making." *Political Studies* 38 (2): 302–322.

Truman, David B. 1971. *The governmental process.* New York: Alfred A. Knopf. As cited in Gilens and Page (2014).

Warren, Mark E., and Hilary Pearse, eds. 2008. *Designing deliberative democracy: The British Columbia Citizens' Assembly.* New York: Cambridge University Press.

Wessel, David. 2015. "The typical male U.S. worker earned less in 2014 than in 1973." The Brookings Institution. https://www.brookings.edu/opinions/the-typical-male-u-s-worker-earned-less-in-2014-than-in-1973/.

Zakaria, Fareed. 2007. *The future of freedom: Illiberal democracy at home and abroad.* New York: W. W. Norton.

Zakaria, Fareed. 2012. "America needs a 2-page tax code." The Global Public Square Blog. http://globalpublicsquare.blogs.cnn.com/2012/03/24/zakaria-america-needs-a-2-page-tax-code/.

Zakaria, Fareed. 2016. "How Trump exposed the corruption in the U.S. tax code." *The Washington Post,* October 6. https://www.washingtonpost.com/opinions/how-trump-exposed-the-corruption-in-the-us-tax-code/2016/10/06/612eec4e-8bf8-11e6-875e-2c1bfe943b66_story.html.

CHAPTER 5

Bringing in the Public

In their study of citizens' attitudes toward democratic governance, Hibbing and Theiss-Morse (2004) confront the conventional view of what Americans expect of their political system. The authors conducted multiple focus group sessions and a custom survey at the national level[1] and gathered important data on how citizens view their government, how they respond to certain legislative proposals, how they perceive the political aptitudes of ordinary people, as well as on their perspectives on the responsibilities of people in government in an ideal polity. Their findings challenge the widespread assumptions that people are more interested in policy results than the processes behind obtaining these results, that they desire to reenter the political arena, and that people would be more satisfied with themselves, their community, and their political system with their deeper political engagement. How then do most people wish their government should work? And, more importantly, what is the thinking that underpins these attitudes? What does this mean for governance and for prospects of democratic change?

We begin with the authors' argument and their less intuitive answers, not the least as they provide much insight into trivialization of politics and its implications. While the authors have used their findings to diminish the value of civic engagement, we take a different perspective on bringing the public into a political forum. Deliberation is not only an integral component of democratic redesigns, as was argued, but it may also facilitate them. Managed deliberation promises to help people appreciate the diversity of viewpoints, the purpose of politics and their

© The Author(s) 2019

O. Bubak and H. Jacek, *Trivialization and Public Opinion*,
https://doi.org/10.1007/978-3-030-17925-0_5

role in it, and to stimulate reflection. It thus leads to critical engagement and learning, requisite to efficacious democratic involvement. Finally, it carries a potential to help change our discursive culture, building new shared meanings, ultimately benefiting our personal and civic choices.

Hibbing and Theiss-Morse (2004) begin with a look at the connection between policy and voting behavior. A major stream of political research has examined the connection between policy concerns and voting preferences, or policy outcomes and voter satisfaction (Alesina and Wacziarg 2000). Scholars have established relationships between policies and attitudes toward the people in power (Nye 1997), yet, due to a number of other factors, these turned out to be weaker than expected, thus decreasing their explanatory value. Many people, for example, have a limited will and capacity to assess how their position on issues stacks up with those of the political candidates (Delli Carpini and Keeter 1996). They may also assume that political parties converge on key issues such as economic stability, or basic education and security, important to all voters. Voters thus use shortcuts such as choosing candidates according to party affiliation, itself often adopted from their parents, or evaluating their candidates on the perceived personal qualities. Also, insofar as the voters have interest in certain policies, these may be limited to one or two issues, frequently of special interest to the individual.

Further, questions on the links between policy outcomes and political behavior, such as one's participation or withdrawal from politics based on disagreeable policies in effect or in the platforms of major political parties, lack adequate answers. "It seems possible that those willing to take to the streets or to turn their backs on the traditional parties would be those most discontented with current policies. However, tests of these ideas have been neither plentiful nor conclusive," write Hibbing and Theiss-Morse (2004, 24). Likewise, there is not much evidence supporting the link between a strong economy and increases in satisfaction and confidence in government (Putnam et al. 2000).

Finally, there are the limits to individual interest in and knowledge of the increasingly complex social and political matters, pointing away from policy issues as the primary determinants of the people's political preferences (Delli Carpini and Keeter 1996). Many of these limits are evident in public opinion polls and observed in research in this area (Chapter 6). In their own study, Hibbing and Theiss-Morse note, for example, that while many people complain that "the vast majority of Congress's members have no idea really what the people's wishes are" (27), the familiar "Washington is out of touch" complaint, their perception of government policies as reported in polls contradict this position. As the authors observe, "the vast majority of Americans (over 70 percent) consider themselves moderate, and these moderates view government policies as right in sync with their own preferences" (29). While we question whether the label "moderate" is interpreted the same way by everyone, the point is that "[m]any people who have no particular problem with the policies produced by the government are tremendously dissatisfied with that government" (34). Given such evidence indicating policy plays a lesser role in citizens' concerns, there must be other reasons for the popular (dis)satisfaction with the government. These come through discussions with participants who talk more of politicians' hidden agendas and undue motivations. As Hibbing and Theiss-Morse note:

> when it is apparent that the political arena is filled with intense policy disagreement, people conclude that the reason must be illegitimate—namely, the influence of special interests. After all, the reasoning goes, people like me could not be the cause of bitter policy disagreements on all those issues because we do not care that much, because we do not see their relevance, and because even when a particular policy goal is important to us we cannot understand why bickering over the details of proposed solutions is necessary. (133)

Hence, as the people assume, or *misjudge*, a general consensus on main issues concerning old age security, fiscal responsibility, or equal access to health care and education, among others, they think differently of the role and purpose of government processes. As a result, rather than specific policy details, they lament the lack of communication and compromise among the parties, the harmful influence of special interests, corruption, or the loss of public servants' principles. So, it is practice rather than policy, and more specifically *processes* of government which have a greater effect on most people's views. That is, the perceptions of *how* a policy was made gain in importance (Hibbing and Theiss-Morse 2001).

People usually do not know what would change, say, drug and education policies for the better, but they do know that special interests, entrenched political parties, and careerist politicians have a stranglehold on the political process. This sentiment is straightforward and manageable. It requires no mastery of the nuances of parliamentary procedure. In fact, it requires remarkably little information at all, it does not pick sides, and the scapegoat (special interests) is vague enough that few people, save perhaps the occasional professional lobbyist, are likely to be offended. In fact, loathing special interests constitutes a unifying belief in modern America. It allows people to talk about politics without a shred of specific evidence and, like the weather, pulls people together against a common, seemingly uncontrollable, enemy,

explain Hibbing and Theiss-Morse (2004, 39). Privy to these trivialized views, we may begin to appreciate why, for example, the "government takeover of health care" framing, discussed in an earlier chapter (2), was employed with such a verve among the opponents of the ACA. The authors thus conclude that given these simple images of privilege, back-room deals, and sold-out politicians, most people are primarily concerned with not being exploited.[2]

And so, although the policy proposals advanced by the political class may seem to match what ordinary citizens want, people will still scrutinize the underlying process. Regardless of the reality, they see changes to term limits, campaign finance, or accountability, among others, as being against the interest of those in power and not amenable to change. Such thinking generates an ongoing dissatisfaction with government and results in calls for the removal of elected officials from their posts as the (only) remedy (Hibbing and Theiss-Morse 2004).[3] This is also why an analytical focus on the perceptions of process, rather than policy and its outcomes, is so important.

The People's View

The people's preoccupation with process over outcomes leaves a larger question, especially important in our context. What government process do most people desire and *why*? As hinted, Hibbing and Theiss-Morse come to conclusions counter to the dominant populist views that see people clamoring to reassert their place at the deliberation table and regain their right to make decisions on important political matters (Kidd 2001, among others). Indeed, while people do not have much confidence in the competence and integrity of the American citizenry, two-thirds of the public prefer to expand the power of the ordinary people and rebalance the decision-making capacity away from the political institutions and their members. At the same time, however, people report disinterest in politics and would prefer to be spared from much involvement. The explanation behind this apparent contradiction, in the authors' view, lies in the people's conviction that the current governance processes are biased and dominated by self-serving elites. Given no other options, people believe they must act to keep checks on the power of this political class. Aside from the people's political involvement, this requires a set of interventions, including an increased use of instruments of direct democracy such as public initiatives and referenda, imposing term limits, shifting power to the state and local governments, or limiting the influence of interest groups.

Yet, if given an option to have a system reflecting the preferences of most ordinary people, Hibbing and Theiss-Morse find it would be, what they call, a stealth democracy: "a system that is instinctively in touch with the problems of real Americans and that would respond with every ounce of courtesy and attentiveness imaginable if those real Americans ever did make an actual request upon the system" (131). This, in essence, rejection of politics reveals how most people think of political problems and their resolution, and how they believe the system should (not) work. What are the roots of such thinking?

First, according to the authors, many people misperceive the level of consensus on the general (dis)interest in politics as well as on particular political issues. The authors, for example, find no semblance of consensus when they asked their survey respondents to identify "the most important problem facing the country." Yet, when asked if "the American people agreed on the most important problem facing the country," 39 and 41% of respondents indicated that most or some did, respectively (132). Rooted in one's lack of political knowledge, perceiving such consensus in turn lessens one's need to seek further information, learn, and engage. The fact that a lack of policy detail accompanied by confident plans to solve major issues with ease—characteristic of the winning candidate of the 2016 US presidential election—did not seem suspect (Chapter 2) can be partly explained by such a posture.

Moreover, such a false reading of consensus ultimately leads to a different orientation toward politics including the views on political conflict and compromise. "Since, according to the people's perceptions, Americans tend to agree on where the nation should go, and since getting there is merely a technical problem, is it any wonder that people have little time for policy debate and compromise?" ask the authors

(133). Perceiving a general agreement on large issues, people interpret conflict as a product of special interests and assign lesser value to democratic processes such as negotiation and compromise.

The responses to the scholars' survey questions on beliefs about debate and compromise provide support for this account. In all, 86% of respondents indicated an agreement with "Elected officials would help the country more if they would stop talking and just take action on important problems;" 43% with "Officials should debate more because they are too likely to rush into action without discussing all sides;" and 60% with "What people call compromise is really just selling out on one's principles" (135–136). While such results are always open to challenge, as we will discuss, there is nevertheless other evidence of decreasing trust in the existing democratic processes and institutions.

Considering then the public's views on debate and compromise, what should governing look like? Numerous polls show the American citizens' deference for apolitical, undemocratic, insular, and non-transparent institutions, such as the military or the police (Bishop 2017),[4] suggesting Americans may be open to giving more power to unelected, expert elites. Indeed, Hibbing and Theiss-Morse find that nearly half of their respondents would agree to give more governing authority to independent institutions and to largely unaccountable officials. This is consistent with the 2011 World Values Survey, for example, where 49% of US respondents agreed that "having experts, not government, make decisions according to what they think is best for the country," up from 36% in 1995 (Foa and Mounk 2016, 13). Recall, on the other hand, about two-thirds of Americans would like more power in the hands of the people. This overlap, the authors believe, lies in the people's simplistic conclusion that given the broad agreement on the larger goals, there is no reason for conflict and thus for much public debate and compromise.

Governing then becomes a technical matter of administration and management that can be entrusted to disinterested bureaucracy. In the end, conflict is a product of special interests which ought to be eliminated from the equation by shifting the power to the people or unelected elite. "It is the same reason that ostensibly populist Americans give a puzzlingly warm embrace to extremely rich candidates" (Hibbing and Theiss-Morse 2004, 143), ones who are thought to be immune from the corrupting effects of money and special interests. Such thinking has been evident most recently in the 2016 US presidential election whose winner did not hesitate to drive such a message.

SPEAKING TOGETHER

To be sure, the above accounts are just some, albeit compelling, readings of a significant proportion of the American public's contemporary attitudes toward politics. While we do not have comparative data, there is little doubt the attitudes of the people have changed over time. This is not the least due to the increased visibility into the legislative processes driven by institutional as well as technological changes, shifts in the way the public is presented and consumes information, or broader politico-economic forces affecting government performance (Chapter 4). As discussed earlier, an alternate analysis sees not the lack of people's knowledge, but the ostensible absence of major social policy conflict—which has stimulated political awareness in the past—as underlying the perceptions of societal consensus. Yet, let us briefly return to our health care example and remind ourselves its defining policy questions. Well-posed by Mahar (2006), these are presented in Box 5.1.

Box 5.1 Difficult questions in health care policy

Is health care a right or a personal responsibility? If it is a responsibility, does that mean that control over health care spending should be turned over to individual consumers? What if consumers don't spend their family's health care dollars wisely—is this society's concern?

On the other hand, if health care is a right, does that mean that it is society's responsibility to guarantee that every citizen has the same level of care? How do we ensure quality? Should we pay certain hospitals and doctors more for better care? Would pay for performance lead to a two-tier system? And if so, what would count as "good enough" at the lower tier?

In the end, given finite resources, must we ration health care, and if so, on what basis: ability to pay? Age? The likely odds of treatment achieving a cure? Or instead of rationing services, should we try to bring down health care prices?

Source Mahar (2006, xvi)

These hard questions, inviting further discussion and argument, are far from settled in the United States, or, for the large part, elsewhere. It is not difficult to see how most of these can lead to intense political disagreements, heightened further by the sensitivity of the topic. And so, we can appreciate the barriers posed by the misreading of political consensus on such issues and many others. First, as discussed, it leads to trivialized views of political conflict as suspect and politics more generally as unnecessary and alters the citizens' view on governance and their role in it. Also, it reduces the perceived need for a public dialogue. Hence, these attitudes pose a challenge to democratic redesigns depending on deliberation at all levels[5] and to arguments of those wishing to treat the contemporary democratic deficits by increasing the political engagement of the public.

Yet, it is the very public deliberation which, if approached properly, can help address these lapses. Before we proceed with making our case for deliberation, it is useful to provide its definition. A good start is Rucht's formulation based on his synthesis of various conceptions of deliberation across literature. The author sees it "as an interaction of speakers who (1) do not exclude other people willing to speak, (2) consider themselves as equal in their potential to reason, (3) present experiences, facts and arguments, and (4) are open to modify their original views, attitudes and opinions in reaction to the perceptions and reasons of others" (Rucht 2012, 114). Thus, deliberation can be described as an inclusive process of open-minded, reciprocal, and reasoned discourse aiming to find better answers to conflicting issues.

There has been an increasing interest in deliberation in the recent decades, particularly in context of deliberative democracy, offering an alternate perspective to traditional conceptions of democratic legitimacy derived chiefly from the aggregation of preferences (Smith 2012). According to one broad definition, deliberative democracy is thus "any one of a family of views according to which the public deliberation of free and equal citizens is the core of legitimate political decision making and self-government" (Bohman 1998, 401). Hence, this view of democracy sees political decisions informed by considered and inclusive argumentation as central to their quality and legitimacy. There are many theoretical and practical questions on deliberation and deliberative governance (Newton 2012), some of which have found answers in the democratic innovations of the recent years as well as through intensified academic engagement. We discuss these along with their travails next.

DELIBERATION IN ACTION

January 1996 witnessed one exceptional, if fleeting, moment in American politics. Reporters, scholars, politicians, subject matter experts, and above all, over 400 randomly selected citizens from across the nation converged on Austin, Texas to join in the first ever national deliberative poll, the National Issues Convention (NIC). The four-day, nationally televised event, as much an experiment as an exercise of an alternate tool of democracy, was on.

A brainchild of a political scholar James Fishkin, the NIC became a venue for a sample of citizens with a variety of views to come together, discuss political issues, weigh information from others, and contemplate their positions. Fishkin and Luskin describe this rare occasion, designed so that representatives of the people get an

> opportunity and incentives to behave more like ideal citizens: to pay attention, to acquire information, to share their views and listen to others, and to think their positions through. ...Instead of getting their information from sound bites, they read briefing materials, listen to policy experts and political leaders, and in many cases are inspired to seek additional information on their own. Instead of passively watching the media in isolation, they share their concerns in small-group deliberations and get to question policy experts and political leaders. (1999, 4)

The nation thus gained an important insight into what public opinion "would be" with adequate information and an opportunity to reach a "considered judgment" (6). The media also got a chance to bring this unique event into the spotlight, provide commentaries, analyses, and ultimately take public deliberation, albeit briefly, to the center of national politics. Finally, it offered social scientists a chance to collect participant and non-participant information prior and after the event, aiming to obtain insight into the efficacy of the process.

The NIC and other deliberative polls have generated many a question and debate among social scientists. Are deliberative polls effective in informing and educating the public? Can they change public opinion? Improve its quality? Do deliberative polls help in creating more discerning citizens, acute to the diversity of views? How do citizens deliberate? Can such polls help overcome ideological divides?

The NIC provided answers to a number of these questions (McCombs and Reynolds 1999) despite a set of challenges such as with the sample representativeness.[6] On the whole, Fishkin and Luskin found the event succeeded in changing political attitudes, fulfilled its informational role, and changed the participants' attitudes toward the political process. More specifically, the authors observed that "on average, participants changed position significantly on 25 of 49 policy issues and on 5 of 10 empirical premises" (25). While the authors did not establish a cognitive function of the NIC, there is some evidence of participant learning. Questionnaires reveal statistically significant increases (7%) in correct answers to 10 knowledge items. In addition, post-event surveys have indicated significant increases in the participants' sense of civic efficacy. On the other hand, others provided a mixed assessment of the NIC. Smith, for example, noted:

> On the positive side, delegates were serious and attentive…the discussions were deeply felt and reflected the core beliefs and life experiences of the delegates. On the negative side, most discussion was general. It was anchored in personal experiences and not closely tied to public policy. When the discussion moved beyond private lives and beliefs, the quality of the information and asserted facts was very mixed, with wrong assertions nearly equaling correct evidence. (1999, 49–50)

Beyond these outcomes, the success of the NIC can be seen in the series of public deliberations it helped to inspire, furthering the case for its public value. The decision of the Public Utility Commission of Texas (PUC), for example, is a well-known case of institutionalizing a deliberative process. Starting in the mid-1990s, the public utilities of Texas were required to involve the public in developing "Integrated Resource Plans," strategies to satisfy the energy demands of their serviced areas (Fishkin and Luskin 1999).

Decisions thus needed to be made on the reliability, stability, environmental impact, and ultimately the mix of energy sources to be developed. Deliberative sessions helped to establish the trade-offs between investments into conservation, renewables, fossil fuels, and infrastructure to import energy from outside the region. An initial set of such sessions across several service areas indicated a shift of focus away from alternative energy and toward conservation, as the participants recognized the "complexities of relying on windmills or solar power as the principal basis for supplying their power needs" (Fishkin and Luskin 1999, 35). What is more, it was found the participants were willing to pay extra for renewable sources of energy (Fishkin and Luskin 1999) as part of an appropriate energy portfolio. The successes of these sessions lead the PUC to update its rules, now expecting "that public participation be statistically representative of customers, that it involve a two-way dialogue, that participants be given access to accurate and balanced information representing competing viewpoints, and that quantitative assessment of their final views be reported as part of the process" (Fishkin and Luskin 1999, 34). As Fishkin later added, "[o]nce the microcosm was seen as a legitimate representation of the views of ordinary citizens, and once its process was seen as transparent and balanced, the conclusions acquired a recommending force. The results were well received throughout the policy community and were even treated favourably in press releases by the utility companies and the Environmental Defense Fund on the same day" (2012, 80). Over time, the results of deliberative polls informed a series of energy programs ultimately making Texas the leading producer of wind power in the United States (Fishkin 2012).

Deliberative polls are among the number of democratic innovations hoped to encourage citizen participation and help address what some view as democratic deficits (Warren and Pearse 2008; Newton 2012). While the list of the new tools is diverse, including community councils, focus groups, or public hearings and submissions, the recent decades have seen experimentation with so-called mini-publics (Goodin and Dryzek 2006). The mini-publics, which include the aforementioned deliberative polls, citizens' juries, planning cells, consensus conferences, and assemblies, have a number of purposeful features: *randomly* selected participants are brought together for one or more day sessions, dependent upon the task at hand; there, they learn from each other and from *experts* who may also be cross-examined; the proceedings are *facilitated* by trained staff ensuring fairness; and the participants have opportunities to *deliberate* in joint or separate sessions (Smith 2012). While various mini-publics have been conducted for decades around the world, recent experiments with Citizens' Assemblies (CAs) have been seen as taking deliberation to the next level.

Particularly notable have been CAs on electoral reform conducted in British Columbia (2004) and Ontario (2006–2007). These have not only demonstrated an alternate, citizen-centric process for "democratic renewal" (Warren and Pearse 2008) but also confirmed some deeper challenges emerging from the above discussion. In a significant departure from the past, the governments of British Columbia (BC) and, later, Ontario (ON) agreed to consider a decision on whether to go away with the single-member plurality electoral system (SMP) whose democratic qualities have long been suspect (Smith 2012; Warren and Pearse 2008). In another first, the governments opted for a novel process centered on a deliberative group of citizens which was to study and decide if and how to change the existing system. Any changes were to be put before the voters in a referendum. "Never before in modern history has a democratic government given to unelected, 'ordinary' citizens the power to review an important public policy, and then seek from all citizens approval of any proposed changes to that policy," noted the Chair of the CA in BC (Blaney 2004). To ensure the body reflected the population at large, the members of the assemblies were chosen in a near-random manner, with stipulations on gender (also age in ON) and representation across electoral districts (Warren and Pearse 2008; Rose 2007). The 160 member BC assembly thus consisted of two individuals from each of its 79 electoral districts in addition to two aboriginal members, while the 103 member ON assembly had one individual from each of its 103 districts including one identified as aboriginal (Warren and Pearse 2008; Rose 2007).

The effort of both assemblies unfolded over three distinct phases. The work began with the learning phase during which the participants studied the properties of different electoral systems as they drew on information from internal and external experts, facilitated discussions, informal conversations, self-study, and a web forum. In BC, the members were given a lesson on the challenges of deliberation, addressing the importance of attentiveness, communication, and receptiveness, among other deliberative qualities (Warren and Pearse 2008). The ON assembly exposed the participants to talk on the functioning of the parliament given by former provincial politicians as well as an opportunity to learn through simulations (Rose 2007). These activities were followed by the public consultation phase, during which the CA participants had a chance to learn from other citizens in public hearings and written submissions. Finally, in the deliberation phase, the participants reviewed information, debated alternatives, reasoned, and voted. In both provinces, the CA participants voted overwhelmingly for change in their current SMP systems and recommended versions of single transferable vote (STV) and mixed member proportional representation (MMP) in BC (Warren and Pearse 2008) and ON (Rose 2007), respectively.

As established, the CAs have concluded with their releases of final reports and their recommendations were readied for referenda. In BC, the question the voters were asked was a binary "Should British Columbia change to the BC-STV electoral system as recommended by the Citizens' Assembly on Electoral Reform?" (Warren and Pearse 2008). In order to pass, the proposal required a supermajority of both district and popular votes. While 77 of 79 districts voted in favor of the proposal, it received 57.69% of the popular vote of the 60% needed. Due to the close result, the BC voters were given a second chance, a referendum which was also unsuccessful (Smith 2012). In ON, the results were clearer, as the proposal found support among only 37% of referendum voters (Smith 2012).

The CAs have been subject to a number of analyses, starting from their designs and their capacities to operate independently from the influence of government (Pal 2012; Pearse 2008), to studies on how participants come to understand their roles (Lang 2008). While some of these are solvable procedurally, we bring up two possible challenges to deliberation as pertinent to our discussion. First, as hinted, the goal in establishing the CAs was to task ordinary citizens, rather than expert politicians, with evaluation of existing provincial electoral systems and, if needed, propose a redesign. Not without a reason, some have been concerned with the citizens' ability to carry out this task on account of their limited awareness and political engagement. In their BC study of participant knowledge and decisions, Blais et al. (2008) found not only that the CA's choice was reasonable and intelligible but also a little evidence "that the most informed had or developed significantly different preferences" or "that the most informed led the group or that the least informed followed their lead" (143). In ON, Rose (2007) observed a "very cautious and methodical way in which the assembly operated" (15). Rose also observed a evidence of participant learning as well as their recognition that learning was critical to the mission's success.

Second, the outcomes of both referenda have affirmed a larger issue. Given that design of an electoral system may create political advantages for one group over another, there is an inherent conflict in keeping this choice within the purview of politicians. Such a decision, however, requires time and resources, which are sparse for most people. Thus, the BC and ON governments decided to delegate this task to a representative sample of disinterested citizens, and with it they hoped to improve the trust in the process and democratic legitimacy. The voters were to have the final say on what was to be assessed as the people's design, one created by ordinary, albeit fully informed individuals. Nevertheless, to make their decision, the voters needed to be privy to the proposal, or at least understand the qualities of the CA.

As readers of this chapter, we may thus be able to appreciate the roots of the outcomes: much of the citizenry is disengaged and people focus on processes, as these can be understood with less effort than policy. In ON, Stephenson and Tanguay (2009) found "that cynicism about government was a factor in the referendum, as the most cynical voters were more likely not to vote, and informed cynical voters were significantly more likely to oppose the electoral change." The authors did not find the discontent with electoral systems and its outcomes to be of influence on the choices of ON voters. In the BC case, Cutler et al. (2008) found that less than 60% of voters did not know anything about either the CA or STV. As Hibbing and Theiss-Morse (2004) would expect, those who did not know anything were ambivalent, whereas those who knew something were preoccupied not with the qualities of the STV but the representative features of the CA (Cutler et al. 2008). In the end, the more voters knew about the CA or the STV, the more likely they were to vote to accept the proposal (Cutler et al. 2008).

WHY DELIBERATION?

In the CA cases above, representative bodies of citizens were brought together to evaluate and decide on their provinces' electoral systems. If they found changes necessary, their proposals were to be submitted to their fellow citizens for an approval in a referendum. There are many trade-off decisions the assembly members had to cope with in assessing their electoral systems,[7] including on the effectiveness and stability of government, equality of vote, fairness, or representation, among others (Warren and Pearse 2008). In BC, the deliberations determined the priorities to be maximizing the choices of the voters, ensuring fairness by proportional conversion of votes to seats, and securing local representation, rather than the traditional schemes of a single-party unimpeded to carry out its agenda (Warren and Pearse 2008). The members needed to consider values and practical needs as they listened to experts, their peers, and the citizens in making their reasoned decision.

While theirs was an uncommon exercise on issues not often discussed or broadly understood, there are other, more familiar judgments to be made. Consider again our health care example and the difficult questions posed in Box 5.1. How do we resolve the conflicts between the rights and responsibilities in this domain? How do we allocate scarce resources? What are the liberties of health care consumers? These are questions of values, evolving with time and social context. Addressing these divisive, moral conflicts adequately, and democratic improvements more generally requires, according to Gutmann and Thompson (1998), a deliberative democracy, an ongoing public dialogue in search for an acceptable common ground, or mutual recognition, enabled by reasoned argument.

Gutmann and Thompson (1998) begin from an observation that moral conflict is continual, rooted not only in persistent scarcity and limited generosity, as argued by Hume, but also in disagreement on moral values and incomplete understanding of the world. Each of these four sources of moral conflict provides the rationale for embedding deliberation into the democratic process. First, deliberation enhances political legitimacy, particularly of difficult decisions on how to distribute limited resources. Scarcity means that there are limits on who gets what or how much, and having a reasoned and transparent process helps to make these choices more acceptable. "Even with regard to political decisions with which they disagree, citizens are likely to take a different attitude toward those that are adopted after careful consideration of the relevant conflicting moral claims and those that are adopted only after calculation of the relative strength of the competing political interests," explain the authors. Importantly, such a process may enhance cooperation and may lead to more resources in the future.

Another benefit of deliberation is its capacity to cope with limited generosity (as altruism is not a common quality) by promoting broader, socially oriented perspectives. The citizens are thus encouraged to go beyond narrow interests and consider a common good. While citizens cannot be expected to change their orientation, the rationale here is to elevate inclusive thinking over the power-driven decision-making processes. The third advantage of the deliberation process, as conceived by the authors, lies in its moral reasoning, helpful in tacking mutually incompatible values. Moral reasoning thus helps to separate different kinds of interests and determine their relative importance. It encourages mutual understanding and appreciation, aiding to resolve conflict or promote respect toward unresolved stances. The final benefit of deliberation derives from its nature as an ongoing process of mutual learning. Unlike in the traditional political bargaining in which parties learn to maximize their prerogatives, the reasoning and justification of deliberation make it more likely to arrive at other, previously unseen solutions, or to acknowledge and correct mistakes.

The above four reasons, according to Gutmann and Thompson, provide grounds for "extending the domain of deliberation within the democratic process." This also addresses the limits of the two dominant views of democracy, the procedural and constitutional, both dedicated to morality and legitimacy, yet lacking in their adequacy of addressing moral conflict. "Procedural and constitutional democrats agree that their disagreement turns on the question whether democratic procedures have priority over just outcomes or just outcomes have priority over democratic procedures," explain the authors, adding their conception has no such a priority. Instead, Gutmann and Thompson conceive of deliberation as an outcome-oriented process guided by a set of six interacting principles.

The first three, reciprocity, publicity, and accountability, regulate the deliberation process, guiding the types, the exposure, and the participants of deliberation. The central principle in deliberative democracy, and also a fundamental moral concept, is reciprocity. Cognizant of lasting moral disagreement, the authors argue for mutual respect and accommodation as set out by reciprocity. "When citizens make moral claims in a deliberative democracy, they appeal to reasons or principles that can he shared by fellow citizens who are similarly motivated. The moral reasoning is in this way mutually acceptable," add the authors. There is also a call for "reliable methods of inquiry," an empirical requirement of reciprocity, and for plausibility, in cases without evidence.

The authors are also mindful of the content of deliberation, or the solutions it seeks. Important to highlight in our context is Gutmann and Thompson's effort to expand the horizons of discourse and keep the solution space less constrained. This means an explicit commitment to going beyond the conversation-ending claims of existing moral theories. The authors observe that

> [libertarians, egalitarians, or utilitarians] often speak as though their claims were decisive independently of a process of deliberation, evidently assuming that the principles are the only reasonable and sufficient standards for resolving the dispute. Acting on this assumption in the face of moral disagreement in politics makes further deliberation appear unnecessary. Deliberative democracy rejects the assumption because its citizens remain open to the possibility of respecting reasonable positions with which they disagree.

The authors thus advance three principles, basic liberty, basic opportunity, and fair opportunity, which make up the content. These "submit themselves to the conditions of deliberative democracy over a greater range than the more comprehensive and single-valued principles of utility, liberty, and equality admit," recognize Gutmann and Thompson. Sitting atop various assumptions, in turn enabled by flawed philosophies we discussed in Chapter 3, such principles have been developed and embraced as shortcuts in dealing with some hard questions arising in complex societies. However, the authors understand addressing moral conflict requires going beyond assumptions, monocultures, and ideas. Mindful of the changing environment, this must be an ongoing search for a balance among a multitude of interacting factors. Rather than reaching to a traditional doctrine, it requires a framework for argument, a model of which Gutmann and Thompson advance.

Conclusion

Recent research challenged the traditional assumptions on how a great deal of people view politics and how they would prefer their government to work. Hibbing and Theiss-Morse's (2004) contribution finds it is the people's misperceptions of consensus that inform their attitudes toward politics and politicians, leading to their misunderstanding of political conflict and affecting their sense of governance and their part in it. People thus favor a "stealth democracy," offering a peace of mind of a system working for the people rather than the elite, yet one needing a little citizen attention. With this understanding, the authors see a solution in a compromise: Policies aiming to reduce the elite's opportunities to be self-serving, and teaching the public that disagreement is a natural part of politics.

While coming to some important findings, Hibbing and Theiss-Morse's research and conclusions neglect two fundamental issues. The first is that their subjects had no exposure to democratic innovations, ones designed to enhance civic engagement and inclusiveness. How would the participants' views of governance change with their experience in a deliberative setting? Without such knowledge, it is difficult to make any meaningful suggestions for a redesign. The second, related problem is the evolving condition of a democratic society. As we discussed previously, pluralist democracy has inherent flaws creating a strong rationale for a new system, particularly when faced with challenges of an increasingly connected, diverse citizenry, and the politico-economic reconfigurations of globalization. We discussed a proposal for governance restructuring to deal with these challenges—a solution which relied on deliberation at all levels. This solution brings the government closer to the people, an area where they are the most knowledgeable and effective. How would the respondents react to such novel demands?

We thus engaged select experiments in democratic renewal, all of which depend on deliberation of representative bodies of ordinary people. These provided evidence that, when given the resources and a proper venue, ordinary citizens have the will and capacity to come to robust decisions. Also, with these opportunities, the citizens' sense of civic efficacy and the importance of learning increases. For example, in the case of CA in ON, an instructor observed that "citizens desire for knowledge – when given the right incentives such as the possibility of changing policy – is great" (Rose 2007, 13).

Yet, to us, deliberation is not just about involving and legitimating, but also a model of a different engagement with practical problems, an effort that leads beyond policy solutions. It pushes people to ask better questions about the surrounding world. A number of participant questions posed at the NIC demonstrate this deeper engagement. For example, instead of raising the generic "Can we narrow that gap?" question on inequality, a participant asked, "Can we narrow that gap and still keep a free-market economy?" A question dealing with a middle-class tax relief was not solely on its extent but rather "How would you structure the tax code and government spending so we can balance the budget and give middle-class Americans a break?" (more in Fishkin and Luskin 1999, 13). As we recognize the value of posing questions (Marquis et al. 2012), even if without immediate or even correct answers (Roediger and Finn 2009), we develop a different appreciation for the normative potentials of deliberation. What is more, if the citizens' false perceptions of consensus are at the core of their misappreciation of governance, deliberation should be a prime place to learn of diversity of opinion and values, helping to change the people's views of politics.

We closed the chapter with a highly visible argument for a new democracy, a view of deliberation as central to coping adequately with the persistent moral conflict. This reconception of democracy has not escaped comments and critiques, whether on its emphases or neglects

(Macedo 1999). But while the greater vision may be aspirational, we appreciate its more fundamental elements, speaking also to our position. Gutmann and Thompson (1998) recognize that moral deliberation must go beyond the predominant "single-value principles," and must, in effect, avoid trivialization of moral questions. Taking exclusively utilitarian, libertarian, or other lenses suggests answers before the conversation has even begun, just as working in the realm of ideas rather than substance is detrimental to discourse more generally. And thus, we hope for more mini-publics and similar instruments of managed deliberation, not only as ways of bringing the public into a dialogue but also as means of finding new shared meanings: an appreciation of nuance and complexity, the necessity for mutual engagement rather than group retreat, and learning. But perhaps there are other limitations that stand in the way. We will explore these in the next chapter.

NOTES

1. Democratic Processes Survey (Hibbing and Theiss-Morse 1998).
2. "The public's suspicions on these points are not entirely misplaced. The amount of posturing in Congress on term limits probably exceeded that occurring on the typical policy issue by a factor of ten. It was an opportunity to voice support for a wildly popular concept, knowing the chances of it seeing the light of day were slim to none," admit Hibbing and Theiss-Morse (2004, 58).
3. These findings offer a new perspective on the strategic questioning of the electoral process by the Republican candidate in the 2016 US presidential race.
4. Although observed has been a steady decline in confidence in most other such institutions, including the Supreme Court (Bishop 2017).
5. As, for example, in the redesign discussed in Chapter 4.
6. As the experiment required travel, there was a level of self-selection. More likely to travel were the younger, politically engaged, and/or educated individuals (Merkle 1996; Fishkin and Luskin 1999).
7. More on electoral systems in Chapter 4.

REFERENCES

Alesina, Alberto, and Romain Wacziarg. 2000. "The economics of civic trust." In *Disaffected democracies*, edited by Susan J. Pharr and Robert D. Putnam. Princeton: Princeton University Press.

Bishop, Bill. 2017. "Americans have lost faith in institutions. That's not because of Trump or 'fake news.'" *The Washington Post*, March, 3. https://www.washingtonpost.com/posteverything/wp/2017/03/03/americans-have-lost-faith-in-institutions-thats-not-because-of-trump-or-fake-news/.

Blais, André, R. Kenneth Carty, and Patrick Fournier. 2008. "Do citizen assemblies make reasonable choices." In *Designing deliberative democracy: The British Columbia citizens' assembly*, edited by Mark E. Warren and Hilary Pearse. New York: Cambridge University Press.

Blaney, Jack. 2004. "Message from Jack Blaney, chair of the citizens' assembly." *Citizens' Assembly.* https://citizensassembly.arts.ubc.ca/public/inaction/chair_message.htm. Also cited in Smith (2012).

Bohman, James. 1998. "Survey article: The coming of age of deliberative democracy." *Journal of Political Philosophy* 6 (4): 400–425. As cited in Smith (2012).

Cutler, Fred, Richard Johnston, R. Kenneth Carty, Andre´ Blais, and Patrick Fournier. 2008. "Deliberation, information, and trust: The British Columbia citizens' assembly as agenda setter." In *Designing deliberative democracy: The British Columbia citizens' assembly*, edited by Mark E. Warren and Hilary Pearse. New York: Cambridge University Press.

Delli Carpini, Michael X., and Scott Keeter. 1996. *What Americans know about politics and why it matters.* New Haven: Yale University Press. As cited in Hibbing and Theiss-Morse (2004).

Fishkin, James S. 2012. "Deliberative polling: Reflections on an ideal made practical." In *Evaluating democratic innovations: Curing the democratic malaise?*, edited by Kenneth Newton and Brigitte Geissel. London and New York: Routledge.

Fishkin, James S., and Robert C. Luskin. 1999. "Bringing deliberation to the democratic dialogue." In *The poll with a human face: The national issues convention experiment in political communication*, edited by Maxwell McCombs and Amy Reynolds. Mahwah, NJ: Lawrence Erlbaum Associates.

Foa, Roberto Stefan, and Yascha Mounk. 2016. "The democratic disconnect." *Journal of Democracy* 27 (3): 5–17.

Goodin, Robert E., and John S. Dryzek. 2006. "Deliberative impacts: The macro-political uptake of mini-publics." *Politics & Society* 34 (2): 219–244. As cited in Smith (2012).

Gutmann, Amy, and Dennis F. Thompson. 1998. *Democracy and disagreement.* Cambridge, MA: Harvard University Press.

Hibbing, John R., and Elizabeth Theiss-Morse. 1998. *Democratic processes survey, 1998.* Princeton, NJ: Gallup Organization.

Hibbing, John R., and Elizabeth Theiss-Morse. 2001. "Process preference and American politics: What the people want government to be." *American Political Science Review* 95 (1): 145–153.

Hibbing, John R., and Elizabeth Theiss-Morse. 2004. *Stealth democracy: Americans' beliefs about how government should work.* Cambridge, UK: Cambridge University Press.

Kidd, Quentin. 2001. *American Government: Readings from across Society.* New York: Longman. As cited in Hibbing and Theiss-Morse (2004).

Lang, Amy. 2008. "Agenda-setting in deliberative forums: expert influence and citizen autonomy in the British Columbia citizens' assembly." In *Designing deliberative democracy: The British Columbia citizens' assembly,* edited by Mark E. Warren and Hilary Pearse. New York: Cambridge University Press.

Macedo, Stephen, ed. 1999. *Deliberative politics: Essays on democracy and disagreement.* Oxford and New York: Oxford University Press.

Mahar, Maggie. 2006. *Money driven medicine: The real reason health care costs so much.* New York: HarperCollins.

Marquis, Elizabeth, Bonny Jung, Ann Fudge-Schormans, Susan Vajoczki, Robert Wilton, Susan Baptiste, and Anju Joshi. 2012. "Creating, resisting or neglecting change: Exploring the complexities of accessible education for students with disabilities." *The Canadian Journal for the Scholarship of Teaching and Learning* 3 (2): 2.

McCombs, Maxwell, and Amy Reynolds, eds. 1999. *The poll with a human face: The national issues convention experiment in political communication.* Mahwah, NJ: Lawrence Erlbaum Associates.

Merkle, Daniel M. 1996. "The polls—Review: The national issues convention deliberative poll." *Public Opinion Quarterly* 60 (4): 588–619.

Newton, Ken. 2012. "Making better citizens?" In *Evaluating democratic innovations: Curing the democratic malaise?,* edited by Kenneth Newton and Brigitte Geissel. London and New York: Routledge.

Nye, Joseph S., Jr. 1997. "Introduction: The decline of confidence in government." In *Why people don't trust government,* edited by Joseph S. Nye, Jr., Philip D. Zelikow, and David C. King. Cambridge, MA: Harvard University Press.

Pal, Michael. 2012. "The promise and limits of citizens' assemblies: Deliberation, institutions and the law of democracy." *Queen's LJ* 38: 259.

Pearse, Hilary. 2008. "Institutional design and citizen deliberation." In *Designing deliberative democracy: The British Columbia citizens' assembly,* edited by Mark E. Warren and Hilary Pearse. New York: Cambridge University Press.

Putnam, Robert D., Susan J. Pharr, and Russell J. Dalton. 2000. "Introduction: What's troubling the trilateral democracies?" In *Disaffected Democracies,* edited by Susan J. Pharr and Robert D. Putnam. Princeton: Princeton University Press. As cited in Hibbing and Theiss-Morse (2004).

Roediger, Henry L., and Bridgid Finn. 2009. "Getting it wrong: Surprising tips on how to learn." *Scientific American,* October 20.

Rose, Jonathan. 2007. "The Ontario citizens' assembly on electoral reform." *Canadian Parliamentary Review* 30 (3): 9–16.

Rucht, Dieter. 2012. "Deliberation as an ideal and practice in progressive social movements." In *Evaluating democratic innovations: Curing the democratic malaise?*, edited by Kenneth Newton and Brigitte Geissel. London and New York: Routledge.

Smith, Graham. 2012. "Deliberative democracy and mini-publics." In *Evaluating democratic innovations: Curing the democratic malaise?*, edited by Kenneth Newton and Brigitte Geissel. London and New York: Routledge.

Smith, Tom. 1999. "The Delegates' Experience." In *The poll with a human face: The national issues convention experiment in political communication*, edited by Maxwell McCombs and Amy Reynolds. Mahwah, NJ: Lawrence Erlbaum Associates.

Stephenson, Laura, and Brian Tanguay. 2009. "Ontario's referendum on proportional representation: Why citizens said no." *IRPP*. http://irpp.org/research-studies/choices-vol15-no10/.

Warren, Mark E., and Hilary Pearse, eds. 2008. *Designing deliberative democracy: The British Columbia citizens' assembly*. New York: Cambridge University Press.

CHAPTER 6

What We Can Learn

There has been much skepticism about people's ability to make good personal choices and of voters' competence to take mindful civic action. Some of the reservations are connected to education. Are people sufficiently knowledgeable to make consequential choices? Others question individual engagement. Are people motivated enough to enhance their decision-making capacity? Still others mention more intrinsic cognitive and affective issues that are systematically impacting our ability to make sound judgments. These are some important questions since their answers point to our prospects for advancement as we make everyday decisions concerning our individual and collective future. In what follows, we begin with a look at select public opinion research. We depart from the discussions in the previous chapters, however, as we are interested to explore *how* individuals come to their opinions rather than what people think. Public preferences have a complex set of determinants in which outstanding is our cognitive engagement. We thus explore select aspects of human cognition, particularly in the context of civic matters, as we move forward in making a case we can do better in the way we make our decisions and solve problems—changing with it discourses, our opinions, and thus our civic and personal decisions.

© The Author(s) 2019

O. Bubak and H. Jacek, *Trivialization and Public Opinion*,

https://doi.org/10.1007/978-3-030-17925-0_6

A Play of Ideas

Views of the public, as revealed through the ubiquitous surveys and polls discussed previously, suggest an uninformed, puzzlingly conflicted, and ambivalent populace. Yet, these conclusions would be hasty as public opinion is reflective of not just of what people report at a point in time, or the limits of their cognitive biases, but also the properties of the surveying processes itself. Consider an observation of a key scholar of public opinion:

> ...more generally, most people really aren't sure what their opinions are on most political matters, including even such completely personal matters as their level of interest in politics. They're not sure because there are few occasions, outside of a standard interview situation, in which they are called upon to formulate and express political opinions. So, when confronted by rapidfire questions in a public opinion survey, they make up attitude reports as best they can as they go along. (Zaller 2005, 76)

And since the respondents are in a rush, "they are heavily influenced by whatever ideas happen to be at the top of their minds," adds the scholar (Zaller 2005, 5) of the salience effects, heuristics people use to help them provide answers and satisfy the interviewers (who, dependant on their goals, often do not offer an "I don't know" option). Hence, scholars have observed, for example, significant variations in survey results based on the order in which the questions were posed, the interviewer's race, or the "priming effects" of news on the television (Zaller 2005).

Importantly, the way the question was framed affects the respondents' answers. Zaller provides an insightful set of examples from the National Election Studies (NES) 1987 pilot study. In one NES experiment, the respondents were divided into three groups, each asked a differently framed question about their support or opposition for drilling on federal lands in Alaska. In the basic and foreign dependency frames, there was no indication that respondents were making a connection between drilling and the economic implications of conservation. Yet, these concerns became notable in the economic costs frame, particularly among the working-class respondents, just as concerns about the environment in this and the foreign dependency frames (2005). Consequently, the questions as formulated *reminded* the respondents of implications beyond those immediately on their mind. Such effects, as Zaller notes, "may be explained by the assumption that individuals do not typically possess 'just one attitude' toward issues, but several opinions ... and that which of these potential opinions they report depends... on the information that has been most recently made salient to them" (2005, 84). This raises questions on the reliability of such opinion and its relevance in democratic governance. How much credence should be given to the views of the public? To some, this becomes especially troublesome when surveys show opinions which are ostensibly contradictory.

Take, for example, the previously discussed contradiction in the public's view on governing authority. As Hibbing and Theiss-Morse (2004) and Foa and Mounk (2016) report, about half of the US respondents would agree to give more governing authority to experts and independent institutions rather than to government officials. On the other hand, about two-thirds of Americans would prefer to have more decision-making capacity in their own hands. This is despite the fact that, in a similar survey, 86% of respondents indicate "[m]ost Americans vote without really thinking through the issues" (Hunter and Bowman 2016). Similarly, most respondents seem to agree with both traditional survey statements: "the government in Washington should do everything possible to improve the standard of living of all poor Americans" and "it is not the government's responsibility, and ... each person should take care of himself" (NORC 2009; Strauss 2012). Revealing too are the 2001 and 2007 Gallup polls on immigration. Asked "whether immigrants to the United States are making the situation in the country better or worse, or not having much effect," majorities or large proportions of respondents in 2007 indicated "worse" or "not much effect." The lowest ratings received economic (52%), social (66%), tax (74%), employment (79%), and crime (88%) dimensions, with the least negative being foods, music, and arts (39%) (Gallup 2017; Strauss 2012). A follow-up immigration question in the same survey "On the whole, do you think immigration is a good thing or a bad thing for this country today?," however, was met with a majority positive response (Strauss 2012).

Intrigued by these apparent contradictions, Strauss (2012) set out to understand how these opinions are formed, with particular interest in immigration and social policy areas. As the author conducted a set of in-depth interviews with subjects representing a variety of backgrounds, including professors, engineers, and a lawyer, she began to discern some important patterns. First, despite the fact most respondents did not know each other, their responses were very similar, with some of their elements being identical. Further, in their responses, the participants drew on a set of ready-made claims, often all over the ideological spectrum. Finally, given the assortment of views they cover, these ready-made points challenge the conventional, reductionist understandings of the American political culture which see people's views informed primarily through the prism of ideology. Strauss calls such "bite sized, easier to mentally grasp and repeat" (337) points *conventional discourses*. For instance, the author identified the familiar "Help Our Own First, Illegal Is Wrong, Jobs Americans Don't Want, Nation of Immigrants, and Employers Taking Advantage discourses about immigration and Government Inefficiency, Personal Responsibility, Work Should Be Rewarded, and Greed of Corporations and the Rich discourses about government social programs," (Strauss 2012, xvi) among others. These are internalized and reproduced through various opinion communities which one may seek out or come into contact with inadvertently. Such communities include social and other media, identity groups, and other social networks.

According to Strauss, the conventional discourses help explain why many people hold seemingly contradictory opinions, ones that do not fit neatly into one ideological corner over another, or ones not representing broad value sets as we expect to see in the world of politics. And, as the scholar explains, discourse-analysis reveals two reasons for what appears as a contradiction in one's opinions: heterogeneous and nonconforming discourses. The former posits

> that people internalize a variety of conventional discourses they encounter in their differing opinion communities. Opinions are built up from these conventional discourses, like a child's imaginative play with figures purchased from kits. All the discourses are somewhat standardized, but the way they are used and their combinations can be unique, just as a child might create a scene combining the astronaut set with the circus performers. (Strauss 2012, 27)

In an alternate possibility, a nonconforming discourse, an opinion may seem contradictory when interpreted in terms of the typical ideological spectrum, as it contains a mix of elements of both left and right beliefs. Yet, in the eyes of a respondent these are not in conflict and capture well his or her position. "In standard political ideologies there is a clear separation: progressive ideologies support government programs that guarantee a good standard of living to all, while conservative ideologies hold that people are only entitled to what they earn through their efforts. For most of my interviewees, however, these are not opposing principles," explains Strauss (2012, 25).

Consider an example relating well to the discussion of moral reasoning in the context of deliberative democracy from Chapter 5. When discussing social policy attitudes with the participants, Strauss identified a combination of "Work Should Be Rewarded," "Help People Be Self-Reliant," "Contributors Deserve Benefits," or "the Incapacity Exception to Self-Reliance" discourses. In these, the respondents expressed that work is important, but hard work must be able to bring a reasonable living standard. They emphasized the importance of trying to be self-reliant but with the understanding that not all individuals can do so. Consequently, they acknowledged the government should help people to be self-reliant through various programs and support those lacking the capacity to be self-reliant. "What looks like muddled ambivalence to the researcher is a distorted impression that results from using elite interpretive lenses to view a differently organized vernacular schema of citizenship that emphasizes reciprocal responsibilities: those of individuals to their society and of society to the individual," concludes Strauss (2012, 26). And engaging moral conflict in a democratic society, as has been argued, requires such a schema.

The above work thus offers an important rationale in understanding public views through conventional discourses which can provide an insight into the foundations and construction of individual opinion. We begin to appreciate why seemingly contradictory answers to traditional survey questions, created based on elite understanding of political culture, may lead us to think of public opinion as inconsistent, rooted in less than informed postures, and thus not very reliable.

It can also help explain the public (mis)perceptions of consensus on various political questions and help answer why the public is seen on the whole as moderate or centrist. Indeed, while individually trivial, the way the broadly shared vernacular discourses on social condition, economy, the role of government, and others combine or build upon each other results not only in opinions richer and more elaborate but also ones transcending ideology. Such amalgams many not necessarily be coherent or correct, yet this is not the reason they attract elite criticism. It is rather as these lead away from politics, or its standard, reductionist conceptions of issues and solutions as conservative or progressive. Locating positions of these views along the political spectrum thus becomes inapplicable in the context of vernacular discourses. Such conclusions may offer some hope to Gutmann and Thompson (1998), who offer a framework for democratic deliberation, seen as needed to cope effectively with moral conflict. In this framework, as we discussed, the authors depart from the single-value principles traditionally used to answer moral questions. These not only narrow horizons and limit the repertoire of solutions but also reduce the need for dialogue. At a high level, the public with its opinions built around conventional discourses may thus be embracing of deliberative democracy. Key questions on accuracy and coherence remain, however.

THE FACTORS IN FORMATION

While helpful, conventional discourses are just one element of the less understood realm of public opinion. In his seminal work, Zaller (2005) teaches us that public opinion is a product of several interrelated determinants: "variations in the information carried in elite discourse, individual differences in attention to this information, and individual differences in political values and other predispositions" (2005, 6). For Zaller, the mass media content, and more specifically the coverage and balance of such content, is fundamental to the formation and change in public opinion. People, in turn, vary in their exposure, attentiveness, and the capacity to understand and retain this information. Finally, people possess a set of predispositions, developed through their experiences as members of society or even based in their traits, influencing which messaging to seek out or reject. These factors interact in various ways and "determine the mix of 'considerations' that gets into people's heads" (39). Ultimately, as mentioned earlier, we learn of people's opinions as they get questioned and reach for an answer most accessible to them.

In a complementary treatment, Strauss sees the people's opinion constituted by conventional discourses, "the public expression of shared mental schemas." Importantly, "[i]dentities, perceived interests, and any beliefs not acquired from conventional discourses, including those derived from personal experience," (2012, 337) not only shape one's opinion but also play a role in deciding which public discourses to consider and assume. As well, conventional discourses may affect one's identity, perceived interests, and personal experiences. Contrary to Zaller, Strauss's conventional discourses are not the same as media or elite discourses. People may be exposed to conventional discourses originating in a variety of settings, while some of these may also be taken up by the elite for political or commercial purposes. Ultimately, the author asks, why do people reach to conventional discourses in constructing their opinions, rather than assuming a distinctive view? Research here is lacking, but cultural, social, cognitive, and linguistic elements may all play a role in these outcomes (Strauss 2012). In the cultural explanation, people seek conformity and thus channel views in line with the majority. People may also join social groups as they agree with their shared discourses which they in turn repeat. To save cognitive resources, people may also internalize views they have heard, sparing them from the need to think again through issues to which there are salient answers. Finally, the linguistic view suggests that adopting conventional discourses is an extension of the process of learning a language, since the repetition and form of these discourses are similar to elements of language transmission (Strauss 2012).

Above, engaging outstanding research on the formation of public opinion, we have sketched some explanations of how the public develops their views. Opinion formation, as we have seen, is a set of interacting processes, including the dynamic elements of public discourse, along with individual predispositions, levels of engagement, and cognitive limitations. These processes unfold within a politico-cultural and, as we will discuss, cultural cognitive context (Chapter 10). While there is variation in the population—as there are well-informed, critically thinking, and politically engaged individuals as well as those who are nearly entirely disinterested and do not follow nor understand politics—scholars have noted some useful patterns and axioms (Zaller 2005) allowing us to explain the roots of and change in public views.

For our purposes, we want to emphasize two key determinants forming a common denominator in the understanding of public opinion: information underpinning discourse and its cognitive engagement. Based on the discussion thus far, it appears the format and content of public discourse, including the dominant conventional discourses as identified by Strauss, meet what most people demand and can manage. That means speaking in ideas, short and easy to understand and communicate, but disconnected from sources and substance—what we call trivialization. This also challenges the integrity of the transmitted information. How can we engage it critically in such a form? Indeed, it has been suggested that this style of discourse, on account of its linguistic character, is perpetuated as a human universal (Strauss 2012). Hence, we ask below, can we overcome this condition and *do better*? Before answering the question in this and the next chapter, we begin with a brief discussion of the relevance of (political) awareness. We emphasize the importance of thinking over knowing, however, shall we find a new discourse, one seeking reality in the age of information.

INFORMATIONAL ASPECTS

Given the disinterest in political matters professed by a great part of the population, the findings of opinion research are perhaps not surprising. In one of the more visible studies of political knowledge, an analysis of over 2000 survey questions in the span of over 50 years, Delli Carpini and Keeter (1996) tested a broad range of knowledge, covering government processes, institutions, substantive matters and indicators, and political actors. The authors found that "political knowledge levels are, in many instances, depressingly low" (269). For example, only over half the respondents could answer 40% of all questions correctly. The authors also noted that Americans "hold fewer, less stable, and less consistent opinions. They are more susceptible to political propaganda and less receptive to relevant new information" (265). The authors surely have a reason for concern, given that "more-informed citizens are more accepting of democratic norms such as political tolerance, are more efficacious about politics, are more likely to be interested in, follow and discuss politics, and are more likely to participate in politics in a variety of ways, including voting, working for a political party, and attending local community meetings" (Delli Carpini 2000, 142). Additionally, more aware public is more likely to have established opinions on key political questions and have opinions which are stable (Delli Carpini and Keeter 1996). Finally, more informed individuals have a greater capacity to hold their representatives to account and vote for those who are more aligned with their interests (Delli Carpini 2000).

However, it is not clear which information is of the greatest immediate benefit. Let us recall several issues we have brought forward. First, the misperceptions of consensus, for example, create fundamental misunderstanding of conflict and politics, with implications to civic behavior. Countering this requires specific knowledge about pending political debates. Second, citizens have the aptitude in making sound and intelligent decisions as well as the interest to do so, given an opportunity for a meaningful engagement. But expecting, for instance, the voters to understand the immigration system or be up to date on the types of electoral systems without such issues being on the agenda may be unreasonable. Third, we may want to leverage citizen knowledge at its best, at the local level. Yet, rather than expanding across the board, information available at the local level is shrinking, given the struggling local newspaper and media markets (Shaker 2009). While this is opening space for civic journalism or other alternates, these lack the resources and editorial control to provide the needed completeness and consistency. Finally, given the informational explosion of the recent decade, it is possible that even the most engaged citizens might end up misinformed, challenging their political efficacy. People, in other words, may have information on issues which is unreliable (Chapter 7).

Let us return to Zaller, who thinks the key question behind news stereotypes, in his view an integral determinant of opinion, is "whether the public is given any choice about them - whether, that is, it is permitted to choose between alternative visions of what the issue is. For in the absence of such choice, the public can do little more than follow the elite consensus on what should be done" (2005, 8). The author provides an apt example of attitudinal change in the support for the Vietnam War. In the early stages of the conflict, the media, including the outlets which were critical of specific choices in policy, framed the US involvement in the war as an effort to contain communism and protect freedom. Accordingly, public support for the war effort was quite strong, especially among people more exposed to this messaging. The situation has begun to change, however, with the increasing salience of an alternative frame—a civil war between two Vietnamese factions, a possibly winnable conflict, and one not critical to US security. While the old messaging was also available, the new line of argument in the media began to alter the opinion of parts of the American public. Liberals were adopting the stance of the elites identifiable as liberal, and conservatives aligning with the apparently conservative pundits.

Zaller's observation and example underscore several important points. The first is the public's reliance on what is presented to them in the media, a more or less accurate report on reality created by others. The second point reminds us how different the modern day world of Internet-driven media is from the media environment of the 1970s. Rather than relying on a few networks or newspapers, the public today may find an overabundance of choices of frames, information possibly tailored to their consumer preferences. Finally, it matters how the information is presented. It may be either through the customary frames, including conventional discourses, or more elaborate and apparently credible narratives, often crafted to achieve a specific goal. Hence, returning to Delli Carpini and Keeter's point, becoming informed under these circumstances hardly points to better informational and efficacious outcomes. In the modern age, crucial is *how* the citizens think. Note, for example, Facebook, a data mining and advertising platform, is a source of news of nearly half of the US adults, with 62% of US adults reporting getting news from social media sites (Gottfried and Shearer 2016). We would hope for a population who thinks differently and understands to go beyond these horizons for news and analyses. This in turn will reshape the discourse while raising the efficacy of each citizen.

In sum, we find ourselves in a complex world of mass information of varied scope and quality. Here, while we cannot be familiar with or hold a preference on every major issue, we are expected to be more aware of how to find, assess, and leverage data. Unlike in the past, we have access to instant information, virtually the same knowledge as those with authority have at their disposal, along with a greater capacity to hold the elite to account. On the other hand, it is a place where it becomes increasingly more difficult to discern and navigate between fact and fiction, particularly if the dominant sources of information are private, profit-seeking, and largely unregulated companies. Dealing with these challenges requires a different style of thinking which in turn yields different discourses. And while a portion of society employs this critical, reflexive thought, which goes beyond ideas and engages substance, majority of people are stuck in the past. Some may see a reason for pessimism in our natural cognitive limitations, others point to a broader inability to learn. We engage these concerns in the next sections.

Meeting the Limits

Our evolutionary history has equipped us to function for the moment in a world with little certainty and much danger. This has served us well until the modern day, where we find more stability and security, yet encounter decisions with different cognitive demands. It is particularly in the present—when faced with questions on how and in what context to invest our time and resources, on which social or economic policies to support, or on how to evaluate contrasting evidence—that our limits are coming to contrast. And so we have begun to shed our assumptions on human rationality and reasoning, as we realize, in the words of Levitt and March, that

> individual human beings are not perfect statisticians...They make systematic errors in recording the events of history and in making inferences from them. They overestimate the probability of events that actually occur and of events that are available to attention because of their recency or saliency. They are insensitive to sample size. They tend to overattribute events to the intentional actions of individuals. They use simple linear and functional rules, associate causality with spatial and temporal contiguity, and assume that big effects must have big causes. (1998, 323)

Scholars have explored such limitations to a great extent in behavioral economics and cognitive psychology, streams of inquiry concerned with cognitive and psychological aspects of individual decision making. We take a closer look at a number of key findings as we engage anchoring bias, overconfidence and the associated treatment of evidence, availability bias, probability neglect, and loss aversion. While there are many other heuristics and biases, these are seen as particularly impactful in the arena of public discourse, including in the formation of individual preferences.[1]

Studies have shown that individuals are influenced by salient values encountered just prior to making their estimates. This *anchoring* effect has been demonstrated in a widely cited experiment in which the subjects were asked the percentage of African countries in the United Nations. Prior to submitting their estimates, the subjects were made to assess whether a number between 1 and 100 (generated by a spinning wheel) was higher or lower than their estimate. The results showed a marked effect, with anchors 10 and 65 yielding estimates of 25 and 45% of African countries, respectively (Kahneman and Tversky 1982). Cognizant of the anchoring heuristic, some argue against providing starting points in a public deliberation (Mandel and Gathii 2006) so as not to bias or limit the outcomes.

Griffin and Tversky (1992) have found individuals tend to elevate the strength or extremeness of evidence and pay less attention to its weight or reliability. This results in either *overconfidence* (in case of high strength and low weight of evidence) or underconfidence (in case of low strength and high weight) in judgment. Further, the authors note, when predictability is low, experts can become even more overconfident than beginners. What is more, this overconfidence impacts the way individuals work with evidence. "[T]he tendency to focus on the strength of the evidence leads people to neglect or underweight other variables, such as the prior probability of the hypothesis in question or the discriminability of the competing hypotheses," note Griffin and Tversky (1992, 430). If overlooked, these biases may carry broad implications, especially when connected to matters such as policy, affecting large segments of the society or the environment.

We further know that individuals are inclined to assess the frequency of a particular category or likelihood of an event based on how easily these come to their mind. Matters that are salient (and thus familiar) or have occurred recently are cognitively *more available* and thus will seem more frequent than other, in reality just as common, events lacking in retrievability (Kahneman and Tversky 1982). Researchers conducted a basic experiment in which the subjects were given lists containing a mix of more or less famous men and women and were asked to compare their occurence. The lists where the men were especially recognizable were judged to have more men, while those with recognizable women names were deemed to be dominated by women (Kahneman and Tversky 1982). This heuristic may explain, for instance, why perceived unemployment often greatly exceeds the actual figures. As media images of the unemployed reinforce individuals' everyday encounters with people out of work, the estimated numbers grow.

Sunstein (2005) also argues that aside from inaccurate judgments on probability stemming from the availability bias, individuals sometimes *avoid* considering likelihood altogether. As well, overtaken by positive or negative sentiments, individuals often disregard the differentials in probabilities. A typical example here is a lottery where the mathematically miniscule chances of winning do not deter people from playing. Yet, as we will explain in later chapters, in some cases talking of probabilities is not even possible. This is true for global phenomena in environmental or social systems, among other complex systems whose properties preclude making any formal predictions altogether.

Challenging the traditional models of rationality, a key finding of behavioral economics is the individual *aversion to loss*. Individuals perceive potential losses from the current condition as less desirable than potential gains. This has been shown in experiments in which some subjects were given items, including coffee mugs, chocolate bars, and binoculars, while others were not. The individuals who were not given such items were asked how much they would be willing to pay to have them. This amount was consistently less than the value demanded by the subjects to give up their items (Sunstein 2005). Such tendencies, Sunstein notes, have implications to social decisions, including the support for public policies, where focusing on losses while neglecting the potential gains may be detrimental. "People will be closely attuned to the losses produced by any newly introduced risk, or by any aggravation of existing risks, but far less concerned with the benefits that are forgone as a result of regulation," explains the author speaking in the context of risk regulation (2005, 24). Further, familiar risks appear more tolerable than unfamiliar risks, even if both risks have comparable probability of occurrence (Sunstein 2005). Smoking, for example, carries familiar health risks that, despite the inherent dangers, are considered tolerable.

Associated with loss aversion is a widespread belief in the "benevolence of nature," where the natural is associated with benign, good, or even healthy, while synthetic or altered is thought to be unsafe and risky (Sunstein 2005). Research finds, for instance, that people underestimate the dangers of natural carcinogens while overestimating those from pesticides. People also prefer spring water, appearing pure and safe, to chemically equivalent purified water (Sunstein 2005). Such views, whether on risk or merits of caution, differ greatly even within societies, making consensus very difficult.

Finally, studies have shown people prefer smaller rewards sooner rather than to wait for greater payoffs collected in a more distant future. Such *time discounting* has been noted in a variety of contexts, including decisions on savings, health, education as well as policy preferences. Moreover, rather than a constant rate of preference, individuals tend to exhibit hyperbolic discounting behavior—where the rate of preference declines with time (see Frederick et al. 2002).

Aside from the fundamental biases and heuristics, individual decision making may be constrained by other, composite factors. Perhaps the most outstanding of the resultant lapses is *system neglect* (Sunstein 2005), a proclivity to overlook the quantity and interconnectedness of social and natural elements, missing thus the second order impacts of system interventions.

Consider a prime example of system neglect: the Australian government's flawed attempts to protect the ecosystem of its Macquarie Island, a World Heritage site. Just as many other islands in the region (and indeed the continent itself), the Macquarie ecosystem has been devastated by nonnative species, dominated by rabbits and cats. These were introduced there by the island's visitors throughout the 1800s, some intentionally as a source of food for the seal hunters working in the surrounding waters. The magnitude of environmental damage caused by the growing rabbit populations forced the government to act. Once under control, the government turned its sights on the cats who, with the lower rabbit populations, switched to native species of seabirds as their main sources of prey. The elimination of cats quickly lead to a massive reemergence of rabbits, who began destroying the island's vegetation, including the foliage used by the seabirds for cover (BBC 2009). What makes this example especially potent is that Macquarie's problem is not unprecedented. Australian governments have had experience eradicating various nonnative species, usually on the heels of their runaway attempts to combat one invasive species with another. "The lessons for conservation agencies globally is that interventions should be comprehensive, and include risk assessments to explicitly consider and plan for indirect effects, or face substantial subsequent costs," concluded a conservationist (BBC 2009) as if Macquarie became *the* lesson, at last.

The individual neglect of the interdependencies among issues also means people pay less attention to the existence of competing alternatives and the necessity of weighing the trade-offs among them (Sunstein 2005). Consider a response to a statement on environmental protection, recurring in US polls since the 1980s: "Protecting the environment is so important that requirements and standards cannot be too high, and continuing environmental improvements must be made regardless of cost." While a large majority of Americans consistently agree with this statement, 52% (asked in the late 1990s) also rejected the Kyoto treaty if it meant each household would have to pay extra $50 a month for the nation to meet its treaty obligations (Sunstein 2005). Only once salient, these costs became part of the individual calculi and lead to different answers.

WHAT CAN WE LEARN?

Above, we have discussed briefly select biases with a question in mind: Are we hopeless captives of these limitations or can we, as individuals or citizens, get past them and make better decisions? A recent study from Jacobs and Matthews (2012) examining citizen policy preferences offers a reason for optimism. Jacobs and Matthews set out to explain citizens' intertemporal decision making—choices requiring the weighing of cost and benefits occurring over time—in the policy arena. More specifically, they wanted to know the reasons and conditions under which individuals time-discount public policy outcomes. It is important to note their hypotheses assumed the participants were privy to policy costs and benefits over time. To satisfy this assumption, the authors exposed them to adequate and clear *information*, which also allowed for a manipulation of timing and causal complexity. More specifically, they tested for what is essentially a trivialized, "low complexity," condition. The respondents in this group "read additional statements citing expert consensus that the reform would be simple to implement and stating that similar plans had been carried out before" (Jacobs and Matthews 2012, 913). On the other hand, respondents in the control group were given no information on process complexity. The policy examined was the US Social Security, a contributory national public pension program funded largely through payroll taxes, expected to come under financial strain with the retiring cohort. In line with the study design, the authors thus provided the subjects with the necessary background, described the financial issues facing this program, and outlined the (future) costs of inaction. They also communicated the trade-offs behind the policy options and reiterated the reforms would not fully address all Social Security issues.

The authors' analysis yields some surprising findings. Contrary to what may be expected from this line of research in behavioral economics and cognitive psychology, the analysis shows little support for positive time preference or consumption smoothing as the discounting mechanisms. Rather, the data indicate that citizens' bias for the short-term policy benefits is rooted in their perceptions of *credibility* of both political commitments and the *reliability* of policy processes. In sum, whether as consumers or voters, people are often subject to various cognitive limitations and biases. Jacobs and Matthews' study points out, however, that *informed* citizens can reason differently. While they manifest time discounting, it is due less to their positive time preference than to the recognition of the complexities of policy processes and their distrust in politics. The importance of these findings goes beyond finance, as "much of human social life—our morality, our relationships—revolves around challenges posed by intertemporal choice" (DeSteno 2018). There is thus hope that information strategies and education may have a key role in helping us overcome many collective challenges, including environmental destruction and sustainability, most of which are intertemporal at their roots (DeSteno 2018).

For completeness, we want to emphasize the decisions we discuss here hope for deliberative, slow thinking rather than the impulsive, intuitive fast thinking. This distinction has been well discussed by Kahneman (2011) in the context of human decision making. The author engages two cognitive systems, System 1 and 2, each with different cognitive demands and subject to different limitations. System 1 is automatic and involuntary, while its counterpart is conscious and calculating.

System 2 articulates judgments and makes choices, but it often endorses or rationalizes ideas and feelings that were generated by System 1...The abilities [of System 2] are limited and so is the knowledge to which it has access. We do not always think straight when we reason, and the errors are not always due to intrusive and incorrect intuitions. Often we make mistakes because we (our System 2) do not know any better,

explains Kahneman (2011). While there is no formula to eliminate biases and replace emotion with reason in our decisions, the research above suggests it *is possible* to do better. Motivation through engagement coupled with adequate information ensuring we "know better" thus becomes essential to making those choices that affect us all. Can we learn?

Outside of what we discussed thus far, surely the reader can think of other examples of startling fluctuations in public views, ill-considered decisions resulting in preventable issues, or good policies which fail upon their implementation, all stemming from limits to our thinking, natural or otherwise. For example, we have discussed that misappreciation of the big picture holds us back from resolving complex issues, often exacerbating them instead. Rather than having a single, consistent cause, these are products of varied combinations of factors unique to each case. Can we make sense of and ameliorate these shortcomings in the interest of our individual and social choices? Perhaps we are predisposed to think for the near term in simple and linear terms and consider only what we can imagine and convey easily. Perhaps our progress depends mostly on trial and error, and the application of the familiar.

Dörner's (1997) outstanding research on the nature of our thinking when faced with complicated problems[2] holds the answers. Inspired by bad decisions common to public and private spheres and the overt confidence people have in their choices, Dörner set out to study failure in planning and decision making. The scholar leveraged the advances in computation and setup "planning games" simulating the struggle for survival of communities in difficult environments. These communities face a number of issues including a lack of water and food, overpopulation, disease, predators as well as conflicts with neighbors. The simulation receives one or more inputs from the study subjects, who, based on their assessment of the situation, may decide to drill wells, make investments into health care and infrastructure, impose a variety of regulations, or reduce pests and predators, among other interventions. The simulation is divided into a series of dynamic sessions, steps in time, updating the players on the conditions on the ground. As in reality, the interventions interact; what was a sensible configuration at the outset may be detrimental as the situation evolves with time. The author is able to observe the strategies, focus, and learning of the players as they respond to complicated problems and thus study the conditions, reasons, and ways to prevent mistakes in these situations.

Dörner establishes that in solving complicated tasks, individuals fail before they even begin as they do not establish proper objectives, do not recognize any contradictions among them, and fail to identify priorities. Individuals are less capable of managing developments unfolding over time, and, curiously, fail to correct their mistakes. The author finds these failings to be predictable, underpinned by a number of elementary causes. These include our cognitive limitations such as the (slow) speed at which we think, the relatively slim amount of information we can process at once, and our limited "inflow capacity," or the rate at which we operationalize new data. Yet, we have other flaws, such as the propensity to seek self-assurance and maintain a feeling of competence. While protecting us from paralysis in analysis, on the one hand, it leads us away from facing our mistakes and encourages *methodism*, the reuse of an established template to solve a one-of-a-kind problem rather than tailoring the solution to particular conditions, on the other. Finally, we also tend to consider problems that are immediate, ones that are salient and in need of attention, while neglecting the possibilities of related issues on the horizon.

We are hence privy to the diverse causes which lead us astray in solving difficult problems. We also appreciate that systems problems are unique, requiring different strategies, levels of input, and styles of execution. Can we overcome these issues and improve our chances of success? Drawing on his analyses, Dörner argues that we can and finds the answer lies in the development of operative intelligence, "the knowledge that individuals have about the use of their intellectual capabilities and skills." This will require a new kind of training, however, an immersion in a diverse set of simulations combined with expert feedback on the participant performance, including on planning and execution and the associated processes. Indeed, Dörner asserts we can learn much from such trainings, as summarized in Box 6.1. And we must, as we hope to show throughout this volume.[3]

Box 6.1 What can we learn?

We *can* learn:

- that it is essential to state goals clearly.
- that we cannot always realize all our goals at once, because different goals may contradict one another. We must often compromise between different goals.
- that we have to establish priorities but that we cannot cling to the same priorities forever. We may have to change them.
- that in dealing with a given configuration we should form a model of the system. We must anticipate side effects and longterm repercussions and not just let them roll over us.
- how to adapt information gathering to the needs of the task at hand, neither going into excessive detail nor stopping too short.
- the consequences of excessive abstraction.
- the consequences of hastily ascribing all events in a certain field to one central cause.
- when to continue gathering information and when to stop.
- that we tend toward "horizontal" or "vertical" evasion and that the tendency can be controlled.
- that we sometimes act simply because we want to prove to ourselves that we can act.
- the dangers of knee-jerk "methodism."
- that it is essential to analyze our errors and draw conclusions from them for reorganizing our thinking and behavior.

Source Dörner (1997)

Conclusion

We began this chapter with a look at select research in the formation of public opinion with an interest to understand how we come to our views. Information flows and discourses, and our cognitive engagement with them, we noted, are the dominant factors. Ultimately, discourses are a reflection of how we think and what we can tolerate within a politico-cultural and cultural cognitive context (Chapter 10). We thus discussed a number of cognitive and behavioral limits affecting the way we perceive and approach issues, in turn shaping the ways we select or formulate our solutions. We made a point these obstacles can be overcome through a combination of individual awareness and collective measures. We engaged Dörner's findings that can explain numerous missteps in our choices, failures of domestic policy initiatives or interventions abroad, whether on the formulation or execution side. The author provides us with an enumeration of capabilities we *can* gain through learning, which we hope to be requisite for anyone in a position of authority.

But in one way, we all are important planners and decision makers. We too make significant choices affecting others. How much should we spend now and save for later? Should we start a business or work for others? Which training, if any, will benefit us the most? We also indicate what policies we want and which candidates we support. And crucially, we are asked to make consequential choices through various referenda or public initiatives. As social and natural problems are increasingly complex, it is neither expected nor feasible to maintain a broad insight into all issues. What we hope for, however, is the collective recognition of their complexity and an embrace of a basic set of orientations toward thinking, learning, and talking about them.

NOTES

1. Recommended here is the seminal work of Kahneman and Tversky (1982). Mandel and Gathii (2006) and Sunstein (2005) elaborate on these biases.
2. Dörner refers to complex problems embedded in situations which have many variables, deep temporal dimensions, and with solutions that may carry extensive and often unexpected consequences. This is different from the term's usage in recent policy scholarship, where complex or wicked problems represent a special class of intractable problems.
3. This is yet another reason to heed the calls of progressive educators to reorient our outdated, industrial age education systems and replace the siloed, information-transfer approaches in favor of integrative development of thinking and problem-solving skills.

REFERENCES

BBC. 2009. "Rabbits devastate island wildlife." *BBC News*, January 12. http://news.bbc.co.uk/2/hi/science/nature/7824153.stm.

Delli Carpini, Michael X. 2000. "In search of the informed citizen: What Americans know about politics and why it matters." *The Communication Review* 4 (1): 129–164.

Delli Carpini, Michael X., and Scott Keeter. 1996. *What Americans know about politics and why it matters.* New Haven: Yale University Press. As cited in Hibbing and Theiss-Morse (2004) and Delli Carpini (2000).

DeSteno, David. 2018. "Intertemporal choice." In *This idea is brilliant: Lost, overlooked, and underappreciated scientific concepts everyone should know,* edited by John Brockman. New York: Harper Perennial.

Dörner, Dietrich. 1997. *The logic of failure: Recognizing and avoiding error in complex situations.* Cambridge, MA: Perseus.

Foa, Roberto Stefan, and Yascha Mounk. 2016. "The democratic disconnect." *Journal of Democracy* 27 (3): 5–17.

Frederick, Shane, George Loewenstein, and Ted O'Donoghue. 2002. "Time discounting and time preference: A critical review." *Journal of Economic Literature* 40 (2): 351–401.

Gallup. 2017. "Americans more positive about effects of immigration." Gallup, Inc. June 28. https://news.gallup.com/poll/213146/americans-positive-effects-immigration.aspx.

Gottfried, Jeffrey and Elisa Shearer. 2016. "News use across social media platforms 2016." Pew Research Center, May 26. http://www.journalism.org/2016/05/26/news-use-across-social-media-platforms-2016/.

Griffin, Dale, and Amos Tversky. 1992. "The weighing of evidence and the determinants of confidence." *Cognitive Psychology* 24 (3): 411–435.

Gutmann, Amy, and Dennis F. Thompson. 1998. *Democracy and disagreement.* Cambridge, MA: Harvard University Press.

Hibbing, John R., and Elizabeth Theiss-Morse. 2004. *Stealth democracy: Americans' beliefs about how government should work.* Cambridge, UK: Cambridge University Press.

Hunter, James Davison, and Carl Desportes Bowman. 2016. "The vanishing center of American democracy." The Institute for Advanced Studies in Culture. http://iasculture.org/research/publications/vanishing-center.

Jacobs, Alan M., and J. Scott Matthews. 2012. "Why do citizens discount the future? Public opinion and the timing of policy consequences." *British Journal of Political Science* 42 (4): 903–935.

Kahneman, Daniel. 2011. *Thinking, fast and slow.* New York: Farrar, Straus, and Giroux.

Kahneman, Daniel, and Amos Tversky. 1982. "Judgment under uncertainty: Heuristics and biases." In *Judgment under uncertainty: Heuristics and biases,* edited by Daniel Kahneman, Paul Slovic, and Amos Tversky. Cambridge, UK: Cambridge University Press.

Levitt, Barbara, and James G. March. 1998. "Organizational learning." *Annual Review of Sociology* 14 (1): 319–338.

Mandel, Gregory N., and James Thuo Gathii. 2006. "Cost-benefit analysis versus the precautionary principle: Beyond Cass Sunstein's laws of fear." *University of Illinois Law Review* 1037–1080.

NORC (National Opinion Research Center). 2009. *General social surveys 1972–2008: Cumulative codebook.* Chicago: Conducted for the National Data Program for the Social Sciences at National Opinion Research Center, University of Chicago. As cited in Strauss (2012).

Shaker, Lee. 2009. "Citizens' local political knowledge and the role of media access." *Journalism & Mass Communication Quarterly* 86 (4): 809–826.

Strauss, Claudia. 2012. *Making sense of public opinion: American discourses about immigration and social programs.* New York: Cambridge University Press.

Sunstein, Cass R. 2005. *Laws of fear: Beyond the precautionary principle.* New York: Cambridge University Press.

Zaller, John R. 2005 (1992). *The nature and origins of mass opinion.* New York: Cambridge University Press.

PART III

Approaching Complexity

CHAPTER 7

Assumptions and Precautions

Earlier, we have discussed key issues in the US health care system while focusing on a recent set of reforms, the Patient Protection and Affordable Care Act of 2010, attempting to address chiefly its problems of coverage and its runaway costs. We also explored the politics behind this deeply contested legislation, a highly trivialized undertaking. Aside from the critics' concerns about the reforms' economic implications or the government takeover of health care, a major controversy plaguing the legislative debates throughout was the issue of short- and long-term budgetary impact.

As mentioned, both sides of the debate drew on a variety of cost estimates framed to support their argument. The Democrats and other supporters mostly used numbers from the Congressional Budget Office showing the ACA did not add to the deficit and emphasized that the costs of insuring 25 million individuals previously without insurance would be covered by lowering Medicare reimbursement rates and by individual and business taxes and penalties (Rawal 2016). The opponents, on the other hand, have employed a variety of projections focusing only on the costs of the expansion of coverage (Rawal 2016). "The government takeover of health care is exacerbating the already dire fiscal challenges our nation faces. If fully implemented, the health care law will cost taxpayers $2.6 trillion, while adding $701 billion to the deficit

© The Author(s) 2019
O. Bubak and H. Jacek, *Trivialization and Public Opinion*,
https://doi.org/10.1007/978-3-030-17925-0_7

in its first ten years," argued Boehner et al. (2011, 12) in their report on economic and fiscal implications of the ACA legislation in which they critiqued the lower estimates provided by the CBO. "The higher numbers—and selective use of certain estimates—was part of the opposition's steady campaign to link the ACA to negative economic impacts" (Rawal 2016). We hence take these figures as products of politics and perhaps do not pay much attention to their outward precision.

According to the Congressional rules, all legislation must be scored by the nonpartisan CBO, an agency established in 1974 to carry out independent economic and fiscal analyses. Based on data from public statistical agencies, surveys, or experts, among a range of other sources, such analyses are used to inform the legislative process and the public. The agency was thus working with the House and Senate Committees in scoring the various versions of the health care bills. In 2010, when estimating the enacted legislation, the ACA, the CBO estimated the cost of the expansion of coverage to be $938 billion for the period 2010–2019. The savings from the cutbacks in Medicare payment rates and revenues from new fees and penalties were estimated to exceed this number, resulting in a projected reduction in the federal deficit by $124 billion over the same period (CBO 2010). These numbers were then widely cited by the proponents and disseminated by the media. The opponents criticized the estimates as low, given they were based on the standard 10-year window including the four years before the coverage expansion went into effect (more in Rawal 2016). The updated 2015 estimates included the expansion and tax credits for the entire 2015–2024 period, bringing the total cost to $1.707 trillion (CBO 2015).

It is not difficult to imagine that different than expected economic situation and enrollment numbers could change these estimates drastically. Hence, just as with the political figures above, peculiar about these point estimates is their apparent exactitude. What is more, CBO's communication (2010) of these scores to Pelosi, the House Speaker at the time, "expressed no uncertainty and did not document the methodology generating the prediction," with uncertainty only acknowledged for numbers beyond the customary 10-year horizon (Manski 2013, 18). Indeed, speaking in the context of public policy, Manski (2011, 2013) observed that certitudes about the outcomes of various policy alternatives and point predictions are common, while admissions of uncertainty are exceptional. "Conclusions may rest on critical *unsupported assumptions* or on leaps of logic. Then the certitude of policy analysis is not credible," notes Manski (2013, 3, emphasis added), who has spent a good part of his career warning against the proclivity in the policy arena to use strong assumptions leading to weak, or less credible conclusions. This is important, in Manski's view, as "consumers of policy analysis cannot safely trust the experts. Civil servants, journalists, and concerned citizens need to understand prediction methods well enough to be able to assess reported findings. They need to comprehend conceptually, if not in technical detail, how predictions depend on maintained assumptions and available data" (2013, 47). Engaging these issues is particularly important in the domain tasked with recommending one policy solution over others, a decision with potentially large social, environmental, economic, or other consequences. Yet this form of trivialization goes beyond the field of policy analysis, economics, or sciences and conditions public discourse, an interaction which too must be taken into account.

Below, we begin with a range of practices, identified by Manski (2011, 2013) as enablers of incredible certitude, and complement them with select examples from the author's work and elsewhere. We would like to encourage further attention to these lapses that remain less salient despite their importance—reminding us again of the general misappreciation of trivialization and its ramifications. We then present a vivid case of certitudes which, upon a closer look, are far from credible yet are of consequence to all of us. Finally, we discuss an important counterweight to scientific certitude, gaining salience not the least due to the lessons learned from history, with the potential to effect change beyond policy making.

Assumptions and Theories

Following Manski, we begin with the discussion of the logic and credibility in empirical research as we return to a study testing the theories of American politics familiar from earlier (Chapter 4). Recall its authors, Gilens and Page (2014), begin from four major theoretical traditions of American politics used to explain the workings of the US political system: Majoritarian Electoral Democracy, Economic-Elite Domination, majoritarian pluralism, and biased pluralism. Rooted in varied assumptions and empirical evidence, these views make different predictions based on which sets of political actors hold the key influence in policy making. Hence, Majoritarian Electoral Democracy, Economic-Elite Domination, and the two pluralisms see policies responding to the wishes of the ordinary people, the affluent individuals, or mass-based and business interest groups, respectively. Supported by more or less sizable scholarly following, such theories have persisted partly as they appear, at least when considered separately, to work. This might change, however, due to the findings of the authors' unprecedented research.

The authors assembled a unique set of data and developed a model with a goal to test the effects each theorized actor has *independently* on policy outcomes. For completeness, Gilens and Page's team gathered information from national surveys administered between 1981 and 2002 on 1779 policy cases which met a set of constraints including policy specifics, relevance to government decisions, categorical phrasing, dichotomous support/not support responses, and respondent incomes. Because these data were gathered from polls, the policies in question could be taken as broadly familiar. To assess the interest group influence, the authors developed the Net Interest Group Alignment index, calculated as a net position on each policy issue assessed for key mass-based interest groups plus business with the biggest lobbying expenditures. The authors and their team also calculated separate indexes for mass-based and business-oriented groups and mapped all numbers to each of the 1779 cases.

Gilens and Page first tested separately the effects of ordinary voters, economic elites, and organized interests on policy outcomes. This step revealed statistically significant relationship between each of these variables and policy change. "Little wonder that each theoretical tradition has its strong adherents," thus noted the scholars (572). However, multivariate analysis in which all the variables were tested together showed that ordinary voters had virtually no independent influence on policy outcomes. These findings, as discussed, not only challenged the existing theories of Majoritarian Electoral Democracy but also brought attention to the long suspect state of American democracy.

This work, however, also highlights the key features and issues in empirical research. The conclusions reached by the major traditions considered by the authors are products of assumptions and empirical evidence, whether quantitative, historical, or observational (Gilens and

Page 2014).[1] Empirical findings may be challenged on the grounds of logic, given the presence of deductive errors or non-sequiturs, or on the grounds of assumptions made (Manski 2011). In terms of the latter, there is an inherent difficulty in working with assumptions, given a trade-off identified by Manski: "Stronger assumptions yield conclusions that are more powerful but less credible" (2011, 2013). Consider the median-voter theorem, a product of rational choice scholarship, and its continued application in majoritarian democracy stream of research. This is partly, per Gilens and Page's literature scan, as this research found evidence that "government policy is consistent with majority preferences roughly two-thirds of the time; that public policy changes in the same direction as collective preferences a similar two-thirds of the time; that the liberalism or conservatism of citizens is closely associated with the liberalism or conservatism of policy across states; and that fluctuations in the liberal or conservative 'mood' of the public are strongly associated with changes in the liberalism or conservatism of policy in all three branches of government" (565). These findings assume, however, that variables including the preferences of the wealthy or interest groups have no independent influence, leading to spurious statistical relationships between public opinion and policy (Gilens and Page 2014). Hence, we have a strong assumption allowing certitude in our conclusions. These, however, become less credible as a result.

Furthermore, this and the like assumptions underpinning the theories considered by Gilens and Page have held (and so have their disagreements) because it has not been possible to test them together in one model for most of their existence (2014). Revised assumptions supported by a hefty data set thus allowed the authors to reach conclusions departing from the traditional assumptions and predictions, namely of theories of Majoritarian Electoral Democracy and majoritarian pluralism. With additional work and contestation in this area, we should learn if such perspectives will retain their following.

We hinted above to the reason these theories have maintained their popularity. But a natural question arises on why such theories based around actors, "or, all too often, a single set of actors," (Gilens and Page 2014, 564) have been advanced the first place. We agree with Manski that one type of support for such a certitude may be found in the prevailing philosophy of science. As discussed, reductionism favored by sciences—namely by the application of Occam's razor in deciding between competing explanations[2] or in simplifying the locus of study—has also been embraced in the study of the social world (Chapter 3). This may be particularly a problem in Manski's field of policy analysis dealing with systemic issues characterized by multicausality, ambiguity, and requiring not one, but several interventions in addressing them (Chapter 6). "Does use of criteria such as 'simplicity' to choose one hypothesis among those consistent with the data promote good policy making?," asks Manski (2013, 15). We hope such a question will be settled with a wider acceptance of a new frame of reference in social sciences (Chapter 9).

Incredible Certitude

As hinted, facilitating incredible certitude is a set of practices particularly evident in the public policy field. The first practice is *conventional certitude*, used by Manski "to describe predictions that are generally accepted as true, but that are not necessarily true" (2013, 16). A good example here is the commonly used scoring of proposed legislation, generated by the CBO for 5 or 10 year periods. Since most legislation is an intervention into a socioeconomic system, an evolving complex of interacting actors reacting to incentives while operating in the condition of imperfect information, the scores are highly sensitive to the initial (best guess) assumptions. Yet, these point estimates are given the appearance of exactitude, while the uncertainty associated with these numbers often goes unquestioned. As discussed, uncertainty is only noted for long-term estimates beyond the arbitrary 10-year window, given "the established CBO practice of expressing certitude when providing ten-year predictions, which play a formal role in the congressional budget process" (Manski 2013, 19). To counter conventional certitude, Manski suggests using ranges, a low and a high estimate, outputs from a sensitivity analysis "describing the sensitivity of predictions to variation in maintained assumptions" (22). Interestingly, aside from a positive reception, the scholar's proposal elicits two responses. The first is that humans are thought to be "either psychologically unwilling or cognitively unable to cope with uncertainty" (14), making it natural for us to embrace certitude; the author provides evidence counter to this supposition. The second response doubts that the Congress, a body guided not by knowledge but politics, would make better decisions with more credible scores. Rooted in game theory, this understanding, as the author notes, does not provide practical or normative insights into using interval scores.

Dueling certitudes are the next practice encouraging incredible certitude. It is quite common to encounter more than one analysis of a proposed policy, possibly very different on account of the concomitant assumptions. To be competitive, these emanate certainty while neglecting to highlight the inherent uncertainty in their assessments. Note the example of the greatly divergent estimates for the costs of the ACA: Speaker Boehner claimed a deficit spending increase of $701 billion over 10 years, while CBO's numbers indicated federal deficit reductions (CBO 2010, 2015), among the number of estimates from other sources circulating at the time.

Further, drawing on his policy experience, Manski offers an example of two very different analyses of policy approaches to cocaine control. On the one hand, RAND produced a study comparing supply and demand-side approaches to drug control, finding drug treatment programs had the greatest impact on drug control per dollar invested. The competing study from the Institute for Defense Analyses (IDA), on the other hand, revised RAND's conclusions and showed it is better to fund interdiction operations. On account of these contradictory findings, a National Research Council committee was approached to review both studies, concluding that neither can be used to inform reliably the policy development. To Manski, the differences between the RAND and the IDA reports are not as notable as their "shared lack of credibility:"

> Each study may be coherent internally, but each rests on such a fragile foundation of weak data and unsubstantiated assumptions as to undermine its findings....What troubles me most about both studies is their injudicious efforts to draw strong policy conclusions. It is not necessarily problematic for researchers to try to make sense of weak data and to entertain unsubstantiated conjectures. However, the strength of the conclusions drawn in a study should be commensurate with the quality of the evidence,

noted Manski adding that "[w]hen researchers overreach, they not only give away their own credibility, but they diminish public trust in science more generally" (2013, 27). Hence, strong conclusions, including those reached in the above case, lead to a diminished trust we have toward people in research and analysis. As well, these reinforce the thinking of scientific results as authoritative and unchanging, and with it the public (mis)understanding of the evolving nature of knowledge, reconfigured or updated in light of new findings.

Wishful extrapolation, "the drawing of a conclusion about some future or hypothetical situation based on observed tendencies and maintained assumptions" (31) when the assumptions are shaky, is another enabler of incredible certitude. Here, assuming invariance, which means that either future conditions will be similar to the present, or that the population at large will exhibit the same response to the treatment as its subset in an experimental setting, is frequently a wishful assumption in the ever-evolving social systems (as the economy, or health care, trade, or governance systems, among others). We will return to this item later in this section.

Another kind of certitude, *illogical certitude*, describes conclusions based on erroneous logic. Such problems range from basic mathematical mistakes to non-sequiturs, conclusions which are not logically connected to the premises. In terms of the latter, a frequent lapse in statistical analysis is to conclude that if null hypothesis, an assumption of no effect, was not rejected it must be correct. Goldberger and Manski (1995), for example, identify this problem in the resurgent *The Bell Curve* by Herrnstein and Murray (1994), where the results of statistical analyses of individual intelligence, environment, and socioeconomic outcomes are used to make the case against welfare. Herrnstein and Murray claimed, for instance, "[m]any studies that seem to be well conducted variations of the successful ones have failed to demonstrate any effect on IQ at all" (1994, 393). In statistical terms, this means the analyses did not reject the null hypothesis of no effect. "But every empirical researcher should know that 'failure to reject' the no-effect hypothesis does not establish its truth. It simply implies that the empirical findings are consistent with the no-effect hypothesis; it may well be that the findings are also consistent with alternative hypotheses which assert substantial treatment effects," note Goldberger and Manski (1995, 775). Indeed, such misinterpretations of quantitative studies are not uncommon, demonstrating the need for a more critical and informed engagement with such claims.

Manski also provides an example of a non-sequitur argument from the debates on nature versus nurture, namely on the heritability of intelligence. These debates gained additional gravity as some of the (illogical) arguments were intended to inform public policy. Specifically, it was argued that if intelligence is mostly heritable—a product of nature and thus just—the government cannot do much to equalize achievement. In this claim, heritability of a trait is understood as a formula, a sum of genetic and environmental factors. To illustrate,[3] consider heritability of height, which is thought to be 80% in the developed world. This means that 80% of height differences in a population can be explained by genes, as people have similar access to nutrition and health care. On the other hand, in developing countries, where environmental factors, such as limited access to good nutrition, prevail, the heritability of height is a significantly smaller number (Hannay 2015). Our discussion of gene-environment interaction in Chapter 3 makes clear this formulation is simplistic since it assumes genetic factors and environment are uncorrelated, or have independent effects on the outcomes. Hence, for instance, it neglects the possibility that people could be (dis)advantaged by their height in regions where hunting and subsistence are more effective due to a particular physique, in turn affecting their nutrition profiles and growth.

Although operationalized differently, the heritability formula is used in *The Bell Curve*. There, the authors find that in economic outcomes (specifically poverty), individuals' cognitive ability is "more important" than their parental socioeconomic status. This high heritability, the authors argue, means diminished effectiveness of social policy, namely of antipoverty programs. Manski emphasizes, however, heritability captures how genes and environment produce observable outcomes, which are not the concern of policy analysis. "Policy analysis asks what would happen to outcomes if an intervention, such as distribution of eyeglasses, were to change persons' environments in some manner. Heritability is uninformative about this," explains Manski (2013, 42). Notwithstanding we now appreciate the nature and nurture argument to be misguided, IQ studies have also meet their limits. "Nobody has the slightest causal account of how or why genes, singly or in combination, might affect IQ, [it is not] because the problem is too hard but because IQ is a specious rather than a natural kind," adds one scholar (Atran 2015). In the end, building an argument around IQ measures may be not only illogical but unfounded altogether.

Still another enabler of certitude in public discourse is the *conflation of science and advocacy*. While the logic of scientific inference proceeds from assumptions and collected data to conclusions, in advocacy the arrow points in the opposite direction. Various advocates begin with conclusions and selectively make data and assumptions to support their needs. This is why, after all, there are conservative and liberal think tanks, or even pollsters of various stripes finding what they need in public opinions through their custom surveys. But even the conclusions of many researchers, particularly in the economic profession as we noted earlier, are predictable.

We thus ask what makes these diverse practices so widespread they can be classified? Most people, including politicians, their support staff, or policy analysts and administrators, get much of their information from mainstream media, which often plays a role in encouraging certitude rather than exercising caution in light of ambiguity. This *media overreach*, the final practice identified by Manski, means research reporting, often commercially or political motivated, is less concerned with scientific rigor, where work must meet a standard of peer-review and scrutiny before it is considered more broadly. Preliminary research that has not gone through these processes is commonly presented with certainty and authority. Consider again *The Bell Curve*, a work which has not gone through an external review and revision as other credible scientific research (Goldberger and Manski 1995). This has not stopped the media from widely publicizing the book. The publication has eventually been subjected to scientific inspection, which was ultimately more "an exercise in damage control rather than prevention" (Goldberger and Manski 1995, 776). Below, we consider a further example of a common matter seemingly resolved long ago, which brings together media overreach with other practices creating a hard to navigate environment of inappropriate certitude.

Quotidian Certitudes

One of the recent issues of the *BMJ* (2013) published two systematic reviews or meta-analyses of the effects of dietary salt on blood pressure and the overall health (Aburto et al. 2013; He and MacGregor 2013). Both identified evidence showing that lower sodium intake reduced blood pressure in adults, while Aburto et al. (2013) further claimed there is some evidence of such effects in children and that reductions in salt intake are also associated with lower risk of stroke and coronary disease in adults. Responding to the articles, Graudal and Gresche (2013) point out these analyses are not only alike, but the latter is also similar to the 2004 Cochrane review (He and MacGregor 2004), itself a nominal update of past research. Also, according to the critics, the latter is nearly identical to a 2009 analysis published in the *BMJ* and the section on sodium intake in children differs by one data point from an analysis conducted in 2006. Graudal and Gresche (2013) argue that the conclusions of the studies are not "justified by the data," continuing their own (Graudal and Gresche 2011) and other such challenges appearing across journals with frequency. Speaking of the *BMJ* in particular, the authors thus ask why the journal "uses so much space on the publication?" and conclude there must be motivations that go beyond science.

Indeed, this is one of many exchanges involving research on salt, a four-decades-long debate over the benefits of lowering the intake of dietary salt. This debate, according to Taubes, a key figure in dietary science and an author of many articles and books explaining its methodological and epistemic limitations, "constitutes one of the longest running, most vitriolic, and surreal disputes in all of medicine" (Taubes 1998, 898). In the public realm, however, there seems to be an appearance of consensus, not the least given the intuitiveness and the confidence of the prevalent message. Peculiarly, "[i]n sharp contrast to this intensifying argument over what the available evidence actually says, public health recommendations at global, national, and local levels have been nearly unanimous in asserting that the evidence is incontrovertible that salt consumption should be reduced" (Bayer et al. 2012, 2739). With direct implications to our well-being, the certitudes over what we should (not) eat, including the recommendations on the consumption of salt as well as fats and carbohydrates, are the quintessential scientific-political issues, where the lines between science and advocacy disappear. And so too, these issues have the potential to undermine our trust in the input of the scientists and the decisions of the policy makers.

Among the first scientists advancing a confident and unambiguous argument for the sodium-blood pressure link was Lewis Dahl, who used evidence from rat studies to make his case. Dahl was invited to testify in front of the Select Committee on Nutrition and Human Needs in 1969 which focused on the content of salt in baby food, also a matter of an ensuing presidential conference on nutrition and health (Bayer et al. 2012). The discussions at the conference, as well as the findings of the National Academy of Sciences committee the following year, have shown a lack of consensus on the evidence (Bayer et al. 2012), an early indication of the brewing controversy. One party to this long-running dispute reads the evidence connecting the current or higher levels of salt consumption to increases in blood pressure as solid. To them, a reduction in dietary salt consumption is the low hanging fruit of health policy, an easy intervention with a potential to save hundreds of thousands of lives. Their opponents, on the other hand, are not only unconvinced by the evidence but also uncertain about the possible negative implications of reducing sodium intake (Taubes 1998), as some research suggests. Yet, as hinted, the government health agencies continue to send a loud and confident message of the benefits of salt reduction. For example, the Department of Agriculture sees salt as a more serious threat than fats, sugars, or alcohol, while the Centers for Disease Control and Prevention (CDC) likens salt reduction to quitting smoking (Taubes 2012).

The nutrition campaigns, including one for a low sodium diet, are effective on account of both strategic advocacy and intuition. We can observe first-hand, after all, that after eating salty foods we get thirsty as our bodies ask for water to rebalance the concentration of sodium in our blood. Until the excess salt is eliminated by the kidneys, the retained water, increasing the volume of fluids in the body, causes a temporary rise in our blood pressure. To this, add a confident statement from a government agency that these fluctuations in blood pressure lead to hypertension and strokes—and it is difficult not to be convinced. Yet, this is merely a hypothesis in need of rigorous testing (Taubes 2012). Similarly intuitive is the simple idea that obesity is a result of an unbalanced lifestyle where energy from consumed food and drinks exceeds the energy expended by the body. A conventional certitude, eating less and moving more, seems a commonsensical way to combat obesity. However, over the past 50 years the incidence of obesity has tripled and diabetes diagnoses are up seven times (Taubes 2014). And thus, as we begin to suspect carbohydrates may be "uniquely fattening" (Taubes and Teicholz 2018), we must consider it may be less the amounts than the *types* of food that lead to obesity and related diseases. Yet, despite the explosion in nutritional research, now producing tens of thousands of articles a year, we have not achieved clarity in our understanding of the causes and, consequently, on the strategies in prevention (Taubes 2014). At the same time, however, the public discourse seems to indicate we have all the answers.

Fuelling this and other contemporary disagreements on public health "is a philosophical clash between the requirements of public health policy and the requirements of good science, between the need to act and the institutionalized skepticism required to develop a body of reliable knowledge," writes Taubes (1998, 898). Consider, for example, the number of existing debates on obesity and its associated disorders. The debates are ongoing as their underlying theories cannot be disproved. Why? We lack reliable evidence, the decisive of which can be obtained through randomized controlled trials. In these studies, the participants are selected at random from the greater population and assigned across treatment and control groups. An analysis then reveals if the interventions had a statistically significant impact on the outcomes. However, as "the hypotheses are ultimately about what happens to us over decades, meaningful trials are prohibitively expensive and exceedingly difficult," explains Taubes (2014). This means that "advice to restrict fat or avoid saturated fat has been based on suppositions about what would have happened had such trials been done, not on the studies themselves" (Taubes 2014). Given such constraints, we have come to settle for alternate methods—including experiments on animals, short-term human studies, or long-term observational studies of certain populations—to make inferences, which, however, often become wishful extrapolations rather than hypotheses that they are (Taubes 2014).[4]

One constructive outcome of the controversies and debates mentioned above is that they concentrate our attention on methodology, particularly given the demands of evidence-based policy making (Bayer et al. 2012). For example, some have questioned the dependence on randomized controlled trials as the only reliable sources of evidence or pondered the value of systematic reviews, others "have sometimes asserted that the 'weight of all the evidence'—including data from observational studies, animal experiments, and clinical experience—should trump the results of analyses that weigh only randomized controlled trials" (Bayer et al. 2012, 2743). It is not difficult then to recognize that methodological pluralism, transparent of the limitations of methods used and coupled with broad appreciation of the ongoing questioning and revision in science, is sensible in informing credible policy.

Revisiting the methodological issues is important, for example, to cope with the increasingly taxing obesity epidemic demanding action with limited knowledge at hand. Consider two-thirds of US adults are either overweight or obese and more than 115 million of Americans have diabetes or prediabetes (Voorhes 2014). While we lack consensus on the causes, we recognize the conventional dietary recommendations have not affected these trends. And because these trends are untenable, we must work within the bounds of available evidence (Taubes and Teicholz 2018) in deciding on policy action. Yet, we face a less apparent obstacle. Taubes, who interviewed over 80 researchers for his 1998 article exploring the politics of the salt policy, quotes then associate director of the Office of Disease Prevention at the National Institutes of Health (NIH), Bill Harlan, lamenting the impatient public's demands for simple, binary answers to public health issues: "They don't want the answer after we finish a study in 5 years. They want it now. No equivocation. … [And so] we constantly get pushed into positions we may not want to be in and cannot justify scientifically" in Taubes (1998, 898). Certitude, thus traditionally expected by the public but countenanced too by the policy makers making strong assumptions to yield powerful but less credible answers, is damaging the efforts to find solutions in the public interest.

It is apparent that addressing these issues is not only a technical matter but also one of public understanding and discourse. We agree with Bayer et al. that "concealment of scientific uncertainty is a mistake that serves neither the ends of science nor good policy. Simplistic pictures of translation from evidence to action distort our ability to understand how policy *is*, in fact, made and how it *should* be made" (2012, 2743, emphasis original). If the goal of policy is to reduce our risk in the face of uncertainty, we must be able to appreciate limitations to our knowledge and possible trade-offs of our decisions. Yet, there exists an attitudinal cross-current, particularly evident in the EU, demonstrating it is possible to change the focus on uncertainty and use it to sanction policy action. This is the core of the precautionary principle we engage next.

The Precautionary Principle

In 2002, the European Environment Agency (EEA) published a volume bringing attention to a number of "late lessons from early warnings," cases of anthropogenic harms to health and environment exacerbated by a delayed regulatory action. Among the cases is radiation, warned to be injurious to humans at the end of the nineteenth century yet not legally regulated in the UK until 1961. Also, benzene, a widely used chemical solvent associated with aplastic anemia already in 1897 and leukemia within the following two decades, did not see a regulatory standard until the 1980s. Asbestos, whose microscopic shards of dust have been found to be injurious in 1898 by HM Medical Inspector with additional reports reaching the policy makers in the ensuing decade, was not banned until 1999 in the EU and its application limited in the US in 1989. Polychlorinated biphenyls have been observed to be toxic as early as 1899 and known to be dangerous to health by its US manufacturer in the late 1930s. These chemicals were banned and their production ceased only in the 1970s. Similarly, despite early concerns, synthetic estrogen diethylstilboestrol, sulfur dioxide, chlorofluorocarbons, antibiotics for growth promotion, and other threats were (or in the last case continue to be) sanctioned until their damage was critical, often until the alarmed public pressed for action (Harremoës et al. 2001).

For some, the above are inevitabilities of technological development, a progress leading to overall reduction of human risks, including the risks created by "inadequate supplies of food; poor access to safe water and sanitation; and insufficient knowledge of basic hygiene, the germ theory, and infectious and vector-borne diseases" (Goklany 2001, 3), especially in the developed world. While creating risks, innovations in science and technology have no doubt touched the lives of nearly everyone around the globe, improving health outcomes, quality of life, and economic opportunities. In this view, new tools, such as risk assessment and cost-benefit analysis (introduced in the 1970s and 1980s), coupled with ongoing scientific advances across fields, allow us to understand better the ramifications of our interventions and to manage possible harms (Raffensperger and Tickner 1999).

Others, pointing to the many lessons from history, recognize that "existing environmental regulations and other decisions, particularly those based on risk assessment, have failed to protect adequately human health and the environment" (Raffensperger and Tickner 1999, 353). In this view, the common tools to identify and quantify risk, successful in situations with known parameters and processes such as infrastructure projects, come short when applied to social and ecological systems, inherently complex and unpredictable (Chapter 9). But because the decisions to regulate activities are taken mostly after "science has established a causal association between a substance or activity and a well defined, singular adverse impact," resource and time intensive activity notwithstanding the neglect of many of the intractable properties of complex systems, "action to prevent potentially irreversible human and environmental harm is often delayed in the name of uncertainty and the harmful activity continues" (Raffensperger and Tickner 1999, 2–3). This approach is particularly problematic when it comes to genetically modified foods, nanotechnologies, or greenhouse gases, whose implications to health or environment are far from understood.

Consider, for example, the uncertainties inherent in the estimates of social cost of carbon (SCC), a valuation of changes to carbon dioxide emissions used in cost-benefit analyses. This number, as do other valuations, depends on a series of assumptions which can yield dramatically different results. Speaking of the cost-benefit analysis of climate change mitigation, Steele notes its recommendation

> depends on which scenarios you think are most likely, on your discount rate, and how far off in the future you think catastrophically adverse effects (e.g., a 50% loss of global economic output) would occur if they happened. For instance, a high discount rate combined with a damage function in which costs of climate change rise very gradually with increasing temperatures is a straightforward recipe for generating low SCC estimates. Given scientific *uncertainty*, then, many distinct specifications of the relevant details may lead to *conflicting recommendations*. (2015, 205, emphases added)

Hence, the traditional cost-benefit analyses run into their limits, offering not much support in deciding on an appropriate path forward. This situation provides one rationale for an increasingly visible concept, the precautionary principle (PP). In one interpretation, the PP rests on two regulatory approaches: "anthropogenic harm to human health and the environment should be avoided or minimized through anticipatory, preventive regulatory controls; and, to accomplish this, activities and technologies whose environmental consequences are uncertain but potentially serious should be restricted until the uncertainty is largely resolved" (Applegate 2002, 13). The assumptions are that harm to health and environment resulting from the application of new technologies can be prevented through proactive regulatory measures; and that protecting health and environment has a priority over "quantitative measures of risk and economic efficiency" (Applegate 2002, 13). With roots in the German law of the 1970s and 1980s, the PP has since become part of health and environmental policies in the EU and a number of international treaties primarily on the environment (Marchant and Mossman 2004).

Over the last two decades, the PP has also been increasingly invoked in North America, where it was brought to prominence by the Wingspread Conference on Implementing the Precautionary Principle in 1998. Motivated by eroding regulations in the face of rising environmental and health challenges, a group of scientists and other stakeholders came together to formalize a new paradigm "address[ing] the limits of science while promoting action to prevent harm" (Raffensperger and Tickner 1999, 8).

> When an activity raises threats of harm to human health or the environment, precautionary measures should be taken even if some cause and effect relationships are not established scientifically. In this context the proponent of the activity, rather than the public, should bear the burden of proof,

concluded the group (Raffensperger and Tickner 1999, 8). This statement became yet another addition to a growing list of formulations of the PP, the most cited of which are included in Box 7.1. And the variety of conceptions, invocations, and applications is a reason for much of the debates and critiques of the PP. Indeed, the PP provides a fascinating case of an evolving idea whose lack of a shared foundation became a boon for its supporters and target for its critics. This is especially when "dissected in an analytical vacuum, considered from a single disciplinary perspective, or treated in a 'plug and play' manner in that its implementation is characterized as simply requiring the inclusion of the principle into policy or a legislative scheme for it to be effective" (Fisher et al. 2006, 1). Such a treatment has thus fueled much debates, controversies, and propositions. We do not intend to review these as they have been much discussed elsewhere.[5]

Box 7.1 Select articulations of the precautionary principle

Principle 15 of the 1992 Rio Declaration of the United Nations Conference on Environment and Development:
In order to protect the environment, the precautionary principle shall be widely applied by States according to their capacity. Where there are threats of serious or irreversible damage, lack of full scientific certainty shall not be used as a reason for postponing cost-effective measures to prevent environmental degradation.

Article 191(2) of the Treaty on the Functioning of the European Union (TFEU):
Union policy on the environment shall aim at a high level of protection taking into account the diversity of situations in the various regions of the Union. It shall be based on the precautionary principle and on the principles that preventive action should be taken, that environmental damage should as a priority be rectified at source and that the polluter should pay.

European Environment Agency (2013, 681, emphases original):
The precautionary principle provides justification for public policy and other actions in situations of *scientific complexity, uncertainty and ignorance*, where there may be a need to act in order to avoid, or reduce, potentially serious or irreversible threats to health and/or the environment, using an *appropriate strength of scientific evidence*, and taking into account *the pros and cons of action and inaction* and their distribution.

For completeness, however, we briefly discuss three key challenges facing the PP and highlight an approach capable of answering them (per Steel 2015). The first issue stems from the range of definitions of the PP, the two extremes of which are often used in critique (Sunstein 2005). At one end is the weak interpretation "according to which uncertainty does not justify inaction in the face of serious threats," while at the other is the strong interpretation "according to which precaution is required in the face of any scientifically plausible and serious environmental hazard"

(Steel 2015, 3). Hence, the weak version is seen as a truism, not very useful in advancing the PP. The strong version is interpreted as irrational given regulations themselves carry risks of negative unintended consequences (Sunstein 2005; Steel 2015). The second issue lies in the variety of seemingly contradictory prescriptions associated with the PP. A reliable system strives for consistency through a unified rather than a disjoint approach to making choices among options (Steel 2015). The third challenge stems from the conflict between the values embodied in the PP and the ostensibly value-free methods of science. What standards should be used to make value judgments on the method in informing policy? (Steel 2015).

According to Steel (2015), addressing these issues that are often considered separate must begin with a realization of their relatedness. The author thus makes the case for an integrated approach bringing together these three aspects. The first, a position that scientific uncertainty of harm should not preclude policy action, bounds the decision rule space: "decision rules that are susceptible to paralysis by scientific uncertainty should be avoided" (9). The second consists of three considerations in justifying regulatory decision: the knowledge condition, harm condition, and recommended precaution. Each of these can have multiple specifications the selection of which requires a close analysis of each precautionary scenario. Finally, there is the principle of proportionality ensuring "the aggressiveness of the precaution should correspond to the plausibility and severity of the threat" (10). A proportional response is one that is consistent and efficient.

The three elements together thus provide a coherent system for the application of the PP, its new interpretation, and a sophisticated underpinning for what has been frequently a challenged idea. With time, we will find whether this or an alternate system will gain a broader acceptance. Currently, however, and namely in the North American context, there has been a significant pushback against the PP, particularly among select scholars and policy makers fearing it replacing "the riskbased, science-dominated, cost sensitive regulatory structures that have come to characterize most of the world's sophisticated environmental regimes" (Applegate 2002, 15). These opponents are thus content with keeping the PP at a general level, allowing them to reshape the specifics (Applegate 2002).

Nevertheless, the PP's growing visibility, compelling various stakeholders to respond, brings their arguments into the spotlight and carries the potential to change not only the way policies are made but also the general attitudes toward scientific certitude. This is particularly the case as we broadly recognize points such as those conveyed in the findings of a publication prepared for the Fourth Ministerial Conference on Environment and Health (Martuzzi and Tickner 2004, 3–4, emphases added):

- "Substantial evidence supports the conclusion that contemporary environmental health risks result from complex interactions among genetic, nutritional, environmental and socioeconomic factors... Many pressing environmental crises ... appear to arise from disruptions of natural systems or cycles, the behaviour of which is *only partially understood...*"
- As we strive for progress in science to help us understand better the risks of our interventions, we also have to seek "ways to make decisions that are based on the best available evidence, while acknowledging the *uncertainties* that remain."
- The PP emphasizes these "uncertain risks and seeks to shift the ways in which science informs policy from a strategy of 'reaction' to a strategy of 'precaution'."
- "There is no single recipe for applying precaution...each decision is different—with different types of risk, evidence, uncertainty, affected communities, availability of alternatives, and technical and financial resources."

Importantly, as the report adds, while we require flexibility in light of the diversity, we must aim for consistency obtained through the use of a shared framework. Above we have mentioned one such a framework capable of introducing logic and coherence into the application of the PP.

CONCLUSION

Examining an argument presented by Pinker in his popular *The Blank Slate* (2003), Robinson notes "it would be reassuring to see a slightly more evenhanded use of evidence... some note taken of the susceptibility of such observations to hoaxing and manipulation ...together with an acknowledgment that those who use such observations are susceptible in turn to overvaluing data that tend to confirm them in their views" (2010, 17). For Robinson, Pinker is one among many science authors tempted by certitude, a confident conclusion glossing over assumptions, evidentiary limits, and balance. This, of course, helps the argument and is appealing to readers uncomfortable with uncertainty. Not unique to popular science, such an attitude is also ubiquitous in areas of greater impact—public policy making. Manski, in particular, has been a vocal critic of such proclivities, observing that

> [t]he scientific community rewards those who produce strong novel findings. The public, impatient for solutions to its pressing concerns, rewards those who offer simple analyses leading to unequivocal policy recommendations. These incentives make it tempting for researchers to maintain assumptions far stronger than they can persuasively defend, in order to draw strong conclusions. (Manski 2007, 7–8)

We opened this chapter with a set of common practices leading to incredible certitude (as described by Manski) in the context of public policy. We have also supplied examples from nutritional science, which is providing guidance with implications to virtually all members of the society, and demonstrated the pervasiveness and the gravity of this form of trivialization.

Such practices, however, go beyond decisions on policy: at issue is the very public trust in the conclusions of scientists and the decisions of policy makers. This is not only important to a functioning democracy but also vital in marshaling support in addressing the modern day risks—risks we do not understand well and cannot predict, yet ones with possibly lasting, global implications. There may be a promise on the horizon in the form of an increasingly salient approach, the PP, recognizing that uncertainty, inherent to complex health and environmental systems, should not be a reason to avoid regulatory action. Its systematic application has the potential to pry open the black boxes behind policy discourses, bringing into light the assumptions and analyses informing the contemporary policy making, and reveal many of the incredible conclusions these offer. At the same time, the PP may be an opening to a new paradigm to be discussed in the next chapter.

NOTES

1. Hence, the logic can be summarized as assumptions + data → conclusions (more in Manski 2011, 2013).
2. The least complicated of which are selected.
3. Example from Hannay (2015).
4. This is why in 2012, Taubes established a non-profit Nutrition Science Initiative. The program has since raised $40 million to conduct rigorous testing of key dietary hypotheses (Horgan 2014; Voorhes 2014).
5. Goklany (2001), Marchant and Mossman (2004), Sunstein (2005), Mandel and Gathii (2006), or Fisher et al. (2006).

REFERENCES

Aburto, Nancy J., Anna Ziolkovska, Lee Hooper, Paul Elliott, Francesco P. Cappuccio, and Joerg J. Meerpohl. 2013. "Effect of lower sodium intake on health: Systematic review and meta-analyses." *British Medical Journal* 346: f1326.

Applegate, John S. 2002. "The taming of the precautionary principle." *William & Mary Environmental Law and Policy Review* 27: 13.

Atran, Scott. 2015. "IQ." In *This idea must die: Scientific theories that are blocking progress*, edited by John Brockman. New York: Harper Perennial.

Bayer, Ronald, David Merritt Johns, and Sandro Galea. 2012. "Salt and public health: Contested science and the challenge of evidence-based decision making." *Health Affairs* 31 (12): 2738–2746.

Boehner, John, ed. 2011. *Obamacare: A budget-busting, job-killing health care law*. DIANE Publishing. https://www.speaker.gov/sites/speaker.house.gov/files/UploadedFiles/ObamaCareReport.pdf. As cited in Rawal (2016).

CBO. 2010. "Letter to the honorable Nancy Pelosi on H.R. 4872, the Reconciliation Act of 2010. Congressional Budget Office. March 20." https://www.cbo.gov/sites/default/files/cbofiles/ftpdocs/113xx/doc11379/amendreconprop.pd.

CBO. 2015. "Insurance coverage provisions of the Affordable Care Act—CBO's March 2015 Baseline." Congressional Budget Office. https://www.cbo.gov/sites/default/files/recurringdata/51298-2015-03-aca.pdf.

European Environment Agency. 2013. *Late lessons from early warnings II: Science, precaution, innovation*. Copenhagen: European Environment Agency.

Fisher, Elizabeth Charlotte, Judith S. Jones, and René von Schomberg, eds. 2006. *Implementing the precautionary principle: Perspectives and prospects*. Cheltenham, UK and Northampton, MA: Edward Elgar Publishing.

Gilens, Martin, and Benjamin I. Page. 2014. "Testing theories of American politics: Elites, interest groups, and average citizens." *Perspectives on Politics* 12 (3): 564–581.

Goklany, Indur M. 2001. *The precautionary principle: A critical appraisal of environmental risk assessment.* Washington, DC: Cato Institute.

Goldberger, Arthur S., and Charles F. Manski. 1995. "The *Bell Curve* by Herrnstein and Murray." *Journal of Economic Literature* 33 (2): 762.

Graudal, Niels, and Gesche Jürgens. 2011. "The sodium phantom." *British Medical Journal* 343: d6119.

Graudal, Niels, and Gesche Jürgens. 2013. "The (political) science of salt revisited." *British Medical Journal* 346: f2741.

Hannay, Timo. 2015. "Nature versus nurture." In *This idea must die: Scientific theories that are blocking progress,* edited by John Brockman. New York: Harper Perennial.

Harremoës, Poul, David Gee, Malcolm MacGarvin, Andy Stirling, Jane Keys, Brian Wynne, and Sofia Guedes Vaz, eds. 2001. *Late lessons from early warnings: The precautionary principle 1896–2000.* Luxembourg: Office for Official Publications of the European Communities.

He, Feng J., and Graham A. MacGregor. 2004. "Effect of longer-term modest salt reduction on blood pressure." *Cochrane Database of Systematic Reviews* 3 (3): CD004937. As cited in Gradual and Gesche (2013).

He, Feng J., Jiafu Li, and Graham A. MacGregor. 2013. "Effect of longer term modest salt reduction on blood pressure: Cochrane systematic review and meta-analysis of randomised trials." *British Medical Journal* 346: f1325. As cited in Gradual and Gesche (2013).

Horgan, John. 2014. "Chewing the fat with diet 'Journalist' Gary Taubes." *Scientific American,* October 7. https://blogs.scientificamerican.com/cross-check/chewing-the-fat-with-diet-8220-journalist-8221-gary-taubes/.

Mandel, Gregory N., and James Thuo Gathii. 2006. "Cost-benefit analysis versus the precautionary principle: Beyond Cass Sunstein's laws of fear." *University of Illinois Law Review* 1037–1080.

Manski, Charles F. 2007. *Identification for prediction and decision.* Cambridge, MA: Harvard University Press. As cited in Manski (2011, 2013).

Manski, Charles F. 2011. "Policy analysis with incredible certitude." *The Economic Journal* 121 (554): F261–F289.

Manski, Charles F. 2013. *Public policy in an uncertain world: Analysis and decisions.* Cambridge, MA: Harvard University Press.

Marchant, Gary Elvin, and Kenneth L. Mossman. 2004. *Arbitrary and capricious: The precautionary principle in the European Union courts.* Washington, DC: American Enterprise Institute.

Martuzzi, Marco, and Joel A. Tickner, eds. 2004. *The precautionary principle: Protecting public health, the environment and the future of our children.* Copenhagen: The World Health Organization.

Murray, Charles, and Richard Herrnstein. 1994. *The Bell Curve: Intelligence and class structure in American life.* New York: Free Press. As cited in Goldberger and Manski (1995).

Pinker, Steven. 2003. *The blank slate: The modern denial of human nature.* New York: Penguin.

Raffensperger, Carolyn, and Joel A. Tickner. 1999. *Protecting public health and the environment: Implementing the precautionary principle.* Washington, DC: Island Press.

Rawal, Purva H. 2016. *The affordable care act: Examining the facts.* ABC-CLIO.

Robinson, Marilynne. 2010. *Absence of mind: The dispelling of inwardness from the modern myth of the self.* New Haven: Yale University Press.

Steel, Daniel. 2015. *Philosophy and the precautionary principle.* Cambridge, UK: Cambridge University Press.

Sunstein, Cass R. 2005. *Laws of fear: Beyond the precautionary principle.* New York: Cambridge University Press.

Taubes, Gary. 1998. The (political) science of salt. *Science (New York, NY),* *281*(5379).

Taubes, Gary. 2012. "Salt, we misjudged you." *The New York Times,* June 2. https://www.nytimes.com/2012/06/03/opinion/sunday/we-only-think-we-know-the-truth-about-salt.html.

Taubes, Gary. 2014. "Why nutrition is so confusing." *The New York Times,* February 8. https://www.nytimes.com/2014/02/09/opinion/sunday/why-nutrition-is-so-confusing.html.

Taubes, Gary, and Nina Teicholz. 2018. "U.S. News is wrong about what constitutes the best diet." *The LA Times,* January 28. http://www.latimes.com/opinion/op-ed/la-oe-taubes-teicholz-us-news-best-diet-problems-20180128-story.html.

Voorhes, Adam. 2014. "Why are we so fat? The Multimillion-dollar scientific quest to find out." *Wired,* August 19. https://www.wired.com/2014/08/what-makes-us-fat/.

CHAPTER 8

Into a New Paradigm

The 2007 burst of the US housing bubble triggered a set of cascading crises that had stormed the globe, each creating different problems and demanding different responses (Kickert 2012; Kickert and Randma-Liiv 2015). The series began with the *banking* crisis in which a number of major financial institutions were saved from collapse by government intervention. This was followed by the meltdown of the financial markets and the ensuing *economic* crisis. The third in the series was the *fiscal* crisis. The massive bailouts and economic recovery packages resulted in drastic budget deficits. Finally, there was the European sovereign debt crisis, or the *Eurozone* crisis of 2010, rooted in the ballooning debts and their costs which became unserviceable for some EU countries. This chain of events revealed not only the interdependent nature of the global system but also its fragility. What happened?

As the turmoil subsided, a number of commissions and enquiries were established by entities ranging from the G30 to the US Treasury with a goal to provide answers to the public (Ciro 2016). Among the more visible was the US Financial Crisis Inquiry Commission (FCIC) report that was made public in the early 2011. The commission concluded

[t]he crisis was the result of human action and inaction, not of Mother Nature or computer models gone haywire. The captains of finance and the public stewards of our financial system ignored warnings and failed to question, understand, and manage evolving risks within a system essential

© The Author(s) 2019
O. Bubak and H. Jacek, *Trivialization and Public Opinion*,
https://doi.org/10.1007/978-3-030-17925-0_8

to the well-being of the American public. ... While the business cycle cannot be repealed, a crisis of this magnitude need not have occurred. (FCIC 2011, xvii)

Yet, notwithstanding the 600-page report's identification of the warning signs, government inactions, and preventable lapses in financial practices and regulations, the explanations and debates on the crises continue to accumulate to this day. This is not only as the crises highlighted slips in morality, responsibility, and regulation, but also as their causes challenged the consensus view of how economy and, more broadly, social systems operate. Let us briefly engage the common explanations to set up the goal of this chapter.

A commonly given story of why the crises occurred begins with cheap credit resulting from investments of strategic savings, primarily of Asian countries, made available to consumers in the USA in the form of loans of various kinds. Interest rates—cut by the US Federal Reserve in the early 2000s to increase liquidity, restore confidence, and forestall economic downturn—made borrowing, particularly in the mortgage sector, broadly accessible (Ciro 2016). The dominant type of credit became the infamous sub-prime, high-interest mortgages, designed for normally ineligible clients, giving rise in relatively short order to a housing bubble. Such mortgages were quickly securitized, or transformed into investment vehicles classified by levels of risk. These securities were held by their issuers or resold to others, oftentimes with inflated ratings given by issuer-remunerated credit rating agencies. To hold more of these lucrative securities and increase their profits, the banks used short-term, low-interest loans on rolling basis. Finally, the securities were insured by credit default swaps (CDSs), innovative financial instruments created to provide additional ways to trade risk. The CDSs were also purchased by non-holders as a bet against the securities (McCarty et al. 2013). The deregulated banks were allowed and incentivized to create and sell more of these securities, creating a fragile risk spiral that soon unraveled.

There exist, of course, a number of alternative perspectives. For example, McCarty et al. (2013) root the global financial crisis in the failure to address a set of three related developments: the proliferation of risky residential debt, its securitization, and the use of novel yet opaque financial instruments. Claessens and Kodres (2014) identify two types of causes. The first set consists of causes common to other financial crises: rapid financial expansion, fast asset price appreciation, creation of novel financial instruments, and financial liberalization (deregulation). Their new causes include the extraordinary increase in household debt and the resulting defaults, financialization of society, and increased complexity aggravated by decreased transparency. Similarly, Davis (2011) identifies five major factors behind the meltdown: unsustainable debt; poor financial sector governance and accountability coupled with incentives to take excessive risks; unmanaged global imbalances; complex financial instruments and shadow banking obscuring and globalizing risks; and public unawareness of the tenuous nature of the financial system. Finally, Varoufakis (2015) offers his six explanations for the crisis: misunderstanding of systemic risk, capture of credit rating agencies and regulatory bodies, greed, the Anglo-Celtic cultural obsession with home ownership, flawed economic theory, and the failings of the free market system.

While there is a common thread in these explanations, including uncontrolled global account imbalances, systemic debt, financialization, as well as failures of governance in the capitalist democracy, they are not the same. The goal here is not to provide an analysis of the crises, which has been done well by these and other authors (Levine 2012), but rather to emphasize the multiplicity of their causes. As other crises, this series happened at a confluence of not one or two, but a set of conditions, accelerated and deepened by the increasingly open global system of finance. Yet, if there is an ultimate reason for these crises, it is the policy makers' assumptions misappropriated from physical sciences and used to understand financial systems and inform policy and regulation. The goal of this chapter is to discuss an alternate perspective—known as the complexity paradigm—slowly finding its way into social sciences. A broad embrace of this view, we believe, holds a promise to remediate our treatment of social and economic systems, to drive the reinterpretation of a variety of concepts and defuse a number of ongoing theoretical clashes, and with these help change our style of discourse.

There has been an intensifying interest in complexity, uncertainty, and systems thinking as manifested, for example, in the work of Jervis (1997), who reaches for systems theory and makes the case for our rethinking of international politics; Taleb (2007) and his influential treatise on the nature of randomness and the unpredictability of critical events; Arthur (2015), a promoter of complexity economics, a framework capable of dealing with the economy in its true form: dynamic and "perpetually computing"; Steinmo (2010) and his cross-disciplinary case to treat political economies as evolving through "as an interactive, interdependent, and ongoing process between the individual, the population, and the broader environment or ecology" (15); or even Esping-Andersen (1989), who, in his classic essay on the origins of welfare state regimes, asserts that our categorical thinking and traditional linear views of power, money, or industrialization lead us to wrong conclusions. And as these and many other scholars from across social sciences including Byrne (1998), Hall (2003), Helbing (2008), Sawyer (2005), or Stacey (2003) recognize nonlinearity, multicausality, emergence,[1] nonadditivity, path dependence—key elements of complexity research—as integral to explanation in their domains, they begin to enter a new paradigm, a transformation whose contours become increasingly discernible. This view is far from new, but its journey has been incremental, steadily advanced through technological progress and persistent academic inquiry, and punctuated by social and economic shocks.

Below, we familiarize the reader with complex adaptive systems (CAS), at once a concept which defines the complexity paradigm as well as a field of inquiry that facilitates it. Setting out to place the new thinking and its implications in a larger context, we chart a series of historical debates leading up to the present intersection. A select overview of complexity research with its questions and answers follows. First, however, building on the chapter's opening, we return to the world of global finance, with a dual purpose in mind.

THE GLOBAL FINANCIAL SYSTEM

Connected in an intricate web, private and central banks, investment houses, international financial institutions, rating agencies, individual buyers and sellers, and numerous local and supranational associations representing a variety of supply as well as demand-side interests are the constituents of global finance networks. Lacking a central authority, these participants are further arranged into *hierarchies*, where they compete and cooperate while *constrained* or motivated by various (dis) incentives, perceived or substantive. Exchange and interest rates as well as rules and regulations set by public or private regulatory institutions—some binding and enforceable, others in the form of voluntary standards without a legal underpinning—are among the control mechanisms in place to minimize variation and provide stability. The participants are sensitive to *feedback*, whether from each other or from within the environment in which they are embedded. The interactions of the participants, limited by their historical trajectories, their interpretation of institutions and the available information, unaware of the intentions of others, and operating within a global economy, give *rise* to the global financial *markets*. Finally, though subject to a number of artificial or natural limits, the markets exist in a state of flux and experience recurring adjustments.

While assumed durable on account of its presumably rational, informed, and distributed actors, this convoluted landscape was quickly brought to its knees with the above-mentioned housing bubble. What followed is the now familiar chain of collapses of major financial institutions, taxpayer-funded bailouts, and a global economic recession. Such sudden and destructive events then beckon a closer study of global phenomena, and namely a better understanding of crises, their roots, effects, and dynamics. Ultimately, we would like to know how to prevent them or at least how to minimize their impact.

This task is mostly left to social scientists, scholars of political economy, economics, political studies, or sociology. Working from a variety of traditions, these scholars study the relationship between social systems and their constituents with hopes of explaining the origins and change of institutions, cultures, and organizations as well as the roots of social and individual lapses, among others. For the structuralists, the key to analysis of this environment is its structural properties. This approach sees material resources, rules, hierarchies, and other social structures as the determinants of actors' behavior. For the individualists, it is the intentions, rationality, and actions of individual actors that are sufficient to the understanding of global characteristics. Others argue that structures and actors are both decisive to analysis and must be considered together. Still, for other scholars, there exists a crucial causal level in between the individual and the structure—the level of interaction. The interaction approach, with its focus on communication, processes, and mechanisms, thus offers an innovation over the deterministic perspectives, as it is better able to deal with contingency and change (Sawyer 2005). In all, these perspectives—which can be classified into the Structure or the Interaction Paradigm (Sawyer 2005)—sit atop problematic, reductionist assumptions and offer at best a partial capacity to explain phenomena arising from complex social interactions as well as the environment within which these interactions take place.[2] Both thus come short in coping with financial crises, conflicts, and other systemic occurrences.

We began with a discussion of the global financial crises and high-lighted their interlinked and multifaceted nature. We then sketched the world of global finance in a deliberate manner, as we emphasized its systemic character, its emergent phenomena, and pointed to its nonlinear properties apparent in an imperceptible change in conditions begetting unexpected system-wide crises. This makes the world of global finance a vivid exemplar of a complex adaptive system. It is this complex environment especially that benefits from a reconsideration of the traditionally held ontologies—which capture our understanding of causal structures—in favor of those intrinsic to CAS where nonlinearity, emergence, or multicausality are fundamental properties. And as we observe the complexity trend—thinking adopted at times inconspicuously and not necessarily completely—we demand its better understanding. In the ensuing sections, we thus take a closer look at CAS and engage the unfolding debates as we help contextualize this development.

Paradigms

As we speak of a new *paradigm*, let us briefly discuss this concept. The common understanding of the term and the associated notion of normal science is due to Kuhn (2012). Normal science refers to solving puzzles within a current paradigm—a scientific tradition encompassing laws, practices, theories, and tools broadly accepted by the scientific community. In this view, paradigm can be "declared invalid only if an alternative candidate is available to take its place. …The decision to reject one paradigm is always simultaneously the decision to accept another…that decision involves the comparison of both paradigms with nature and with each other," explains Kuhn (2012, 78). According to Kuhn, progress in science is not driven by proactive scrutiny but through problem-solving that continues until the paradigm eventually meets its limits.

Social science paradigms similarly comprise "a set of factual and explanatory knowledge claims, in other words, theories, that are widely accepted by adherents [and] structure further research: determining which facts are theoretically salient; defining what constitutes a paradox and what questions urgently require answers; identifying which cases need to be examined and what kinds of evidence are considered meaningful" (Geddes 2003, 7). Yet, the social world is different from the physical, in its tangibility, variety, and fluidity, in turn reflected in its paradigms—an unruly mix of macro-, mid-range, and micro-theories which often conflict with each other. Also, because social science research is not "shaped only by discourse within the community itself" (Kohli et al. 1995, 3), its paradigms may follow a different path than in science.

While there exist a range of paradigms based on their scope and specificity, here we are concerned with the most general of paradigms, a *meta-theory*. Over the past three centuries, the sciences have operated from what may be called the Cartesian-Split-Mechanistic scientific paradigm (Overton 2015). It was borne with Descartes' splitting of the world into independent parts, "one constituting a fixed immovable foundational Reality, the other a derived appearance of reality," ultimately resulting in "'either/or' propositions, and the selection of one or the other of a forced choice." Knowledge was hence created "according to the categories of materialism or idealism, subjectivism or objectivism, body (e.g., brain) or mind," among others (Overton 2015, 17–18). Newton, building on Descartes' categories, established a set of assumptions on the nature of matter (its inertness and atomicity) and with it methods of inquiry. Explanation, according to Newton, thus involved a reduction of the object of study to its smallest constituents and, based on direct observation of stimuli and responses, an induction of fundamental and universally applicable laws (Overton 2015).

As hinted earlier (Chapter 3), not the least due to its successes in natural sciences, the same paradigm began to inform inquiry across sciences. Yet, it was not long before some scientists outside of the physical sciences began to realize the inadequacies of this conceptual framework in studying biological or social systems. Sawyer (2005) described several features unique to the social world, quickly revealing its kind of complexity. First, unlike in many natural systems with clearly delimited loci of discourse, there is an inherent ambiguity to social systems' boundaries and so to their constituents and relations. In many circumstances, this openness is not amenable to reductionist approaches. Also, in social systems, the interconnections between the elements are not physical and thus not observable. Moreover, the information exchanged over such connections is qualitatively different from the relatively simple physical or chemical signals in physical systems as it is mediated by language and symbols. Finally, while biological systems are complex and self-organizing, "[n]eurons do not have interpretations, meanings, and intentional action" (Sawyer 2005, 26). But people do and carry with them representations of structural patterns, evolving templates applied to interaction, greatly increasing the relative complexity of social systems. Assuming away feedback, context, and causally important global properties has limited our capacity to explain and understand change, behavior, and systemic effects—and not only in social sciences. Next, we will describe the field of study concerned with properties and behaviors of complex systems, which informs the new frame of reference.

COMPLEXITY RESEARCH AND ITS IMPRINTS

There exist multiple perspectives on complexity, not the least due to its relative novelty and the inherently transdisciplinary application. We observe a persistent confusion over chaos theory, a formal study of behavior in deterministic dynamical systems, and complex systems research or CAS, referenced above. There are historical reasons for this as systems thinking has made it into social sciences in three different waves (Sawyer 2005). Parson's cybernetics-inspired structural functionalism, and systems and chaos theories defined the first and second waves, respectively. The third wave is the contemporary CAS-driven focus on emergence and the relation between the individual, social, and interaction levels of analysis (more in Sawyer 2005).

Hence for clarity, it is important to describe and differentiate CAS class of systems from those complicated, chaotic, and closed. A key starting question here is: What is the structure of a complex system and how does it behave? Complex systems are composed of *many* networked objects or agents that are *interacting*. The large number of agents as well as their interactions are fundamental—necessary but not sufficient, however—features setting complex systems apart from those that are merely complicated. The interactions may be physical or informational, taking place primarily among neighboring agents or groups of agents. Extended interactions are possible with signals generally transformed, i.e., attenuated or intensified en route. The interactions are *nonlinear*, where the output is disproportional to the input, and *recurrent*, where the feedback involving one or more agents can occur in reinforcing or inhibiting loops. Also, the agents' actions are constrained on account of their histories and thus their present choices cannot be understood apart from their past ones (Cilliers 1998; Johnson 2009). This path dependence, as we will discuss, is among the key insights of this line of research. Given the nonlinearity, feedback, as well as temporal considerations, the behavior of the agents, and by extension of the system, is sensitive to *initial conditions*. Note the characteristics presented thus far could be subsumed under *chaos theory*, a stream within dynamic systems theory seeking deterministic models of systems behaviors, which provided an impetus for the study of complex systems.

There are several important properties distinguishing CAS from the above perspectives. First, complex systems lack a clear boundary separating them from their environment and other systems, rendering them *open*. Unlike closed systems, assumed to be self-contained for analytical convenience, the environment becomes a critical determinant in CAS. Second, CAS operate in states that are far from equilibrium, moving in parts or as whole between disorder and order. Such transitions are crucial as they allow us not only understand change, but also to manage and possibly control CAS (Johnson 2009). Third, the interactions between the system components, each individually unaware of the totality of the system in which it operates, give rise to a variety of unpredictable, *emergent* phenomena. "When we look at the behavior of a complex system as a whole, our focus shifts from the individual element in the system to the complex structure of the system. The complexity *emerges* as *a result of the patterns of interaction* between the elements," explains Cilliers (1998, 5, emphasis added). Importantly, this implies there is no "invisible hand" or central coordinator that organizes the agents and orchestrates emergence (Johnson 2009). Finally, CAS have a capacity to self-organize which "enables them to develop or change internal structure spontaneously and adoptively in order to cope with, or manipulate, their environment" (Cilliers 1998, 90). This self-organization is itself a property emergent from the interaction of networked agents, and their ability to retain information and learn through feedback loops. Hence, we say the systems are adaptive.

We have introduced key structural and behavioral features of CAS, which we can discern in the financial system as sketched earlier. A natural question is how can CAS analyses enhance our understanding of such systems? A process that involves mapping the system's actors and their interactions, identifying its behavioral properties, and determining external factors that impact but are not impacted by the system, reveals a number of important dynamic features (Helbing 2015). Under particular conditions, including targeted interactions and external interventions, the system remains stable; at a certain point, however, changing conditions may shift the system to a new regime, a dramatic adjustment in the behavior of the system (Helbing 2015). "The corresponding systemic processes often occur in a cascade- or avalanche-like manner, and the frequency of such extreme events is *much higher* than expected. It typically follows a so called fattailed distribution rather than a normal distribution," explains Helbing (2015, 29, emphasis added). The financial crises, the likelihood of which was minute according to traditional models, are an example of such a regime shift.

CAS hence focuses our attention at *robustness*, the capacity of a system to resist regime shifts, no doubt of top concern in the world of finance. Indeed, Helbing (2015) argues that considering the essential features of robustness is central to the understanding and management of complex systems. The author describes several such properties[3] and shows how a number of destabilizing factors diminished the robustness of the financial system and lead to crisis. One destabilizing factor is self-organized criticality where the system components reorganize to adapt to some conditions while reaching a critical state. This is especially problematic if this happens en masse. A robust system copes with self-organized criticality through compartmentalization, a partition of the system into a number of mostly independent subnetworks. And deregulation and monetary policies lead to less barriers and greater interdependencies. Another destabilizing factor is lower transparency, diminishing the ability to understand and hence manage the system. Here, Helbing points to the growing complexity of financial instruments which was not met with adequate analytical capacity, challenging "the robustness criteria of variety (in terms of different approaches to risk assessment) and redundancy (requiring that different experts investigate the same risks)" (2015, 32). Hence, robustness analysis as enabled by CAS steers attention to these and other factors, allowing for an enhanced understanding of financial systems and their regulation.

While complexity research was invoked explicitly in the case above, we may recognize CAS imprints across political research, even if scholars do not reference CAS directly. Let us briefly consider select cases from institutional research, where scholars early recognized path dependence and feedback as central to explanation of institutional development. Ostrom (2007), for example, points to several main difficulties facing institutionalist scholars. For one, institutions, as shared rules, norms, and strategies, often exist as implicit knowledge rather than codified directives, raising questions about how to delimit and assess them. Also, given institutions are social constructs, which are context dependent as they must be understood relative to culture, language, shared understandings, their study is inherently transdisciplinary. Institutions may be economic, familial, political, juridical, etc., and thus their study requires a broad theoretical purchase. Further, institutions are of layered nature as rules at one level may affect or are affected by rules or norms at another level. Working at multiple levels of analysis is thus necessary to fully appreciate the origins, interactions, and the effects of institutions. Finally, institutions produce effects that are not additive. Rather, society and its institutions combine and interact, requiring a systems analysis. Responding to these challenges, Ostrom thus advances the Institutional Analysis and Development (IAD) framework, a meta-theoretical construct reminiscent of CAS analyses: multilayer design encompassing structures, actors, interactions, and interpretations while emphasizing feedback dynamics from outcomes toward the elements of the environment.

Mahoney and Thelen's (2009) model of gradual institutional change reflects similar themes. Their approach recognizes that institutional outcomes may not be reflective of ideas or goals of any particular group but rather an unintended consequence of their conflict. Aside from the balance of power among actors, which may be borne endogenously or exogenously via feedback, the authors introduce a compliance variable. Departing from the mainstream view of self-enforcing institutions, they separate compliance as an independent variable allowing to capture the discursive (hence political) aspects of institutional dynamics. Recognizing the causal importance of political context, institutional characteristics, and actors struggling for change, Mahoney and Thelen develop a model capturing their relationships. Specifically, a type of institutional outcome is linked to the characteristics of the political and institutional context, which, in turn, determine the type of the dominant change agent. Despite its criticisms, the framework—embracing the evolutionary, multidimensional, nonlinear, and emergent features—is nevertheless a step toward the complexity treatment of institutional change.

Pierson's work (2000a, b) is also mindful of the complex nature of social systems and institutional development. In a high-impact contribution, Pierson (2000b) points out the shortcomings of the predominant explanations of the origins of formal institutions—mostly viewed as useful products of intentional, far-sighted actions of rational agents. The author shows that even if we concede the (unlikely) instrumental behavior of institutional designers who plan for the long term,[4] institutions carry extensive unintended consequences. "[W]e should expect that social processes involving large numbers of actors in densely institutionalized societies will almost always generate elaborate feedback loops and significant interaction effects which decision makers cannot hope to fully anticipate," explains Pierson (2000b, 483). The author also points to the difficulties with the functional views of institutional evolution and shows that institutional learning and enhancements are not only difficult but also constrained by the grip of path dependence, self-reinforcing feedback mechanisms limiting available options. "Actors do not inherit a blank slate that they can remake at will when their preferences shift or unintended consequences become visible," adds Pierson (2000b, 493). Thus, to make progress in the understanding of institutional origins and change, Pierson calls for a new approach taking into account "dynamic processes that can highlight the implications of short time horizons, the scope of unintended consequences, the emergence of path dependence, and the efficacy or limitations of learning and competitive mechanisms" (2000b, 494). This is the essence of CAS. Next, we will place in context this potentially transformative meta-theoretical shift.

Debates, Paradigms, Innovations

The last century has seen some ebbs and flows in the evolution of thought in political scholarship. In one view, the development of mainstream political research has experienced several theoretical clashes. The first debate was concerned with knowledge and institutions, in the idealist view essential in achieving the world stability and order. The realists questioned the scientific reliability of idealist claims and argued science held the key to explaining the social world (Dunne et al. 2013). The dominance of this stream of thinking became evident in the work of social scientists in the 1950s and 1960s. This was the case particularly in the USA and other Anglo-Saxon countries, attesting to its ideological rather than substantive foundations. Ciepley confirms that the contemporary agendas were rooted in "assumptions that were highly polemical in origin, born of the encounter with totalitarianism" (2000, 200). Any consideration of the powerful, encompassing, and controlling state apparatus was, as Ciepley observes, wiped out from the image of democratic America. Preferred hence became those explanations of political outcomes which have elevated *observable and measurable* actions of autonomous actors and their relationships while suppressing the role of the state, its ability to act with independence, or the relationships between its institutions. Behavioralist research agendas thus assumed the center stage; but this was not to last.

The frequent policy failures brought by the increased intensity of policy making activity in the 1960s and 1970s lead to demands for better solutions (Immergut 2008). The subsequent search for answers resulted in a theoretical refocus toward norms, rules, laws, regulations, and, at a higher level, states and structures. "Institutions have affected policies, and policies have changed our understandings of institutions. Indeed, policy studies have led to an institutionalist interpretation of politics, and new *theories* about democratic governance," comments Immergut (2008, 557, emphasis added). The emergence of this new institutionalism (and its rational, historical, and sociological variants, all with different assumptions and goals) can be seen as a critical moment opening up space for the establishment of new fields of inquiry such as International Political Economy (IPE) (Keohane 2009) while setting the tenor for the consequent debates. It is this development that in time enabled the post-positivists to challenge the tenets of positivism: the assumptions that systematic *observation* is necessary and sufficient to explain social outcomes. *Meaning* and beliefs, the post-positivists claim, are essential to understanding of social realities (Dunne et al. 2013). While this debate was epistemological—drawing a distinction between interpretation and observation, understanding and explanation—the ensuing debate is largely ontological.

In this dispute, primarily between the rationalists and reflectivists, the nature of reality takes the center stage. Embracing the theories of rational choice, the rationalists view reality with a logical structure, one in which actors make strategic choices in response to various (dis) incentives. The reflectivists, on the other hand, caution that all choices are relative and dependent on context rather than a universal formula. Here, some authors (such as Wiener 2006) add the constructivists, who see reality as created socially through language and symbols, as a separate party to the debate. This debate was echoed in economics-oriented stream of scholarship, where views of preference formation and of *natural* markets were met with resistance from scholars arguing to consider the social aspects of the international economy.

The debates presented thus far involved two opposite, yet equally *limited* views. One, rooted in the traditional philosophies of science, strives to find general explanations to social and physical phenomena. The other, privy to biases and ambiguities inherent to the *social* world, relies on intuition in deconstruction and critique. The complexity paradigm, arising from transdisciplinary inquiry, is a significant departure from the past debates. Particularly, the science of complex systems "confronts the postmodern challenge to modernist metanarratives to address issues of diversity and complexity more adequately and responds without giving up the quest for explanation and analysis of causation," notes Walby (2004, 1). Indeed, as we will discuss, the paradigm integrates elements of both camps. And it is this new thinking that provides a foundation for the developing transformation.

Earlier work identified the cleavage between linear and nonlinear paradigms as the "fifth debate" (Kavalski 2007). Such a characterization is only a part of the CAS picture and casts various postmodernist views out of consideration, however. We posit the shift to be from reductionism toward adaptive complexity. *Reductionism* is an analytical drive in either downward direction, to an individual level as in the rational choice theories, or upward toward larger abstractions as in the structuralist approaches (Walby 2004). *Adaptive complexity*, in our definition, is a view that components and their behavior must be understood in context of a larger system and the environment, given they may exhibit *global* properties analytically irreducible to their components or subsystems.

Indeed, sitting atop these debates is one of the essential, if for many conceded, questions of social science—the emergence of social phenomena. Do social structures exist? How do they develop and change? What is the relationship between interactions at the individual level and macro-properties? are among these questions. The answers here have mostly[5] depended on the reductionist assumptions of individual (rational) choices aggregating to collective outcomes, informing the methodologically individualist accounts of emergence rooted in microeconomics. The alternate, postmodernist views offer no resolution, as they do not consider social phenomena real and hence causally relevant. While there exists a variety of theoretical views of emergence supported by a range of philosophies,[6] they lack in their capacity to ultimately explain the *mechanics* of social emergence (Sawyer 2005). According to Sawyer, this will demand an "[a]ccounting for causal relations between structure, interaction, and individual" (2005, 207). And with its meta-theory and innovative methodological tools, CAS is well positioned to help address these questions. At the same time, as we will discuss, with its capacity to synthesize features of competing paradigms, CAS holds the potential to resolve some outstanding debates.

QUESTIONS AND ANSWERS IN COMPLEXITY RESEARCH

Below we explore select transdisciplinary research that both engages and draws on CAS. Rather than to present a literature review, the goal here is to show the broad span of CAS work, ranging from theoretical and applied research to practical applications of CAS.

In their outstanding work, a complexity scholar Helbing and his collaborators (Helbing et al. 2015) demonstrate how CAS research can lead to new insights and solutions in the study of crowd disasters, crime, terrorism, wars, epidemics, and other issues involving populations and their dynamics. The scholars note that the prevalent approaches to managing these social issues are concerned with *controlling* behavior at an individual level, neglecting their systemic aspects. This "'linear thinking' and classical control approaches fail to overcome or mitigate such problems efficiently due to the non-linear, non-equilibrium and therefore often counter-intuitive nature of these problems" (736). The CAS view thus brings into consideration systemic instabilities, where, for example, small variations in the behavior of each actor are amplified as they get transmitted throughout the system resulting in a regime shift. Traffic jams and "crowd turbulence," where forces transmitted from involuntary body contact reverberate, jolting the crowd around, are examples of these cascade effects. While unpredictable, they are preventable given we know they occur at high densities under particular conditions. As well, our updated understanding of population dynamics allows us to discern signs of critical transitions and predict escalating conflicts or spreading infections, and take action reducing their impacts. Finally, the authors find that in complex systems "too strict control attempts may actually cause a loss of control... as it tends to undermine the natural capability of complex systems to self-organize" (774–775). It is hence more effective to steer rather than control. Such findings inform new approaches to enhancing the effectiveness of regulation and policy in the age of complexity (Chapter 9).

Among the more salient concepts rooted in complexity research is the Black Swan that has been developed by Taleb (2007). A metaphor, the Black Swan describes an unpredictable, probabilistically unquantifiable event of high impact. Such events are characteristic of CAS, in this case social domains made up of many interdependent, interacting parts embedded in various hierarchies, including government institutions, public, civil and private organizations, parties, media groups, and others. These systems experience unexpected, disruptive "blowups," more intense and frequent under particular conditions. While Black Swan events may be understood only in retrospect and are unknowable, the authors note some situations increase their potential as well as their impact. Among these is the artificial suppression of variation, through the altering of various institutional and informational channels. The risks become hidden, with the system *appearing* cohesive and stable.[7] "Making an economy robust in the face of business swings requires allowing risk to be visible; the same is true in politics," argue Taleb and Blyth (2011, 150). The authors thus advance a set of, at first sight counterintuitive, prescriptions: rethink the foreign (and domestic) policies aimed at containing fluctuations, as they lead to severe, persistent, and undesirable flare-ups.

Jervis (1997), a scholar credited with setting the complexity research agenda in International Relations (IR), explored similar themes. Jervis recognized early that "[t]wo or more elements produce results that cannot be understood by examining each alone; the fate of an actor's policy or strategy depends on those that are adopted by others; behavior alters the environment in ways that affect the trajectory of actors, outcomes, and environments" (1997, 60). This contingent landscape is thus replete with unintended consequences, the dynamics of which, as Jervis shows, cannot be adequately addressed with the available methodologies. What are the methodological solutions? is the question left on the author's table, however.

Inspired by the work of these and other authors, Geyer takes CAS scholarship into the field of political economy. Geyer examines the "third way," both a concept and a strategy of a middle way between capitalism and communism, using his complexity framework. The author finds that the typical, linear conception of left and right may not be analytically nor normatively appropriate, not the least due to "new manufactured uncertainty... further complicated by the increasing social reflexivity of individuals in the postmodern world" (2003a, 13). Complexity framework in this sense does not endorse nor point to the third way but looks beyond it "by recognising that the third way is only a small indication of a much more fundamental shift in the social sciences and society, a complexity shift" (2003b, 15). Geyer also studies the European integration and the nexus between the EU and the British welfare state (2003b). The author promotes his complexity framework arguing that traditional positivists and postmodern methods fail to deal with the combination of "orderly, complex, and disorderly elements," and makes clear that finding a universal answer or a law describing or predicting social policy development is not possible. And just as Jervis, Geyer stops short of providing a methodological offering.

Yet, it was new technology-driven tools and methodologies whose results inspired some outstanding CAS research with a promise to change the way we understand and study social phenomena as well as the way we conduct social research more generally. Sawyer (2005), cognizant of the inadequacy of the predominant paradigms in dealing with the fundamental questions of social science—what is the relationship of the individual to the collective, and, more specifically, how are social structures constituted—set out to address this gap. Sawyer (2003, 2005) surveyed a set of simulations enabled by multi-agent systems (MAS) technology, a powerful innovation over the prior simulation approaches in modeling social systems.[8] These *artificial societies* model interactions of a large number of autonomous agents and enable the study of the emerging, macro-structural phenomena (more in Helbing 2012). And despite their limited features, the experiments were revealing. In artificial societies, "objective structures can emerge, and the existence of those structures can constrain individual agents (via changes in patterns of local interactions), even when agents have no internal representations," observed Sawyer (2005, 161). Moreover, they demonstrate "that when the agent communication *language* changes, the processes of emergence change, and the global properties that emerge often *change* as well" (2005, 170, emphases added). These are important findings as they challenge both the predominant, methodologically individualist explanations of emergence and the postmodernist views of social structures.

Sawyer thus concludes that "individual-society relation cannot be explained without recourse to sophisticated theories of communication and of emergence from communication" (2005, 191) and advances the Emergence Paradigm, a synthesis of the widely used, but lacking Structure and Interaction Paradigms. The Emergence Paradigm introduces two intermediate levels of social reality between the individual and structure,[9] capturing the mechanisms and processes of emergence. Consistent with CAS, Sawyer's paradigm does not generate predictions, it is a meta-theory. Importantly, it proposes a methodology centered around two parallel activities: the analyses of interactions and the resulting emergents.

We have explored select research in international politics and beyond that both engages and draws on CAS. Rather than to conduct a review of the existing work in the field, we hoped to demonstrate the range of CAS applicability, spanning theoretical, applied, and practical areas. The growing amount of research and its diversity opens a variety of questions, some of which we will explore in the next chapter.

CONCLUSION

Above, we discerned a rising meta-theory driven by an increasing trans-disciplinary engagement, technological innovation, as well as necessity and sensibility. We argued this complexity shift has been measured, unfolding gradually and organically, often without a broader awareness of its implications. We added that this development is unlike those borne of the disciplinary debates, which, at their core, share the same philosophy of inquiry—reductionism—limiting their capacity to explain phenomena in the increasingly complex social systems. While some social scientists point at the repeated successes with reductive explanations in physical sciences made possible with advancements in physics and mathematics, MAS research points away from these arguments. The complexity of human communication makes social systems distinct from those in nature, raising questions on the commensurability of natural and social sciences. Novel technologies offer the potential to explore these questions and test the fundamental theories of social science.

Hence, this is not only an important time bringing the potential to dislodge the deeply seated conceptions of the social world, but also one offering a promise of advancement in how we study the systems-rich environment around us, make policy, and how we lead our discourse. We explore these prospective transformations in the next chapter.

NOTES

1. While the use of the term as well as the assumptions behind emergence in social sciences remains contested, it will be used here to mean the formation of macro-social phenomena irreducible to individual properties or behaviors.
2. Specifically, these are unable to theorize micro- to macro-links and social emergence, and neglect the properties of such systems including nonlinearity and unpredictability.

3. Helbing lists "variety, redundancy, compartmentalization, sparseness (i.e. a low degree of interconnectedness), and mutually adjusted time scales of processes in the system" (2015, 29).

4 These assumptions are mostly challenged in politics. In economics and international relations, scholars have drawn on the mechanism of "credible commitment" (North 1993) to support the feasibility of bargains for the long term (Pierson 2000b).

5 We acknowledge there has been a rich body of work dedicated to this topic resulting in a whole ecosystem of theories. Nevertheless, we proceed in our discussions with the prevailing views, those which were of the most consequence in the real world.

6 These have been discussed at length in Mitchell (2012), Sawyer (2005), or Wendt (2015). Wendt (2015) advances a novel account of emergence informed by quantum mechanics. "[W]hat social structures actually are, physically, are superpositions of shared mental states—social wave functions," explains Wendt (2015, 258). How these states become shared is less clear, however.

7 "Variation is information. When there is no variation, there is no information," add Taleb and Blyth (2011, 158). Note that allowing for variation, or fluctuations in regimes, politics, or orientation, are part of robustness design, an important CAS *practice* highlighted later.

8 It must be noted that while MAS is an advancement over the traditional equation-based modeling (EBM), each approach has its application. The key difference is the unit of analysis. In the case of EBM, this is the modeling of macro-level variables by evaluating equations, while in MAS it is a microsimulation of individual actors. Contrary to EBM, MAS allows modeling cognitive processes of individuals and changing the behavior of these heterogeneous actors. See Helbing (2012) and Sawyer (2003, 2005).

9 These are *ephemeral* and *stable emergents* encompassing interactional frames of conversation analysis, and culture and language, respectively.

REFERENCES

Arthur, W. Brian. 2015. *Complexity and the economy*. Oxford and New York: Oxford University Press.

Byrne, David. 1998. *Complexity theory and the social sciences: An introduction*. London and New York: Routledge.

Ciepley, David. 2000. "Why the state was dropped in the first place: A prequel to Skocpol's 'bringing the state back in.'" *A Journal of Politics and Society* 14 (2–3): 157–213.

Cilliers, Paul. 1998. *Complexity and postmodernism: Understanding complex systems*. London and New York: Routledge.

Ciro, Tony. 2016. *The global financial crisis: Triggers, responses and aftermath.* Farnham, UK and Burlington, VT: Ashgate.

Claessens, Stijn, and Laura Kodres. 2014. "The regulatory responses to the global financial crisis: Some uncomfortable questions." International Monetary Fund Working Papers. WP 14/46.

Davis, Kevin. 2011. "Regulatory reform post the global financial crisis: An overview." The Australian APEC Study Centre. RMIT University.

Dunne, Timothy, Milja Kurki, and Steve Smith, eds. 2013. *International relations theories: Discipline and diversity.* 3rd ed. Oxford: Oxford University Press.

Esping-Andersen, Gosta. 1989. "Three political economies of the welfare state." *Canadian Review of Sociology and Anthropology* 26 (1):10–36.

Financial Crisis Inquiry Commission (FCIC). 2011. *The financial crisis inquiry report, authorized edition: Final report of the National Commission on the Causes of the Financial and Economic Crisis in the United States.* Washington, DC: US Government Printing Office.

Geddes, Barbara. 2003. *Paradigms and sand castles: Theory building and research design in comparative politics.* Ann Arbor: University of Michigan Press.

Geyer, Robert. 2003a. "Beyond the third way." *British Journal of Politics and International Relations* 5 (2): 237–257.

Geyer, Robert. 2003b. "Europeanisation, complexity, and the British welfare state." Paper presented to the UACES/ESRC. University of Sheffield.

Hall, Peter. 2003. "Aligning ontology and methodology in comparative research." In *Comparative historical analysis in the social sciences,* edited by James Mahoney and Dietrich Rueschemeyer. New York: Cambridge University Press.

Helbing, Dirk, ed. 2008. *Managing complexity: Insights, concepts, applications.* Berlin: Springer.

Helbing, Dirk, ed. 2012. *Social self-organization.* Understanding Complex Systems. Berlin and Heidelberg: Springer Berlin Heidelberg. http://link.springer.com/10.1007/978-3-642-24004-1.

Helbing, Dirk. 2015. *Thinking ahead—Essays on big data, digital revolution, and participatory market society.* Cham: Springer International Publishing.

Helbing, Dirk, Dirk Brockmann, Thomas Chadefaux, Karsten Donnay, Ulf Blanke, Olivia Woolley-Meza, Mehdi Moussaid et al. 2015. "Saving human lives: What complexity science and information systems can contribute." *Journal of Statistical Physics* 158 (3): 735–781.

Immergut, Ellen. 2008. "Institutional constraints on policy." In *The oxford handbook of public policy,* edited by Michael Moran, Martin Rein, and Robert Edward Goodin. The Oxford Handbooks of Political Science. Oxford: Oxford University Press.

Jervis, Robert. 1997. *System effects: Complexity in political and social life.* Princeton, NJ: Princeton University Press.

Johnson, Neil F. 2009. *Simply complexity: A clear guide to complexity theory.* London: Oneworld Publications.

Kavalski, Emilian. 2007. "The fifth debate and the emergence of complex international relations theory: Notes on the application of complexity theory to the study of international life." *Cambridge Review of International Affairs* 20 (3): 435–454.

Keohane, Robert O. 2009. "The old IPE and the new." *Review of International Political Economy* 16 (1): 34–46.

Kickert, Walter. 2012. "State responses to the fiscal crisis in Britain, Germany and the Netherlands." *Public Management Review* 14 (3): 299–309.

Kickert, Walter, and Tiina Randma-Liiv. 2015. *Europe managing the crisis: The politics of fiscal consolidation.* New York: Routledge.

Kohli, Atul, Peter Evans, Peter J. Katzenstein, Adam Przeworski, Susanne Hoeber Rudolph, James C. Scott, and Theda Skocpol. 1995. "The role of theory in comparative politics: A symposium." *World Politics* 48 (1): 1–49.

Kuhn, Thomas S. 2012. *The structure of scientific revolutions.* Chicago and London: University of Chicago Press.

Levine, Ross. 2012. "The governance of financial regulation: Reform lessons from the recent crisis." *International Review of Finance* 12 (1): 39–56.

Mahoney, James, and Kathleen Thelen, eds. 2009. *Explaining institutional change: Ambiguity, agency, and power.* New York: Cambridge University Press.

McCarty, Nolan, Keith Poole, and Howard Rosenthal. 2013. *Political bubbles.* Princeton, NJ: Princeton University Press.

Mitchell, Sandra D. 2012. *Unsimple truths: Science, complexity, and policy.* Chicago: University of Chicago Press.

North, Douglass C. 1993. "Institutions and credible commitment." *Journal of Institutional and Theoretical Economics* 149 (1): 11–23.

Ostrom, Elinor. 2007. "Institutional rational choice: An assessment of the institutional analysis and development framework." In *Theories of the policy process,* edited by Paul Sabatier. Boulder, CO: Westview Press.

Overton, Willis F. 2015. "Processes, relations, and relational-developmental-systems." In *Handbook of child psychology and developmental science,* vol. 1, edited by Richard M. Lerner, Willis F. Overton, and Peter C. M. Molenaar. Hoboken, NJ: Wiley.

Pierson, Paul. 2000a. "Increasing returns, path dependence, and the study of politics." *American Political Science Review* 94 (2): 251–267.

Pierson, Paul. 2000b. "The limits of design: Explaining institutional origins and change." *Governance* 13 (4): 475–499.

Sawyer, R. Keith. 2003. "Artificial societies: Multi agent systems and the micro-macro link in sociological theory." *Sociological Methods and Research* 31: 37–75.

Sawyer, R. Keith, 2005. *Social emergence: Societies as complex systems*. Cambridge, UK: Cambridge University Press.

Stacey, Ralph D. 2003. *Complexity and group processes: A radically social understanding of individuals*. New York: Routledge.

Steinmo, Sven, 2010. *The evolution of modern states: Sweden, Japan, and the United States*. New York: Cambridge University Press.

Taleb, Nicholas. 2007. *The Black Swan: The impact of the highly improbable*. 1st ed. New York: Random House.

Taleb, Nicholas, and Mark Blyth. 2011. "The Black Swan of Cairo: How suppressing volatility makes the world less predictable and more dangerous." In *The new Arab revolt: What happened, what it means, and what comes next*, edited by Council on Foreign Relations. New York: Council on Foreign Relations.

Varoufakis, Yanis. 2015. *The global minotaur: America, Europe and the future of the global economy*. London: Zed Books Ltd.

Walby, Sylvia. 2004. "Complexity theory, globalisation and diversity." Lancaster: Department of Sociology, Lancaster University. Paper presented to a conference of the British Sociological Association, University of York, April 2004.

Wendt, Alexander. 2015. *Quantum mind and social science*. Cambridge, UK: Cambridge University Press.

Wiener, Antje. 2006. "Constructivist approaches in international relations theory: Puzzles and promises." *SSRN Electronic Journal*. https://doi.org/10.2139/ssrn.1939758.

CHAPTER 9

Transformations

Previous chapters hinted to Western cultural history and discerned its imprints not only in the way we view and study our world and society but also in our discourse. Much of this history has its roots in ancient Greece and the legacy of its thinkers, who have pondered on the nature of matter, motion, time, and change, on sources of knowledge, or the purpose of being, among other themes. Prominent have become the views of Plato and his followers, who believed humans, intrinsically different from other types of existence, were more than just a part of the natural world (Hutcheon 1996). Reflecting his era's embrace of dualism, Plato drew a distinction between the world as observed through senses, and what he called the Form, its essential qualities to be obtained solely by logic and reasoning. Reinforcing the essentialist thinking, Plato's student Aristotle believed objects had intrinsic, unchanging qualities in addition to their changing, accidental properties. This view also saw "matter as particulate and separate—formed into discrete objects," and based its analysis on examining objects separately from each other and the environment (Nisbett 2003, 10). Placing objects at the center of inquiry invited naturally a systematic process of analysis. The process begins with an observation of the object and its properties, which in turn "become the basis of categorization of the object; the categories become the basis of rule construction; and events are then understood as the result of objects behaving in accordance with rules" (Nisbett 2003, 10). Moreover, analyses of Plato and Aristotle would be teleological, seeing

© The Author(s) 2019

O. Bubak and H. Jacek, *Trivialization and Public Opinion*,
https://doi.org/10.1007/978-3-030-17925-0_9

"all natural processes only in terms of some end toward which an external purpose is propelling them" (Hutcheon 1996, 9), demanding further assumptions on order and the existence of different types of "causes."

These prevailing philosophies all had implications to the understanding of causes and effects and thus to explaining change. They also carried deep consequences for Western civilization. In one view, "[t]he Greeks' discovery of nature made possible the invention of science" (Nisbett 2003, 21). For Nisbett, the ancient philosophers' systematic categorization of the world based on essential properties of its objects enabled theorizing and explanation. As we hinted in the previous chapter, such dualism and division of the world into independent parts by Descartes, inspiring in turn Newton's assumptions on the qualities of matter, lead to the institution of modern science. Yet, while this legacy is mainly of Plato and Aristotle, not all their ancient contemporaries shared their views.

There was a philosophical "road not taken," with potential costs to our cultural and scientific development (Hutcheon 1996, 16). As Hutcheon explains, this path was briefly illuminated by the genius of Democritus and his mentor Leucippus, and later Epicurus. Leucippus theorized that all matter is constituted of minuscule, indivisible elements he called atoms. Building on this work, Democritus envisioned atoms existing in a state of constant motion in "the void," a space where these atoms collide and cluster into various arrangements giving rise to different compounds. Rejecting dualism of body and mind, Democritus thought "that sensation and thought are both alterations of the body, operating as a continuous process" (8). Such thinking allowed Democritus to go beyond teleology and develop a sophisticated theory of causality not relying on a notion of an external mover; reconceive time as an "impression made upon living things of the succession of natural events like light and darkness" rather than a cyclical phenomenon; and propose "that humans once lived like other animals, in caves, and only slowly and gradually developed social institutions" (9). Democritus' cosmology was thus in many aspects far ahead of his contemporaries and more scientific than even the future generations of Hellenistic philosophers.

Generations later, Epicurus took what he understood to be the best explanation of the world—as given by Democritus—and aimed for its synthesis with the humanism of Socrates. Contrary to the then prevailing metaphysics of dualism, Epicurus believed in free will rather than external design and that truth could be found in reasoning on information collected by the senses. Importantly, the philosopher rejected the essentialism of the dominant school. Justice, for Epicurus, was "never a thing in itself," but instead "a condition which emerges in the dealings of human beings with one another, based on a commitment to be fair to others" (13). Assuming these views lead to an unwelcome departure from the contemporaneous conceptions of ethics, social order, and system of rule, no less relevant today than in the past. Unfortunately, just as with the revolutionary writings of Democritus, much of the work of Epicurus was destroyed to the detriment of our cognitive and cultural progress (Hutcheon 1996).

Where would we, as a civilization, be had the Greeks followed the path of Democritus and Epicurus? What would happen had the late Hellenistic society turned away from dualism and embraced universality of cause and effect, rejecting ideas of supernatural interference and with it justifications of a certain social order? And how would our approach to science differ had Democritus' advanced views of matter, causality, and change prevailed? Of course we cannot know the answers to these questions given the contingencies of history, yet outlines of one alternative are now coming into focus. In this world, we break out of the Cartesian-Split-Mechanistic scientific paradigm (Overton 2015) and begin to build knowledge and make decisions within a new frame of reference—one toward which we have been progressing, if in a roundabout manner, since the days of early science. In this world, our cultural and scientific legacies will come into contrast with the new perspectives while we begin to see the flaws in our discourse. In what follows, we take a systematic look at the prospective transformations and continue with a discussion of their more fundamental implications.

Catching Up

We noted the impact the prevailing views of early philosophers had on the ensuing developments of culture and scientific thought. Influenced by these views, scholars' attempts at reducing the physical world to its basic elements and searching for universal laws have seen success. To a point, organizing the world based on an assumption of some essential qualities of its objects has also helped the scientific inquiry. Yet, as became evident, these views were deficient in the study of life, where the attempts at finding model species in order to develop various taxonomies proved to be an obstacle to progress. It was Darwin's refocus from an individual to a population and from an intermittent change to a process of continuous selection and adaptation that allowed the formulation of the theory of evolution. To be sure, ideas of this kind have been explored throughout the history of natural philosophy, as "various thinkers have seen that we must include within that natural flow the emergence and development of life, of animal forms and sentience and ultimately of a consciousness" (Hutcheon 1996, 483). But Darwin's revolutionary theory at last opened doors to a new thinking as scholars of human development, psychology, and social behavior realized the evolutionary view of causality, that is causality "after the fact, with effects being contingent on the environmental conditions as altered by the consequences of previous actions," was applicable in their domains (Hutcheon 1996, 485). Thinking in evolutionary terms thus meant an awareness of the connections between elements, of the relationship to the environment, and of the novel (and causal) properties arising from their interactions, and thus of importance of time and history. It meant to appreciate adaptive complexity.

In time, the technological and scientific progress has not only brought to light formerly underestimated complexities across domains (Chapter 3), but also lead to an increasing complexity of existing socio-technical systems and to a rise of previously non-existent complex systems. Yet, it was not until two key developments in the twentieth century that complexity science saw its establishment. The first was the Gödel-Turing-Post discoveries of "incompleteness and algorithmically unsolvable problems, where, for the first time, the logical impossibility limits to formalistic calculation or deductive methods were established" (Markose 2005, F160). To show the limits to computability meant to explain that novelty production (and self-organization more generally) in CAS was an emergent process that could not be understood by an appeal to individual parts (Markose 2005). The second development was advancements in computing technology enabling Holland-Bak-Arthur to employ computer models in simulating interactions of many autonomous agents and to obtain insights into unpredictable, system-level properties (Markose 2005).

Thus, we have begun to study the structures, patterns, and at times seemingly chaotic behaviors and counterintuitive outcomes not only in biological and climate systems but also in social and communications networks, human organizations, financial and equity markets, traffic and transportation, or technological and innovation systems. And so, as detailed previously, scholars and practitioners are finding

[d]eeply interconnected systems behave in ways that surprise. Whether it is the economy, large organizations, energy policy or ecosystems, the interconnected nature of systems leads to emergent behaviour not obviously triggered by a single cause. These complex systems can trip across thresholds into sudden transitions and they can react disproportionately to seemingly small triggers, or change out of themselves, endogenously. They have collective or emergent properties that cannot be traced back linearly to the underlying components. (Kupers 2014, 13)

Hence, the CAS view takes what were once considered "accidents" or "boundary conditions" to the center of inquiry (Mitchell 2012, 13), forcing us to revisit our assumptions on causes and effects, change, control, and predictability.

Are we just catching up by adding tools to represent, probe, and explain reality, and with these merely expanding our model of science? Or are we entering a different paradigm ushering a new era of thinking? The answers depend on one's point of view and conceptions of paradigm and change. Below, we offer one way of navigating the transformations.

Navigating Change

As apparent from Chapter 8, due to the nature, breadth, and the pace of adaptation of CAS thinking, many questions remain, including on how we may orient about and engage any unfolding change. Here, we introduce a framework providing a starting point for understanding CAS-driven transformations. At its core, the framework directs attention to key issues including: What are the ontological assumptions? What are the methodologies at hand? Is the relationship congruent? How are uncertainty and risk treated in practice? What tools are used? The framework thus induces its users to consider a wider picture and begin to understand the state of play across the area of interest.

We begin with an understanding that ontology has historically been either ahead or behind the contemporaneous methods available to make inferences in social sciences. "Some of the most prominent theories in comparative politics now understand the world in terms that do not conform to the assumptions required by standard regression analysis," observed Hall (2003, 384). In line with this insight, the framework recognizes that the constituent components of research paradigms may develop separately and asynchronously. It is thus constructed around

Table 9.1   The framework separating *meta-theory*, *methodology*, and *practice*

Meta-theory	Methodology	Practice
A singular way to capture reality, universally applicable across disciplines. Reduction of complexity (upward or downward) is the goal	Quantitative (correlational, survey, causal comparative, etc.)	Assuming a modeling culture
	Qualitative (case study, historical, ethnographic, etc.)	Designing for robustness
Multiple ways to describe reality composed of objects as well as images. Systemic depth and emergence. Epistemic dynamism	Methodological pluralism (comparative, integrated methodologies)	Improving insight
		Managing risk
		Developing scenarios

meta-theory, *methodology*, and *practice*, capturing the (mis)alignments among the conceptions, the means, and the needs. Table 9.1 depicts the framework whose dimensions are separated to emphasize their potential incongruence at a point in time. We discuss each in turn.

Meta-Theory

No doubt scholars across time have recognized the inherent complexity of the physical, social, and biological world. However, reducing the object of investigation into elements at a level of abstraction where they bring to bear their causal essence has been key to explanation, and often taken as the aim of scientific study (Mitchell 2012). "Whether the atoms of inquiry were the material *particles* of the early physicist, the *genes and DNA* of later day molecular biologist, the *neurons* of the neurophysiologist, the *elements of consciousness* of the early structuralist psychologists, the *responses* of the later behavioral psychologists, or the *output* of contemporary cognitive psychologists, these were the bedrock material elements that, interacting in linear combination with causal forces, generated the illusion of transformational change and complex organization," explains Overton (2015, 15, emphases original). Note then, the logic is the same for an atom as the constituent of matter as it is for an individual as the constituent of a market or a social movement.

The underlying assumption here, as discussed, is that ultimately "all compositionally complex structures and systems can be explained, without remainder, by appeal only to the properties of their simplest components" (Mitchell 2012, 24). More fundamentally, this reductionism assumes the "existence of a privileged level of description in which all levels of complex structure and behavior can be restated and thus reduced," a problematic view given that representations are inherently partial or incomplete (Mitchell 2012, 23). While these approaches have proven fruitful and supported much progress namely in physical sciences, the commitment to them across domains has shown its limits (Chapter 8).

Hence emerged a line of research attuned to special properties of complex natural and social systems, CAS. It sees such systems as networks of elements, whose micro-interactions at once effect and are affected by macro-phenomena, evolving within a larger, causally relevant context. The complexity paradigm encompasses a set of rules and principles defining "what is acceptable and unacceptable, meaningful and meaningless as theory—the means of conceptual exploration of any scientific domain—and these rules place constraints on theoretical and observational discourse" (Overton 2015, 15). Hence, CAS does not make predictions, it is a worldview, a meta-theory. Broadly, CAS and other meta-theories "transcend (i.e., *meta*) theoretical concepts and theories in the sense that they constitute the conceptual context within which theoretical concepts and theories are constructed" (Overton 2015, 13). Meta-theories may be distinguished by their level of generality, with those capturing ontological and epistemological fundamentals occupying the most general level. In this light, as shown in Table 9.1, the framework distinguishes the principles of the emerging complexity paradigm from those of the dominant reductive, universalist paradigm.

In contrast to the traditional research paradigm discussed above, what may this revised epistemology and ontology look like? Mitchell (2012) suggests a new approach, "integrative pluralism," recognizing complexity can be understood but requires expanded assumptions and a different approach to analysis. The scholar begins from a pluralist-realist stance toward ontology, a view that rather than a single true representation of reality, there exist "multiple *correct* ways to parse our world, individuating a variety of objects and processes that reflect both causal structures and our interests" and argues for explanatory pluralism, pragmatism, and the acceptance of "dynamic and evolving character of knowledge" (13). When we recognize that complex systems exhibit emergent, system-level phenomena defying explanation by reduction, we need to be able to integrate a variety of theories and tools aiding in explanation. Also, as we accept there exist other types of things beyond "fundamental physical particles, and there are more kinds of laws than naturally necessary, universal, exceptionless ones," we also need to enlarge "the conceptual space of laws to reflect the different degrees of contingency, stability, and scope of the causal structures science represents" (15).

Further, once we are free from the absolutist insistence on a singular description of the world, we begin to work with a multiplicity of accurate but incomplete representations. Given our needs and possibilities, we determine pragmatically which representation, such as the level of abstraction, is suitable. Mitchell uses an example of combating malaria in a population. Do we want to eliminate malaria plaguing a particular locality, or do we want to understand its pathophysiology and be able to prevent it? Our goals will drive the approach taken.

Finally, as we hinted above, our world is continuously changing—whether by natural processes, by human intervention, or a combination of both—creating with it new causal structures. This also means our knowledge of the world is not static; it must evolve, changing with it in turn our decision-making strategies. As we appreciate the inherent unpredictability and causal complexity in CAS, "[c]ertainty or even estimable probability of predicted outcomes gives way to representations in terms of multiple-scenario projections" (17). To be sure, not all systems are complex[1] and much of science benefits from reductionist approaches. Complexity meta-theory thus has room for both understandings (Mitchell 2012).

Methodology

Contrary to conventional disciplinary inquiry, CAS research involves an *integrated* study of interactions, the environment, and properties emerging from these interactions. With an aid of modern computer tools in the study of complex systems, each of which is unique, we expect to produce "a host of contingent, domain-restricted generalizations that describe more or less stable causal structures," rather than "eternally true universal laws applicable to all space and time" (Mitchell 2012, 18). And social systems are even more complex, as they involve human communication, a transmission of information through language and symbols subject to evolving interpretative processes.

Recall artificial society experiments demonstrate not only the emergence of objective structures out of the interactions of autonomous agents, but also the structures' capacity to influence the agents' actions. Further, the mediating language has been shown to affect emergence processes and frequently to alter the emergent properties at the macro-level. It is not difficult to appreciate that these findings were the result of bringing together various streams of research, countering the trend that saw the creation of disciplinary silos, each with its questions and methodologies.

To be sure, some authors, including many historical comparativists, have long been on the vanguard of methodological and theoretical pluralism (Kohli et al. 1995, for example). Engaging difficult, often uncommon puzzles, they understood that systems thinking, historical analyses, and integrative approaches were essential to explaining complex social outcomes. In the transforming inquiry into social systems and beyond, we expect qualitative or quantitative methods, corresponding to the two debated visions on how to study social and political outcomes, to be giving way to such approaches.

As hinted, complexity science and its study of behaviors and properties in complex social and natural systems were made possible by advances in computational simulation. While a range of such technologies has been developed, multi-agent computer simulations stand out as they "provide a methodology to study the *mechanics of the micro-macro* relations underlying social dynamics" (Sawyer 2005, 150, emphasis added).[2] Given the centrality of communication to social emergence, MAS tools offer "a way to experiment with different conceptions of symbolic communication and explore how these conceptions change the micro-macro relation" (Sawyer 2005, 25). This line of research would thus draw on and integrate results from macro-analyses such as institutionalism and, at the micro-level, ethnomethodology, symbolic interactionism, or conversation analysis, among others (Sawyer 2005), holding too a promise to alter the boundaries between disciplines.

At the same time, many research questions on complexity can be answered without MAS, or other integrated methodologies. Nevertheless acknowledging a multiplicity of causal structures (Mitchell 2012) means openness to using a mix of methodologies in studying them. Thus, in our framework, the *methodology* dimension captures the two broad methodology streams (quantitative and qualitative) and adds methodological pluralism, an essential strategy of the complexity paradigm. It also recognizes methodological development in CAS is a joint, transdisciplinary endeavor sharing the meta-theoretical underpinnings, which may occur asynchronously from theoretical efforts.

Also, as methodologies are tied to concepts, their definitions would also change in line with the CAS paradigm. Consider a reconceptualization of terms such as *state* or *globalization*, for instance. In the new view, we expect state to be defined as an actor, depending on the analysis either centrally coordinated or with an internal structure and hierarchy. The actor then receives and generates feedback—based on its histories, incentives, and interpretations—from other actors and from its environment. Globalization, in turn, becomes a phenomenon arising from the interaction patterns of actors at various levels of the global system and the broader context. Rather than a deterministic process, it is an *emergent* phenomenon.

Practice

Privy to the debates on the divide between theory and practice (Dunne et al. 2013), we accept the close relationship between the two not the least for pragmatic reasons. We thus see *practice* as the strategies available to and the decisions made by policy makers, administrators, and scholars operating in the newly found world of pure (unquantifiable) uncertainty, evolutionary processes, emergence, nonlinearity, path dependence, and other systems effects. This dimension is important as practitioners may use inconsistent or incongruent terminology; assume a particular modeling culture where both linear and nonlinear models may be appropriate (Richardson 2002, 2007); use different heuristics when designing for system robustness, for example, when balancing connectivity and information flow (Helbing 2015); assume different views on forecasting based on timeframes; or have varying conceptions of the purpose and goals of policy, among others.

For a peek into the emerging possibilities and the challenges in practice, let us turn to Linstone (1999) and discuss some specific tasks of concern to managers and technological planners who use CAS insights to help move their organizations forward. They appreciate that CAS reveals the limits to forecasting—which informs strategy and investment, and long term competitiveness in public and private sectors alike—but recognize that progress stems from "the conjunction of order and chaos, stability and instability, self-organization and chance" (1999, 88). It follows that with tools and experience forecasting can be improved and processes can be shaped to stimulate innovation.

In recent decades, the S curve, a nonlinear growth model, gained popularity as a forecasting tool, particularly useful in describing the evolution patterns of technology. It was found that unpredictable behavior occurs at each end of the curve, as "[i]ncreasing obsolescence or inadequacy of an established pattern leads to a critical situation where a minor event can suddenly push the system into chaos" (80). It was also observed that progress is a cyclical process, which can be expressed by a series of S curves "with stable growth followed by bounded randomness followed by stable growth, and so on" (82). We learn we can expect the onset of a chaotic phase with a declining growth pattern, but cannot predict its start or duration; on the other hand, the closer the system is to its stable phase, the better the predictive capacity (Linstone 1999). In light of these findings, the practitioners are faced with a new set of questions and decisions. Linstone's (1999, 88) analysis suggests, for instance, they:

- "Try to understand and map the domains of stability, stable oscillation, chaos, and instability." The practitioners want to be able to identify the phases correctly but also to know the conditions under which transitions occur. Especially important is a better grasp of what happens during the innovation-determining chaotic phase. For example, in cases of early competing technologies we know the winning product is not necessarily the best product, but one which can leverage "network externalities" such as its greater compatibility with existing products (Arthur 1994). How can these externalities be leveraged (namely within ethical and legal bounds)?
- "Recognize that random-appearing data may not be random and, conversely, a perceived pattern may actually be produced by chance." Randomness is important to innovation as "it creates

fluctuations that act as natural seeds from which new patterns and structures grow." Hence choices resulting from its misidentification can impact progress.

- "Find ways to circumvent the limitations to provide improved insights." As mentioned, a better understanding of the patterns of change can enhance forecasting capacity. At the same time, practitioners' ability to explain the systems dynamics can support planning and action even when prediction is not possible. This means precautionary measures can be developed and taken in face of uncertainty, inherent to new technological, geopolitical, or natural systems.
- "Recognize means to stimulate" or "to delay or forestall a phase change." As innovation is a product of chaos yet also may be its victim, the practitioners can learn to use strategic interventions to direct phase changes. This may be done by altering the flows of information and the density of feedback loops in the system.

Importantly, the practitioners and policy makers recognize that human organizations, such as states or companies, also evolve through stages of stability (alternating between centralization and decentralization) and instability, and information technology is now inextricably tied to this development (Linstone 1999). Understanding such coevolution and making changes to optimize the organizational structures has the potential to enhance innovation and competitiveness. And thus "technology policy must mirror this complexity and adaptability if we are to compete effectively…It means constant organizational learning and adjusting behavior as well as abandonment of *reliance on general or universal rules* of management," explains Linstone (1999, 87, emphasis added). Indeed, these insights go beyond technology planning and management and force us to rethink the role of policy and policy makers altogether, as discussed next.

Transforming Governance

The global financial crisis has energized debates on financial regulation and policy and on designs to avert another systemic failure. In a departure from the debates on what rules have to be changed or added, Paul Romer (2012) advances a different solution. The proposal is partly inspired by Myron Scholes's observation that "[a]symptotically, any finite tax code collects zero revenue" (2012, 112). This, what Romer calls,

Myron's Law describes a reality where a set of fixed rules will always be rendered ineffective by the actions of opportunists quick to find loopholes to their advantage. Romer thus argues for a regulatory system which *evolves* in response to the fast-changing world, shaped by the adoption of "new technologies, increases in the scale of social interaction, and opportunistic attempts at evasion" (2012, 112). This is especially important in domains which are global, large scale, and highly technical. Hence, rather than taking a process-oriented approach, which provides a codified set of processes to be followed (and which are open to being gamed), the regulatory rules in finance should be centered on *goals*. Indeed, this is not a new model as there are domains which have used these alternate systems with success. We can thus find inspiration in aircraft manufacturing, for example, where the Federal Aviation Administration (FAA) specifies outcomes and holds individuals responsible for decisions leading away from these outcomes.

> The general requirement that the FAA places on a new plane is that the manufacturer demonstrate to the satisfaction of its examiners that the new airplane is airworthy. The examiners use their judgment to decide what this means for a new type of plane. Within the FAA, the examiners are held responsible for their decisions. This changes the burden of proof from the regulators of a new technology to the advocates of the technology and gives FAA examiners a large measure of flexibility,

explains Romer (2012, 116). There are no checklists to follow for the FAA nor the manufacturer, but rather a set of requirements: to demonstrate the airplane is and *continues to* be safe to fly.

Similar systems, as Romer notes, are implemented to ensure combat readiness by the US Army or economic stability by the Federal Reserve. These organizations share the same type of hierarchical structure designed to promote responsibility. People at lower levels of the hierarchy have the authority and responsibility to respond quickly in order to meet the stated goals. Instead of relying on courts to challenge the enumerated processes, a time and resource consuming effort, individuals closest to the issues are given the authority to decide if acts meet intended outcomes. The superiors in turn make judgments and decide on the adequacy of their performance. Finally, at the top of the hierarchy are appointed administrators accountable to the people through the Executive and Legislative branches of government (Romer 2012).

While there are cases in which the predominant, process-centric approaches are suitable, "we need to recognize that this approach is not the only alternative and that it has obvious disadvantages," concludes Romer (2012, 123). The disadvantages become quite obvious when taking the CAS point of view. Modern communications networks and open economies are creating an increasing number of connections and interdependencies giving rise to complex systems of actors at various levels. As mentioned, the nonlinear nature of the interactions results in unpredictable and non-intuitive behaviors in these systems, challenging our ability to understand and control them. Due to feedback loops and network interactions, large interventions may have negligible or unintended effects while small changes may trigger various cascade effects and result in a regime shift, making predictions unreliable (Helbing and Balietti 2010). Moreover, given the "interaction-based systemic instabilities, the system behaviour may get out of control even if all system components behave close to optimally" (Helbing and Kirman 2013). What does this mean? "What people believe affects what happens, and what happens affects what people believe!" explains Allen (2003, 348) speaking of the feedback loops driving herding or other collective phenomena. This, as Allen adds,

> severely affects the outcome of 'free markets', as we have seen repeatedly in commodity cycles, land speculation and the prices of almost anything of which there is a limited supply. Instead of market dynamics necessarily leading to a sensible and effective allocation of investment and resources, we will often find that it leads to massive misallocations of resources and much waste. (2003, 348)

And, based on the standard analyses, the frequency of these events is underestimated, while our ability to control the systems is habitually overestimated (Helbing and Balietti 2010). Some scholars, including Romer, have found the traditional top-down, rule-centric approaches to policy informed by reductionist worldviews to be lacking, namely when faced with the implications of the growing social and technological complexity.

Colander and Kupers (2014) are among those arguing for fundamental rethinking of the purpose and goals of policy, including on the role of policy makers and the government, and offer their view on reframing policy. The authors recognize that our thinking about policy as well as the behavior of people and organizations has been influenced by economics and its assumptions on individuals making rational choices; economic systems exhibiting linear, predictable behavior amenable to control; markets operating independently of governments; or unchanging institutions. These simplifications inform, what the authors call, the standard policy frame giving rise to two ideational centers of gravity and setting the boundaries for all discussions about policy. Hence, debates on policy revolve around two contrasting views: market fundamentalist position which sees self-organizing and efficient markets working ideally without state interference, and the dominant government control position where government intervention becomes essential to functioning markets (Colander and Kupers 2014). In the latter view, the government is needed to address market failures such as negative externalities, informational asymmetries, lack of competition, or public goods, and to stabilize the economy.

Given our discussion so far, the reader may appreciate that both of these views are lacking. The complex and adaptive nature of markets means they are unpredictable and resist control, rendering the customary interventions problematic. While this is in line with the market fundamentalist perspective, markets do not and cannot function as self-contained entities as it assumes. The underlying problem here, as Colander and Kupers note, is that both views neglect crucial realities, including not just the nonlinear dynamical qualities inherent to economic systems but also the institutional characteristics, norms and morals, various feedback effects (such as herding mentioned by Allen above), irrational behaviors, and the idea welfare may have other than material dimensions.

Cognizant of these shortcomings, the authors advance the *complexity frame*, a new paradigm for thinking about economics and policy more generally. It is based on a recognition that the institutions of the state "developed to assist the market, and theoretically are as necessary to the functioning system as the market" (46). If markets and governments are functionally and analytically inseparable, we must revisit our approach to control and regulation. Assuming the complexity frame, according to Colander and Kupers, thus means a change of thinking along several dimensions. First, complex social systems cannot be fully understood nor controlled but rather *influenced*, not only through traditional incentives but also through a conscious approach to shaping the institutional development. Also, as hinted, markets and governments are complementary rather than opposite systems, and, by extension, properly operating markets are the result of properly developed market institutions overtime. Yet, rather than the development of *specific* policies and rules, the aim is the creation of the right *ecostructures*, an environment "within which people operate and the normative codes that they follow" (182). The focus is on evolution of both top-down policies establishing the ecostructures and bottom-up policies emerging from them. Hence, there is no policy prescription to advance or a preferred policy model, as decisions are always made in context of the changing environment. Finally, path dependencies, nonlinearities, and lock-ins, inherent to social systems, are recognizable and can be managed through an appropriately designed policy approach (Colander and Kupers 2014).

Let us return to Romer and his proposal for a new model of regulation of the financial system, an approach reminiscent of the complexity frame. Here, rather than to produce specific rules and regulations—whose mere interpretation might permit undesirable behaviors—the government would establish a set of goals to be met. At the same time, it would create an environment of empowerment and accountability ensuring the practices and outcomes were aligned with the desired goals. In these examples many of the key goals, such as flight safety or trading system stability, are straightforward. Others, however, may be less clear and evolve depending on the circumstances. "Actual goals emerge from vague conceptions of goals, and a too early formal specification of goals, as top-down control structures require, can undermine the emergence of society's actual goals," recognize Colander and Kupers. Complexity frame is thus "also about a better way to determine what those goals actually are" (2014, 215).

Consider the case of a large technology company, Facebook, a vivid example of the limits of the conventional approach to policy and regulation in the age of rapid socio-technical change. "We believe building tools to help people share can bring a more honest and transparent dialogue around government that could lead to more direct empowerment of people, more accountability for officials and better solutions to some of the biggest problems of our time... We believe that a more open world is a better world because people with more information can make better decisions and have a greater impact," stated the company's founder in a letter released a upon the company's initial public offering (Zuckerberg 2012). Yet, as this proclamation was made in 2012, Facebook was allowing a massive experiment during which its users were unknowingly exposed to manipulated news feeds containing various mixes of positive or negative content. The study found that social networks are capable of changing its users' emotions on a large scale (Booth 2014), pointing to an enormous responsibility of Facebook and other such firms in presenting information to their users. Unfortunately, there is evidence that rather than embracing this responsibility, the provider abused its position, for example, in tracking and targeting vulnerable youth (Tiku 2017). Then, more recently, came the Cambridge Analytica scandal involving a firm in the possesion of private data on nearly 90 million Facebook clients (Roose et al. 2018) (a fact which Facebook did not disclose to its users at the time), which it used in their analyses to help influence the elections. Not to forget, there are much more consequential uses of Facebook in politics in vulnerable regions outside of Europe or North America. For instance, as a major source of news for people of Myanmar, Facebook has had a role in facilitating the persecution of the local minority population (Roose 2017). It is likely there will be more disclosures of Facebook's problematic practices given the increasingly public dissatisfaction of its employees concerned with the firm's unethical behavior (Roose et al. 2018).

The story of Facebook and other broad-reaching technology companies provides a strong support for the complexity frame. First, as such technologies emerged, their potential social, psychological, and (geo)political impacts were unclear, and any attempts at setting rules, in short order outdated or subverted, unproductive. If we opt instead for a goal-based regulation, we face another challenge. As we learn of the implications of technological (mis)use by these evolving companies and their clients, our regulatory goals may shift too. What began as an innocuous platform for sharing may be designated a publisher, a media company, a virtual forum, or a special type of public interest entity, changing with it the regulatory strategies. Getting these right, which is difficult to do in the conventional top-down manner, is important in satisfying the broader social aims and developing institutions capable of ensuring compliance and accountability (Colander and Kupers 2014). Importantly, while the company has articulated its vision containing a number of socially oriented aspirations, its notorious "growth-at-all-costs" mindset (Roose et al. 2018) quickly undermines any such designs. Unsurprising, this development is reflective of a deeper issue: "the current institutional structure doesn't encourage the social side of people to emerge," as the policy paradigm supplies the assumptions on norms and preferences (Colander and Kupers 2014, 220). A bottom-up policy supported by appropriate institutional environment opens avenues to other possibilities, which, as we understand from Chapter 6, may be far from ideologically delimited.

Transforming Discourse

Above and in the previous chapter, we have begun to explore some dimensions of a promising trend: The reemergence of a view of the world whose early rejection carried inestimable consequences to our development. We highlighted a series of scientific milestones building on each other and advancing us toward new horizons. We pointed out that the findings from biology (evolutionary theorists), mathematics (Gödel-Turing-Post), and computer simulation (Holland-Bak-Arthur) made possible the establishment of a new field of inquiry. This in turn has lead to a rich body of transdisciplinary work influencing the thinking of scholars and practitioners across disciplines. As a result, as evident through our discussion thus far, there has been an intensifying intellectual activity in the meta-theoretical, methodological, and practical spaces as scholars revise our epistemologies, expand our methodological toolkits, or develop new strategies to stimulate innovation, manage high-density events, or cope with conflict. It is no coincidence we are increasingly aware that financial crises, the palpable changes in our ecosystems, or the fallouts of our indiscriminate application of technology have been exacerbated by our conventional worldviews and witness a growing number of calls for change. For example, the increasingly visible precautionary principle (Chapter 7) is focusing the attention on the limits to prediction in complex systems and sparking animated debates on the current assumptions and approaches to regulation.

To some, the conceptual breakthroughs constitute "a major revolution in human knowledge, comparable to those of Copernicus and Darwin" (Hutcheon 1996, 486). No doubt, their potentials go beyond an expanded understanding and explanation of social and biological systems. For example, applied complexity research promises to help save lives, minimize the occurrence or impact or various systemic calamities such as financial crises, or help organizations manage change and companies grow. As well, the new view may lead us to redesign our systems of regulation and governance more broadly. Indeed, we have discussed above the complexity frame for policy with a purpose: It reveals more fundamental aspects of complexity thinking with broad sociocultural implications.

In one view, complexity thinking leads us away from ideologies driven by wishful assumptions capturing static, oversimplified view of people's values, preferences, and behaviors. Hutcheon, for example, points to three dominant ideologies—humanistic psychology, Marxist-based socialism, and libertarianism including laissez-faire capitalism and the social libertarianism—difficult to sustain once faced with the continually evolving, interrelated, and adaptive nature of the social world (1996). The trouble is that some of these ideologies (rather than science) continue to steer policy debates. As Colander and Kupers explain,

> economists often come to diametrically opposing policy views; some support market fundamentalism and others support government intervention. If their arguments come directly from the same scientific theory, both can't be right. The answer to this puzzle is that economists' policy views don't come from scientific theory—they come from different interpretations and assumptions of the same scientific theory. (2014, 68)

Such assumptions are ideologically based and result in biased policy prescriptions, whether toward laissez-faire solutions or government intervention. This is quite apparent in the debate on climate change, for example. Colander and Kupers share their experience from a climate conference: "Almost without fail, supporters of rapid climate change action were highly skeptical of the market, and those who felt less of a sense of urgency were highly skeptical of government" (2014, 270). Even more alarmingly, people toward the right of the ideological spectrum are more skeptical of anthropogenic climate change or unconcerned with its implications altogether (McCright and Dunlap 2011). Taking the complexity perspective means to reject ideologically determined assumptions, not only opening up the solution space but also allowing a productive debate.

Complexity paradigm brings out other virtues derived from its understanding of social world in a state of perpetual adaptive change. Let us return to Hibbing and Theiss-Morse's (2004) research finding most people preferred stealth democracy, or democracy on demand (Chapter 5). In light of their data, the authors recommended some policy adjustments in preventing regulatory capture and encouraging civic education, and were all but ready to recommend the implementation of the desired system. These conclusions, of course, supposed citizens' values and views would not change, for example, with the increasing use of mini-publics and other tools of democratic renewal. Hence, while not ideological, the conventional assumptions here could exacerbate rather than solve the problems of democratic malaise (Chapter 4).

Finally, in time, a broad embrace of complexity promises to effect a deeper transformation yet—that to our discourse. In this volume, we have hinted at an emerging worldview antithetical to trivialization. As the reader may recognize now, this perspective is not an admission much of the world is so complex it is beyond our capacity to describe, understand, and mend it—which itself leads to trivialization. We argue that the complexity view challenges the three enablers of trivialization, reductionism, essentialism, and relativism (Chapter 3), thus steering us toward different ways of thinking and understanding.

As already indicated CAS views emergent phenomena, system properties arising from the interaction of its elements, as *irreducible* to the behaviors and properties of the elements, and recognizes dynamics of social systems are nonlinear. An outcome may not be a product of a singular, identifiable cause, but a set of interrelated conditions. Attempts to intervene in these systems may have disproportionate consequences. CAS hence challenges our understanding of causes and effects, compromising the conventional reductionist explanations in politics built around a small number of clear and intuitive actors or stimuli (Chapter 3); the assumption that collective behaviors are aggregates of individual actions (Chapter 8); or the popular reductionist heuristics such as Occam's razor (Chapters 3 and 7).

Further, the new paradigm sees systems and their constituents as *continually* evolving, being influenced by each other, the environment, and the system emergents. This means there are no intrinsic, essential qualities we can point to in explanations of systems and their elements. Thinking otherwise leads us to separate fundamentally related and coevolving entities, such as genes and environment, nature and nurture, or governments or markets, leading us astray in science, policy, and social discourse (Chapter 3).

These assumptions have not only shaped our discourse but also fueled overconfidence in our ability to determine causes and predict outcomes, and skewed our understandings, in turn leading to various social, cultural, and policy failures. These lapses helped to stimulate the rise of counter philosophies increasingly skeptical toward authority and power (Chapter 3), a development surely exacerbated by the certitudes—(mis)taken as backed by science—permeating most popular press, policy debates, and even public recommendations of government agencies (Chapter 7). The adherents to these views embrace various forms of relativism which sees knowledge as dependent on context, and science (however, it is understood) as no better than other conceptual systems.

The complexity view could help reduce such anxieties, as we explain. Recall CAS are open systems since there is no discrete boundary between them, their environment, and other systems (Chapter 8). This means that scientists studying such systems have decisions to make. One is related to boundaries whose selection requires making a subjective judgment, creating with it subjective uncertainty; another is inherent to "the modelling of the system itself, as random fluctuations create bifurcations to a large number of future states," a source of objective uncertainty (Kupers 2014, 20). Contrary to Newtonian science, we cannot know the future state of the system on account of these uncertainties. While we lose the possibility to predict, we retain the capacity to *explain*. Science, in its dominant conception as predictive science, thus gives way to an expanded, holistic science accommodating multiple goals of inquiry (Lemons and Brown 1995). The complexity paradigm then brings subjectivity (in delineating the boundaries) and "irreducible uncertainty" (in CAS behavior) to the foreground (Kupers 2014, 20), forcing us to make explicit our assumptions and make pragmatic judgments while, at the same time, surrendering certitude.

CONCLUSION

Assuming the new frame of reference, the complexity paradigm, means to begin thinking differently about our capacities to predict and alter the behavior in social systems. This leads us to revisit a range of issues from how we understand and depict problems to how we do regulation. Impervious to ideology, complexity paradigm encourages openness, humility, and caution, surely needed to renew the trust and credibility of the skeptical population toward those in charge. We are thus faced with a prospect of change reshaping the thought, institutions, and ultimately the society. While we cannot predict how it will unfold, we can look into history and study the evolution of thought and understand better the barriers and potentials. This is the objective of the following chapter.

Notes

1. Not all systems exhibit emergence. The systems where emergent phenomena are more likely have a large number of components linked into dense networks; their system functions are not performed by dedicated subsystems, and, by extension, their useful functional decomposition is not possible; and their system components are interacting in a complex language (Sawyer 2005).
2. The value and formalism of this "new methodology will *replace* the mathematics of *utility maximization* because those formalisms cannot be expanded to model symbolic communication and emergence mechanisms" adds Sawyer (2005, 229, emphases added). This, according to Sawyer, would place sociology rather than economics at the center of social sciences.

References

Allen, Peter. 2003. "Knowledge, ignorance and the evolution of complex systems." In *Frontiers of evolutionary economics: Competition, self-organization, and innovation policy*, edited by John Foster and J. Stanley Metcalfe. Cheltenham, UK and Northampton, MA: Edward Elgar Publishing.

Arthur, W. Brian. 1994. *Increasing returns and path dependence in the economy*. Ann Arbor: University of Michigan Press.

Booth, Robert. 2014. "Facebook reveals news feed experiment to control emotions." *The Guardian*, June 30. https://www.theguardian.com/technology/2014/jun/29/facebook-users-emotions-news-feeds.

Colander, David C., and Roland Kupers. 2014. *Complexity and the art of public policy: Solving society's problems from the bottom up*. Princeton: Princeton University Press.

Dunne, Timothy, Milja Kurki, and Steve Smith, eds. 2013. *International relations theories: Discipline and diversity*. 3rd ed. Oxford: Oxford University Press.

Hall, Peter. 2003. Aligning ontology and methodology in comparative research. In *Comparative historical analysis in the social sciences*, edited by James Mahoney and Dietrich Rueschemeyer. New York: Cambridge University Press.

Helbing, Dirk. 2015. *Thinking ahead—Essays on big data, digital revolution, and participatory market society*. Cham: Springer International Publishing.

Helbing, Dirk, and Alan Kirman. 2013. Rethinking economics using complexity theory. *Real-World Economics Review* 2013 (64): 23–52.

Helbing, Dirk, and Stefano Balietti. 2010. "Fundamental and real-world challenges in economics." *Science and Culture* 76 (9–10). http://dx.doi.org/10.2139/ssrn.1680262.

Hibbing, John R., and Elizabeth Theiss-Morse. 2004. *Stealth democracy: Americans' beliefs about how government should work*. Cambridge, UK: Cambridge University Press.

Hutcheon, Pat Duffy. 1996. *Leaving the cave: Evolutionary naturalism in social-scientific thought*. Waterloo: Wilfrid Laurier University Press.

Kohli, Atul, Peter Evans, Peter J. Katzenstein, Adam Przeworski, Susanne Hoeber Rudolph, James C. Scott, and Theda Skocpol. 1995. The role of theory in comparative politics: A symposium. *World Politics* 48 (1): 1–49.

Kupers, Roland. 2014. *The complexity frame for policy and management: Introductory tome*. PhD diss. http://repository.nyenrode.nl/search?identifier=12404.

Lemons, John and Donald A. Brown. 1995. "The role of science in sustainable development and environmental protection decisionmaking." In idem. *Sustainable development: Science, ethics, and public policy*, 11–38. Dordrecht: Springer.

Linstone, Harold A. 1999. Complexity science: Implications for forecasting. *Technological Forecasting and Social Change* 62: 79–90.

Markose, Sheri M. 2005. Computability and evolutionary complexity: Markets as complex adaptive systems (CAS). *The Economic Journal* 115 (504): F159–F192.

McCright, Aaron M., and Riley E. Dunlap. 2011. The politicization of climate change and polarization in the American public's views of global warming, 2001–2010. *The Sociological Quarterly* 52 (2): 155–194.

Mitchell, Sandra D. 2012. *Unsimple truths: Science, complexity, and policy*. Chicago: University of Chicago Press.

Nisbett, Richard. 2003. *The geography of thought: How Asians and Westerners think differently... and why*. New York: Simon & Schuster.

Overton, Willis F. 2015. "Processes, relations, and relational-developmental-systems." In *Handbook of child psychology and developmental science*, Vol. 1, edited by Richard M. Lerner, Willis F. Overton, and Peter C. M. Molenaar. Hoboken, NJ: Wiley.

Richardson, Kurt. 2002. "Methodological implications of complex systems approaches to sociality: Some further remarks." *Journal of Artificial Societies and Social Simulation* 5 (2): 1–11.

Richardson, Kurt. 2007. "Complex systems thinking and its implications for policy analysis." In *Handbook of decision making: Public administration and public policy*, edited by Göktuğ Morçöl. Boca Raton: CRC/Taylor & Francis.

Romer, Paul. 2012. "Process, responsibility, and Myron's Law." In *In the wake of the crisis: Leading economists reassess economic policy*, edited by Olivier Blanchard, David Romer, Michael Spence, and Joseph E. Stiglitz. Cambridge, MA: MIT Press.

Roose, Kevin. 2017. "Forget Washington: Facebook's problems abroad are far more disturbing." *The New York Times*, October 29. https://www.nytimes.com/2017/10/29/business/facebook-misinformation-abroad.html.

Roose, Kevin, Cecilia Kang, and Sheera Frenkel. 2018. "Zuckerberg gets a Crash Course in Charm: Will congress care?" *The New York Times*, April 8. https://www.nytimes.com/2018/04/08/technology/zuckerberg-gets-a-crash-course-in-charm-will-congress-care.html.

Sawyer, R. Keith. 2005. *Social emergence: Societies as complex systems.* Cambridge, UK: Cambridge University Press.

Tiku, Nitasha. 2017. "Get ready for the next big privacy backlash against Facebook." *Wired*, May 21. https://www.wired.com/2017/05/welcome-next-phase-facebook-backlash/.

Zuckerberg, Mark. 2012. "Founder's letter." Facebook. https://www.facebook.com/notes/mark-zuckerberg/founders-letter/10154500412571634.

PART IV

Shifting Cultures

CHAPTER 10

Beyond Folklore

In the film *The Invention of Lying*, Ricky Gervais portrays a character in a peculiar universe, a modern society in which everyone is truthful and sincere and concepts such as lie, deceit, fact, or credulity have no meaning. In this culture, there is no fraud, fiction, pretense, or hyperbole. Nor there is art, philosophy, or religion. The only media content is news and documentaries which are, from the protagonist's experience, increasingly harder to produce. One day Gervais's character has an epiphany and gains the ability to "say things that aren't," transforming not only his individual fortunes but the world as it had been. Conceived as a love story, the movie explores the intrinsic dilemma about how this "gift" should be used, if at all. We thus see a series of untruths be told with no broader consequence. Yet we also witness a birth of a myth, a new meaning that quickly finds appeal throughout that society and reveals its mixed blessings. The movie has stirred some debates and found its following for a number of reasons, but perhaps the most intriguing is its depiction of a world unlike anything we have ever known. For in our world, we began with myth and have had a difficult relationship with the truth. Below, we take a look at this story from a perspective less common as we examine the development of thought at the individual and social levels. Our goal is to visit our cognitive history to understand the present condition and any prospects for the future.

© The Author(s) 2019
O. Bubak and H. Jacek, *Trivialization and Public Opinion*,
https://doi.org/10.1007/978-3-030-17925-0_10

Individual Development

Human history can be told from a variety of views and many different starting points. Yet, such a tale is never complete without including what happens when people get together in increasing numbers and begin to communicate, solve collective challenges, and organize into social structures, all the while building shared meanings—the evolution of human culture and society. To obtain a larger historical understanding of such developments, some scholars begin in a place less likely as they reach to the work of Jean Piaget and his studies of individual cognitive development (Piaget 2005; Piaget and Inhelder 2013, among other work). Based on extensive psychological research, Piaget formulated the seminal stage theory according to which one's cognitive competence changes qualitatively with development. We briefly discuss his stages below, before explaining their greater applicability.[1]

The first stage, lasting from birth until up about two years of age, is the *sensorimotor* stage, during which a child gains a basic capacity to integrate perception and movement and to apply generalized patterns of behavior when dealing with external entities. The child then enters the *preoperational* or representational stage[2] lasting until about six or seven years of age. Throughout this stage, the child learns the basic properties of the surrounding environment but lacks the capacity to distinguish between fact and fiction. The child receives information about the world and guidance on what to do in it through language and example; these can be challenged by other ideas, appealing or familiar. As well, "[t]he child comes to represent the external world through the medium of symbols, but he does so primarily by generalization from a motivational model e.g., he believes that the sun moves because 'God pushes it' and that the stars, like himself, have to go to bed," explains Parsons (in Piaget and Inhelder 2013, xii). The child thus understands and explains new or strange phenomena in terms of their symbolic similarity with familiar things, often involving magical thinking (Barnes 2000).

The next stage, throughout which the child develops the ability to perform concrete operations, lasts from the age of 7 until about 11. At this *concrete operational* stage, the child not only develops the ability to discern between thoughts and reality but also begins to classify and relate real-world objects. The reality is thus interpreted in terms of specific images and stories rather than higher-level abstractions, and primarily in the context of one's culture. One develops the capacity to handle narratives of increasing complexity. This also means one can, with time, comprehend books consisting of a set of interrelated chapters, if such materials are produced by the attendant culture (Barnes 2000). It is important to note that developed at this stage is intuitive, commonsense thinking, successful and sufficient in quotidian tasks, yet very different from scientific thinking and often contrary to it (Wolpert 2006).

Entering the *formal operational* stage around the age of twelve, the child begins to gain the capacity to logically formulate hypotheses about the elements of reality and to test them. This involves "reflecting systematically on all the interrelations among data in order to mentally devise and test some basic explanatory scheme or theory that will tie it all together in a new way, to devise alternative theories for the same data, and then to test the various alternatives against other data and other seemingly well-supported theories, to arrive at a logically sound conclusion that is consistent with the evidence," explains Barnes and adds this capacity includes the ability to understand similar sentences (2000, 22). Such thinking is facilitated by systems of thought that exist within a particular culture, which provides not only the principles and context but also their education and training. Mastering these tools allows one to reflect upon the traditionally held beliefs and question and contest them. However, the newly gained confidence may result in dogmatic rationalism, "relying on the logical and hypothesis-forming workings of the mind to arrive at clear and correct truth" (Barnes 2000, 22). Needless to add, such an orientation limits dialogue and forestalls advancement.

Finally, beyond the formal operational thought of adolescence, one may begin to appreciate the limits to knowledge and recognize its conditionality. At this *late formal operational* phase, one applies the same logic in search of the truth, but understands the theory to be subject to continuous scrutiny and, with new discoveries and evidence, revision. This most advanced style of thinking is far from common, yet essential in both science and everyday decision making, as we will discuss.

While the ensuing research in developmental psychology revealed that children, especially in the preoperational stages, had in some aspects greater cognitive and conceptual faculties than previously thought (Gelman 2003), Piaget's stages continue to be very influential, even outside of the psychology field. This is partly as Piaget, seeking to establish the relationship between individual learning and knowledge building processes at the social level, early suggested "an isomorphism between the child's evolving grasp of space, time and causality, and that of early humans as reflected in mythology and the first crude stirrings of scientific thought" (Hutcheon 1996, 375).[3] Piaget argued that just as children emerge from their egocentric world as they leave the preoperational stage, so too science, during the Copernican Revolution, experienced a shift away from a geocentric model of the cosmos. As Hutcheon explains:

> [c]hildren no longer experience themselves as the centre of the universe, and objects that move beyond their view can still exist. Just as early humans conceived of surrounding objects as living and endowed with spirits, so too does the young child in the animistic stage see intention in the marble's movement, or in the wall that "hits" them. Just as early primitives saw purpose and design in every occurrence, with human-like gods in total control, so too does the child see no chance or coincidence in nature. (1996, 375)

Piaget also recognized the parallels between how children perceive time as they develop and the gradual refinements in the concept of time in physics. During the preoperational stage, time is understood as a localized phenomenon, duration is related to distance traveled, and velocity is connected to other moving objects irrespective of their initial positions. Space and time are absolute as in the Newtonian model. Gaining access to portable clock, and hence the ability to measure durations of events separately, allows us to decouple velocity from concrete events in space. The child thus begins to understand simultaneity, "the intuition that when two objects begin and stop moving at the same instant, the one which has gone the farthest has moved the fastest" (Hutcheon 1996, 376). This comparison is a requisite step in the thought process as we can now question our assumptions: Does simultaneity work under all conditions? "Einstein's refinements of the concept of time bear solely on non-simultaneity at a distance...simultaneity, in the case of great velocities, depends purely on the relative motions of the observer and the phenomena he observes as well as their distance apart...the measurement of duration itself will depend on the coordination of these velocities," explained Piaget (1971, 306). Hence, Piaget showed that Einstein's updated notion of time was just an extension of a fundamental principle behind how people come to construct physical and psychological time.

Whether drawing on Piaget or working independently, scholars, interested in the development of human thought in philosophy, science, or religion, have come to identify patterns similar to Piaget's. Barnes's work (2000), in particular, makes a case for the value of Piaget's schema in interpreting macro-changes in the process of cultural evolution in the cognitive method. The author provides a compelling account of cultural development highlighting cognitive changes in science and religion. We follow with the requisite sociohistorical context before looking closer at these important arguments.

The Social Trajectory

Evolution is defined by change, a set of processes unfolding over extended periods of time and, regardless of its biological, social, or cultural variants, involving large numbers of interacting elements within a larger context. It is never easy to make generalizations and establish useful analytical patterns, especially as the task involves going back in time which has never been kind to evidence. Moreover, the change is gradual, nonlinear, replete with interdependencies and feedback effects, not readily apparent and difficult to isolate.

Nevertheless, four changing features of society—population size, subsistence, political centralization, and social stratification (Diamond 2013)—have been useful in understanding some broader, interrelated trends.[4] As a primary means of subsistence, hunting and gathering can support only small, often nomadic, groups of no more than several dozen individuals. The members of these *bands* know each other well, and, as there is no formal leadership and little wealth, are all of relatively equal status. The advent of basic farming and herding allow for groups to settle and morph into a more evolved social order, a *tribe*. Tribes[5] depend on joint decision making and thus retain their mostly egalitarian character.

The gradual intensification of and the innovations in agriculture and storage practices provide for a further population growth. Made possible by irrigation systems, tools, and animal power, increasing yields and efficiency allow more people to spend their time in other ways, leading to social specialization. Hence created are new roles supporting the emerging needs of the growing society. When such collectives reach the size of a *chiefdom*—a group of several thousand where it is no longer possible for everyone to know each other and where it ceases to be practical for all to come together and weigh in on courses of action as well as implement and administer them—new social issues surface and demand resolution. Taking a predominantly functional perspective, Diamond writes:

> [f]irst, strangers in a chiefdom must be able to meet each other, to recognize each other as fellow but individually unfamiliar members of the same chiefdom, and to avoid bristling at territorial trespass and getting into a fight. Hence chiefdoms develop shared ideologies and political and religious identities often derived from the supposedly divine status of the chief. Second, there is now a recognized leader, the chief, who makes decisions, possesses recognized authority, claims a monopoly on the right to use force against his society's members if necessary, and thereby ensures that strangers within the same chiefdom don't fight each other. The chief is assisted by non- specialized all-purpose officials (proto-bureaucrats) who collect tribute and settle disputes and carry out other administrative tasks, instead of there being separate tax collectors, judges, and restaurant inspectors as in a state. (2013)

Thus, we can trace the roots of many of the familiar facets of our social and cultural order—such as social stratification, socioeconomic specialization, and resource redistribution—to chiefdoms, thought to have existed as early as 5500 BCE. The top of the social hierarchy is occupied by chiefs and their families claiming their hereditary status, while commoners and slaves are at the bottom. Some societies stratified further, creating castes based on factors such as occupation, status, language, and others. Chiefdoms have also seen increased specialization, with artisans, warriors, priests, and bureaucrats all having a particular social or economic role. Also, the chiefs demand food and labor from their subjects, redistributing it in turn strategically to the direct servants as well as the laborers employed in the chiefs' works. This in-kind taxation was an early implementation of a redistributive economy.

Finally, further increases in population demand and are made possible by steady food and water supplies, order, and security. This is realized in social organizations of the highest order, *states*, providing the decision making, executive, and administrative capacities needed to support the needs of mass populations. Modern states, with their complex political and economic systems and complex administrative hierarchies, all embedded within an international order, have evolved from state-like societies first appearing in Mesopotamia about 4000 BCE.

We have briefly discussed types of societies which have emerged over time and some drivers of their change. This basic developmental trajectory supplies context as we examine related developments integral to our understanding of the present condition. In a nutshell, "[t]he continuum of increase in population size, political organization, and intensity of food production that stretches from bands to states is paralleled by other trends, such as increases in dependence on metal tools, sophistication of technology, economic specialization and inequality" (Diamond 2013). Not to be forgotten here, however, is a crucial aspect of evolving societies, the development of culture, shared meanings which at once arise from and shape these processes.

CULTURAL DEVELOPMENT

When compared to the millions of years of human evolution, its cultural counterpart unfolded over just a blink of an eye. Despite the process's uneven and slow nature, some find our development of tools; mastery of fire for cooking, safety, and heating; parietal art, ritual burials, and artifacts for tracking the phases of moon; and the use of language as medium for cross-generational transfer of information—all in place by about 20,000 years ago—together as evidence of early development of culture.[6] And as hinted above, scholars of culture have long identified patterns in its evolution and have found Piaget's work particularly apt in their analyses. Below, we review the four stages of one such an analysis.

The most basic of cognitive styles is prevalent in *primitive culture*. Such cultures are common in hunting and gathering, pastoral, or rudimentary horticultural societies, whose members live in smaller groups of settlements. Lacking writing, the members rely on spoken word and memory to pass on their stories, thus making these relatively short and simple. Reality is thought to be composed of people, objects, and events which can belong to one or more possibly overlapping language categories. As what is seen and known is determined culturally—informed by traditions, beliefs, and assisted by language—there is not much clarity about what is a fact or fiction. Primitive cultures can thus be characterized by the combination of preoperational and concrete operational style of thought. As in children throughout the preoperational stage, there is much magical thinking. Importantly, these cultures' supernatural beliefs are reflective of their classless quality; rather than a few dominant gods, there are important yet ubiquitous spirits and magic.

"Belief in gods, 'polytheism,' apparently begins to develop only as the culture develops clear social class structure. When chiefs come to rule among people, then gods also rule in the spirit world," observes Barnes (2000, 53). Such beliefs, borne of the increasing social complexity of the early cities and states, intensified in the next stage of the evolution of thought, *archaic cultures*. Given their reliance on mostly concrete operational thought, archaic culture appear closer to primitive cultures resulting in their frequent conflation. Nevertheless, given their social innovations and the associated growth of sophistication in the style and content of thought unfolding over thousands of years, some have assigned them to distinct stages. As hinted above, the advancements in food production supported dense settlements, cities, the functioning of which required specialized social roles and hierarchies. The emerging inter-city trade also meant the inhabitants began to appreciate the existence of a world beyond their immediate surroundings. These changes in turn began to reshape the prevalent beliefs; more powerful, god-like figures now dominated the world of spirits.

Even more critical to the evolution of cognition, however, was the advent of writing systems and literacy in the latter part of the archaic stage. It was now possible not only to produce registries or transactional records but also to capture histories, legends, and liturgical content. Writing meant that these informational artifacts could now be longer and more complex, in turn requiring specially trained individuals capable of working with them. Formal education was needed, and bureaucrats and priests became its first beneficiaries. While highly exclusive, literacy nevertheless had a deep impact on the development of thought as writing enabled consistency, accumulation and transmission of information, and more extensive mappings of the objects of reality. But, perhaps most significantly, literacy encouraged scrutiny and questioning.

The ensuing rise of great civilizations in China, India, Greece, and parts of the Middle East saw a major evolution of thought, the era of axial or *classical cultures*. A significant addition to the past cognitive styles, the emerging thinking went beyond the tradition and common sense and contemplated "causes that were not only hidden to the eye, as were the traditional magical powers and spirits and gods, but were also the universal structures or forces that accounted for all the individual happenings of the universe" (Barnes 2000, 26). Hence, seeing a natural world with a stable, unified, and logical constitution, people began to apply logic in search of the one, true explanation. The multiple and possibly contradictory stories which have accumulated overtime and been accepted by convention could now be questioned more formally, thus allowing the development of new understandings. Even as logical thinking in everyday situations was not uncommon to primitive or archaic cultures, it is their classical counterparts' formal and accepted quest in finding the universal order that becomes the distinguishing feature. The traditional identities reflecting group or family membership, or norms derived from status, are thus challenged by universalist views, in turn opening debates on justice, morality, truth, and government, among other issues of universal import.

Notably, similar patterns of thinking emerged within a relatively short period in India, China, and Greece, where philosophers established systems of formal logic, formulated rules of analysis, or looked for an underlying form or essence. These intellectual efforts, all driven by a desire to find truth, were supported by and required gathering, categorizing, and connecting large amounts of information, generating hypotheses and testing them against evidence and each other—efforts ultimately leading to an establishment of contemporaneous theory. Such type of thinking is characteristic of Piaget's formal operational stage. The use of formal operational thought was also reflected in the broader, spiritual search for the ultimate meaning. Here, "[n]o merely supreme god among lesser gods would do. Only a Reality that transcends the gods and all else could satisfy the searchers. In China it was the formless and incomprehensible Tao, in India the Brahman beyond categories or the incomprehensible Atman, in Greece the 'One' of Plato and eventually of Philo Judaeus and then of Christians," explains Barnes (2000, 93). These were the roots of the major universalist faiths lasting to this day.

Developing over the last few centuries has been the most evolved of cognitive styles, the *empirical-critical* thought. Analogous with the late formal operational phase of cognitive development, empirical-critical approach recognizes that knowledge, whether a product of common-sense observation, logical theorizing, or systematic research, is not final. This means that regardless of the apparent strength or appeal of what we know, we must be open not only to continuous scrutiny and new questions but also to revision of our theories in light of new findings. It was precisely this thinking which had driven the Scientific Revolution and made science a key transforming force. But science carries within it a contradiction. "While it has been extremely successful in discovering things about this universe that had long eluded the most insistent questionings of humankind, at the same time its continuing successes have been dependent on a willingness to doubt all observations and theories, to leave them open to further testing by any critic, to treat them as models for interpreting reality rather than as simple truth," explains Barnes (2000, 28). Scientific skepticism thus fueles progress.

Enabled by the empirical-critical culture, the advancements of the scientific era have been characterized by an uneven, interactive process that has not only broadened the existing culture but also opened new horizons of inquiry. Diamond (2015), speaking of how ideas come and go in the context of scientific inquiry, complements the view on progress. The author admits new theories and approaches often supplant the old, offering some examples: "the replacement of biogeographic theories assuming a static Earth by the acceptance of continental drift, from the 1960s onward; the rise of the taxonomic approach termed cladistics at the expense of previous taxonomic approaches, also from the 1960s onward; and the rise in the 1960s and 1970s, followed by the virtual disappearance, of attempts to make use of irreversible (non-equilibrium) thermodynamics in the fields of population biology and cell physiology." Yet, Diamond makes clear there are also instances where *new* ideas fill a space not previously covered by any coherent idea and identifies two drivers of such developments: "new ideas responding to new information made possible by new measurements, or else responding to new 'outlooks.'" These outlooks, or *worldviews*, provide contexts in which new lines of questioning make sense.

There are a number of illustrative examples provided by Diamond, but a two stand out in particular, one for each of the drivers. One of the most visible cases where new measurements opened space for new ideas was the discovery of the double-helix molecular structure of deoxyribonucleic acid (DNA). This feat was made possible by a combination of two essential measurements: the findings from X-ray crystallography and the analyses of physical chemistry of nucleic acids. As there was no established theory in this space, a previously empty knowledge space was filled with the acceptance of the double-helix model.

In the case of a new *worldview*, or what is better termed by German *Fragestellung*, opening possibilities for new ideas, Diamond points to the founding of a number of modern sciences including biogeography, taxonomy, evolutionary biology, or ecology. The fundamental findings across these fields are based on measurement, observation, and basic calculations, without much need for equipment. For the most part, such research could have been conducted by the classical Greeks over two millennia ago.

> The Greeks were eminently capable of patient, accurate, quantitative observations of planets and other features of the natural world. Aristotle could similarly have examined Greek animals and plants and arrived at Linnaeus' hierarchical taxonomy. Herodotus could have compared the species of the Black Sea with those of Egypt and thereby founded biogeography. And any ancient Greek could have grown and counted pea varieties as did Gregor Mendel in the 1860s, noticed the differences between Willow Warblers and Chiffchaffs (a related warbler species) as did Gilbert White in the 1780s, watched young geese as did Konrad Lorenz in the 1930s, and thereby founded genetics, ecology, and animal behavior,

adds Diamond (2015). But the Greeks, working within the confines of their classical thinking, lacked the essential *Fragestellung* which would provide an inspiration for asking these questions. It was nearly two thousand years later that a new *Fragestellung* provided meaning to such questions and drove empirical-critical scholars to collect data and attempt to answer them. These data gave rise to new ideas, opening again possibilities to fill previously void spaces in our knowledge.

The recent decades, however, have seen a number of thinkers and like-minded movements question the validity of objective truth, argue against the existence of an observer-independent reality, and view science, supposedly a Western invention, to be merely one of many valid ways of knowing the world. Yet, as Barnes shows, the elements of empirical-critical thought, including the application of logic and the skeptical philosophy, have been present in India and China as early as they were in ancient Greece. So, although scientific fields were established and inquiry was made effective in the West, science's roots are not solely Western, nor is science valid only there. Thinking otherwise neglects not only our "common humanness"[7] but also our common potential along with the possibilities of unlocking it.

Box 10.1 The cultural development thesis

1. There are different fundamental styles of thinking, different cognitive techniques, each recognizable in the way it manifests itself in daily work, in religious beliefs and thought forms, in scientific approaches, in philosophical reasoning, and in other cognitive activities.
2. The more difficult of these styles of thinking will appear only later in any individual's development because of a need for experience, training, and continuing brain maturation.
3. Piaget's description of the sequence of development of major cognitive skills is a fairly accurate guide to the basic styles of thinking that people learn as they develop.
4. A culture may maintain a simpler, easier style of thought as its dominant style for many centuries or even millennia, even if some individuals go beyond the culture's general achievement. (The simplest style may function as the common denominator of general social communication, among children and adults, the learned and unlearned, the very bright and the mentally slow.)
5. Though people everywhere share in the same basic human intelligence, some cultures have discovered cognitive tools to promote more complex and difficult cognitive styles and to educate an increasing number of people in their use.
6. The most difficult cognitive styles are skills mastered in any culture only by a relative few (for whatever reasons) who nonetheless have significant impact on the general nature of the culture.
7. The actual history of religious thought in major cultures exhibits a sequence of development of thought styles suggested by the prior six points, a development in which science has shared.

Source Barnes (2000)

GAINING GROUND

Above we began with a sketch of the history of social organization, a process of growing population and social complexity, made possible by innovations in food production and storage, accompanied and reinforced by a number of technological, economic, social, and cultural developments. We took a particular interest in cognitive evolution at the cultural level and the respective adaptations in scientific and religious thought, an interpretation we find especially useful in studying the present condition. Some scholars, we noted, find Piaget's stages or their analogues useful in navigating these developments. Among such scholars is Barnes (2000), who offers his cultural development thesis (Box 10.1), especially insightful in understanding the evolution of religion and science and, with these, the society's orientation toward reality and truth. We discuss and expand upon its select points in turn.

First, as discussed above, we can identify different styles of thinking of increasing difficulty corresponding to Piaget's stages of individual cognitive development. These styles, which influence the way the world and its constituents are perceived and interpreted, are discernible at individual as well as collective levels. To review, at the preoperational stage, individuals understand their surrounding as a collection of distinct elements, which they begin to classify into elaborate categories. Associations among these categories are made at the concrete operational stage. The ability to think systematically, generate competing explanations, collect evidence, and apply logic in adjudicating them develops during the formal operational stage. Finally, in the late formal operational stage, individuals begin to appreciate that truth claims are not final and thus subject to continuous testing and revision. These stages, as Barnes (2000) teaches us, are also differentiated by increasing "reality discrimination." The preoperational thought is the least discerning of what is real and what imagined, particularly when the ideas are attractive. With the concrete operational style of thinking, individuals begin to seek evidence to distinguish between truth and fiction, although there is often deference to authority in making these judgments. Logical and systematic, formal operational thinking seeks truth in coherence and unity. Much of the agency in determining the truth is thus placed into the hands of the individual. The late formal operational thought embraces the conditionality of truth claims and is motivated by continuous refinement of knowledge. These styles of thought are also apparent at the cultural level, evident in the collective posture toward knowledge, in discerning reality, and the understanding of ethics and morality.

Second, while a long historical view reveals a positive trend toward more advanced cognitive styles across cultures, this process has been uneven and often experienced extensive setbacks. Take, for instance, the classical culture of Greece and later the Roman Empire, dating back as far as the fifth century BCE and flowering for hundreds of years before its eventual decline. What was a culture of great philosophers and artists producing lasting artifacts of history, literature, philosophy as well as art, eventually gave way to archaic culture, a thousand-year long retreat in cognitive, and with it social, progress. More specifically, formal operational thinking of the classical era embraced a reality which could be known through systematic inquiry, a method in determining the truth, and an interest in accumulating reliable knowledge, and supported universalist views of human nature, social relations, and moral standards. What followed was a gradual reemergence of concrete operational thinking, evidenced in an acceptance of an unpredictable world "best described by a myth-style narrative plot rather than systematic analyses" (Barnes 2000, 124), in a preference for tradition and authority in separating truth from fiction, and in a pessimism in the ability to obtain knowledge. This, in turn, was reflected in an elevation of status and honor over "interior uprightness," a deference to a leader and authority as a source of stability, and the a sense of oneself as a member of the collective rather than as an individual (Barnes 2000). While there are ongoing debates on the reasons for these shifts, it is important to recognize the arrow of cognitive development of culture does not always point forward (Chapter 3).

Third, the evolution of cognitive styles across cultures can be described as an increasing mastery of more advanced cognitive techniques by the *influential* portion of the population. But rather than displacing the previous cognitive styles, more advanced ones begin to dominate the toolkits of these cognitive elites. Speaking of the English Renaissance, Thomas captures this situation well:

> Tudor and Stuart England may have been an under-developed society, dependent upon the labours of an under-nourished and ignorant population, but it also produced one of the greatest literary cultures ever known and witnessed an unprecedented ferment of scientific and intellectual activity. Not every under-developed society has its Shakespeare, Milton, Locke, Wren and Newton. The social élite was highly educated. It has been calculated that by 1660 there was a grammar school for every 4,400 persons, and that two and a half percent of the relevant age-group of the male population was receiving some form of higher education, at Oxford and Cambridge, or at the Inns of Court. (1971)

And so we remember this period as the time of the Scientific Revolution, a return to logic, systematic observation, search for laws of the universal order, and problem-solving, opening the door to the Age of Reason. Driven by the elite, much of this cognitive progress went unnoticed to the commoner steeped in magical beliefs and living in a world filled with elves, fairies, and goblins, among other creatures of great diversity and powers. Passed from generation to generation, these fear and superstition-evoking beliefs were deeply ingrained in the contemporary society. Indeed, it was the archaic culture, with its predominantly concrete operational thought, which has enabled such beliefs:

> For one striking aspect of fairy-beliefs was their self-confirming character. The man who believed in fairies could, like the astrologer or the magician, accept every setback and disappointment without losing his faith. He knew that he could never count on actually seeing the fairies himself, for the little people were notoriously jealous of their privacy and would never appear to those who were so curious as to go looking for them,

explains Thomas (1971). Driven by urbanization, the rise of science, and the idea, increasingly endorsed by religion, of reliance on self rather than the supernatural, magical thinking saw its eventual decline (Thomas 1971).[8] Yet, whilst the belief in fairies, observed even in the early twentieth-century Ireland (Thomas 1971), is now the stuff of children's stories, elements of concrete operational thinking perpetuate various types of folklore in the form of legends, myths, or superstitions to this day. Also, as hinted above, this style does not pay much value to systematic analyses, preferring to defer to the customary and familiar in determining what is real. While for an ordinary person this thinking did not matter much in the Dark Ages, it is of much consequence in modern-day democracies, particularly in cases where the citizens get a chance to bypass the layer of representation and decide directly on their future. As well, channeling this thinking, politicians may appeal to their naive voters as they boast a reliance on instinct, invoke tradition, and spread myth.

CONCLUSION

Can we get beyond folklore? We thus ask if we, as a society, can get past the thinking which perpetuates myth and is fond of trivialization and embrace substance, logic, and critical thought more broadly. Can we have a larger part of our society assume a systematic approach in probing and questioning the reality around us? To answer these questions, we first note there is no evidence that humans, throughout the aforedescribed cultural history or across cultures, differ fundamentally in their intelligence (also in Diamond 2013). Hence, we acknowledge as we all share the same cognitive abilities, our cultures evolve with changing *cognitive styles*. As we recognize the human mind has the capacity for the most difficult of styles of thought, it follows it is the *culture* that serves either as a barrier or as a facilitator in developing these qualities more broadly.[9] The reader has surely noticed there have been novel thinkers, much ahead of their time, whose contributions became appreciated only when the society caught up with their thought. So "if the culture does not have the language and social structure *publicly* to support ideas of a new level of complexity or sophistication, then the thinking of the innovators will likely go unnoticed, be rejected, or revised into simplicity," notes Barnes (2000, 18, emphasis added). On the other hand, if the society develops a shared meaning around the importance of imparting difficult cognitive skills in its members by implementing advanced systems of education, it not only facilitates innovation but also enables further transformation.

But in empirical-critical cultures only "*some* people have learned to use formal operational thought when their culture educates them in tools for such thought, … [t]hese tools are cultural products, not self-evident practices… that have had enormous impact on the societies that educate their young in the use of these tools," adds Barnes (2000, 96, emphasis added). While we have experienced quite a progress within a comparatively short time, one may recognize that empirical-critical thinking exercised by the few is insufficient in the contemporary open society in which citizens, administrators, or consumers are expected to adjudicate between claims, assess tradeoffs, and make choices mindful of their possible consequences. Consider, for example, while the empirical-critical approach is fundamental to science, it appears uneasy in general, particularly to those immersed in classical or even archaic thinking. Bateson makes a strong point:

> Most people are uncomfortable with the notion that knowledge can be authoritative, can call for decision and action, and yet be subject to constant revision, because they tend to think of knowledge as additive, not recognizing the necessity of reconfiguring in response to new information. It is precisely this characteristic of scientific knowledge that encourages the denial of climate change and makes it so difficult to respond to what we do know in a context where much is still unknown. (2015)

It is for these reasons we must aim to establish the broadest collective capacity to reflect systematically *and* critically on the world around us. Only then we can productively question what we hear, read, and want. This includes, for example, reassessing the long-for-granted systems of governance, including representation and accountability, and deciding whether they meet the modern-day tradeoffs between local and global, the demands of increasingly technical nature of policy, and the needs for diversity, among others. And this also means learning more about political issues and understanding them better, changing the condition which has remained virtually constant for the past half a century despite the enormous growth in our access to the tools of information (Delli Carpini 2000).

Returning to our question above, we hope to get beyond folklore. To start, we, and this includes primarily those in the positions of influence, must first have the will to take the lead and begin to reshape the culture from within. Once we do, we will hear clearer the calls for a new education, a system that does more than teaching and testing of numerical and literacy skills, traditionally sufficient in preparation for industrial employment. And it is not just an updated education system, but a new, innovative approach to public engagement (Chapter 5) which involves, tackles preconceptions, and demonstrates the variety of values, perspectives, and the depth of issues around us. This new system must develop advanced cognitive skills (Chapter 11), not just in preparing people for the new age but also in cultivating new shared meanings.

NOTES

1. Drawing on primarily on Barnes (2000) and Piaget and Inhelder (2013).
2. We note Piaget reacts to the Anglo-Saxon tradition in psychology emphasizing the verbal features of intelligence as he employs the term *operation* which includes direct or internal actions and manipulations (Piaget and Inhelder 2013).
3. The following discussion of Piaget is based on Hutcheon (1996).
4. The ensuing historical discussion draws on Diamond (2013).
5. The word tribe has been conflated with chiefdom in the popular discourse. The oft referenced Native American "tribes," for example, are technically chiefdoms (Diamond 2013).
6. This and the ensuing paragraphs on stages of culture are based primarily on Barnes (2000).
7. Well expressed in Barnes (2000, 13). More on relativism in Chapter 3.
8. Thomas observes "men emancipated themselves from these magical beliefs without necessarily having devised any effective technology with which to replace them" (1971), noting that magical thinking was on the decline before more effective medicine, methods of prediction, or new technological tools were available.

9. For completeness, notable here is Nisbett's (2003) work in cultural psychology. The author presents a compelling case "that Easterners and Westerners differ in fundamental assumptions about the nature of the world, in the focus of attention, in the skills necessary to perceive relationships and to discern objects in a complex environment, in the character of causal attribution, in the tendency to organize the world categorically or relationally and in the inclination to use rules..." (190). The differences in the systems of thought shape and are shaped by the respective social practices.

REFERENCES

Barnes, Michael Horace. 2000. *Stages of thought: The co-evolution of religious thought and science.* New York: Oxford University Press.

Bateson, Mary. 2015. "The illusion of certainty." In *This idea must die: Scientific theories that are blocking progress,* edited by John Brockman. New York: Harper Perennial.

Delli Carpini, Michael X. 2000. "In search of the informed citizen: What Americans know about politics and why it matters." *The Communication Review* 4 (1): 129–164.

Diamond, Jared. 2013. *The world until yesterday: What can we learn from traditional societies?* London: Penguin.

Diamond, Jared. 2015. "New ideas triumph by replacing old ones." In *This idea must die: Scientific theories that are blocking progress,* edited by John Brockman. New York: Harper Perennial.

Gelman, Susan A. 2003. *The essential child: Origins of essentialism in everyday thought.* Oxford and New York: Oxford University Press.

Hutcheon, Pat Duffy. 1996. *Leaving the cave: Evolutionary naturalism in social-scientific thought.* Waterloo, ON: Wilfrid Laurier University Press.

Nisbett, Richard. 2003. *The geography of thought: How Asians and Westerners think differently... and why.* New York: Free Press.

Piaget, Jean. 1971. *The child's conception of time.* Translated by A. J. Pomerans. New York: Ballantine Books. As cited in Hutcheon (1996).

Piaget, Jean. 2005. *The psychology of intelligence.* New York: Routledge.

Piaget, Jean, and Bärbel Inhelder. 2013. *The growth of logical thinking from childhood to adolescence,* vol. 84. Abingdon: Routledge.

Thomas, Keith. 1971. *Religion and the decline of magic.* London: Weidenfeld & Nicolson.

Wolpert, Lewis. 2006. *Six impossible things before breakfast: The evolutionary origins of belief.* New York: W. W. Norton.

CHAPTER 11

Thinking Change

In *On Dialogue*, a theoretical physicist David Bohm (2013) recounts a story of a changed relationship between Albert Einstein and Niels Bohr. The two famed scientists were once amicable, talking, and sharing their findings. As their ideas evolved, however—Einstein's view was informed by his theory of relativity, Bohr's was fixed in quantum mechanics—they grew estranged, despite a number of attempts at reconciliation of these views. Years later, during a social event at Princeton, the two had a chance to meet again. There, Bohr and his colleagues socialized on one side of the room, while Einstein with his associates remained on the other side. "They couldn't share any meaning, because each one felt his meaning was true," comments Bohm on their lack of interaction (2013, 43). Stories such as this, not uncommon to science, inspired Bohm's series of essays discussing the virtues, necessities of as well as obstacles to an open and sustained dialogue. Yet, these stories are familiar outside of science and academia, in politics, critique, and the general discourse.

The biggest of issues facing us today, according to Bohm, is incoherence, a lack of shared meaning. Getting to a proper dialogue holds a promise to build coherence while establishing new shared meanings, ultimately allowing us to change how we think and act. "Bohr and Einstein probably should have had a dialogue, [one in which] they might have listened properly to each other's opinion. And perhaps they both would have suspended their opinions, and moved out beyond relativity and beyond quantum theory into something new," added Bohm (2013, 43). That leading scientists could not get past their ideas and engage with

© The Author(s) 2019

O. Bubak and H. Jacek, *Trivialization and Public Opinion*,
https://doi.org/10.1007/978-3-030-17925-0_11

each other's arguments suggests a deeper problem, one that continues to plague our broader discourse. In *Trivialization and Public Opinion*, we set out to explore this class of fundamental issues, obstacles in dealing with personal and social challenges—negating the advantages of the information age. While not insurmountable, they require our attention from multiple perspectives, and actions lead by those with the awareness and capacity to take them.

On Trivialization

We began with an observation that for most of our history, the access to knowledge and information was privileged, limited to a learned minority who used this asymmetry to their advantage. The advent of the printing press, the communication tools such as the telegraph and the telephone, the democratization of reading, followed in turn by the mass embrace of radio and television, informed, educated, and altered the public's awareness of the contemporaneous social order, stimulating demands for greater equality, justice, and liberty. Extensive social and political transformations thus came on the heels of major milestones marking the broadening of access to information. The age of the network, however, has brought into contrast the limits to these trends. With some exceptions, virtually everyone in the democratic world with an Internet connection enjoys the *same* unparalleled access to news, research, raw or analyzed data, commentaries, critiques, expressions of culture, and much more. At the same time, with this unprecedented spread and importance of information and communication technologies, people across the globe are expected not only to stay abreast of these tools but also to make use of them to inform the progressively demanding personal and civic decisions. Yet, as we highlighted through some uneasy examples, the discourses surrounding public choices and ultimately the votes cast, appear, in the age of information, rather uninformed. While some critics, speaking particularly of the Internet generations, have seen the network as detrimental to individual knowledge outcomes (Bauerlein 2008), others have not observed much change, concluding

> that, despite concerns over the quality of education, the decline in newspaper readership, the rise of soundbite journalism, the explosion in national political issues, and the waning commitment to civic engagement, citizens appear *no less* informed about politics today than they were half a century

ago. The bad news is that despite an unprecedented expansion in public education, a communications revolution that has shattered national and international boundaries, and the increasing relevance of national and international events and policies to the daily lives of Americans, citizens appear *no more* informed about politics today than they were half a century ago. (Delli Carpini 2000, 136–137, emphases original)

As we are no longer limited by the availability and access to information but have not been able to make much progress in what we do with it, there must be something else holding us back. Our treatment of information and our construction of knowledge are constrained by the prevalent styles of thinking, the evolution of which has been outpaced by technological progress. Such limits are also apparent in the daily discourse manifesting, in our view, a fundamental lapse inhibiting our collective ability to engage, discuss, and address contemporary challenges.

It is in this environment it becomes possible, indeed welcome, to advance simple, appealing, and intuitive prescriptions to inherently difficult problems; exude certainty over the conclusions while glossing over logic and assumptions; focus on the obvious or convenient while neglecting the larger picture; or reduce complex social and political arrangements to what are often binary choices—all of which can be easily conveyed in a few sound bites. Our world, an evolving complex of systems with interdependencies, histories, feedback effects, and intrinsic uncertainties, and its dilemmas, multifaceted and contextual, become reduced to a few categories and options. While this may have been sustainable in the simpler times of the centuries past, given our modern capacity to alter the environment on a global scale, or change the health outcomes of tens of millions of people at a time—both possibly based on unspoken assumptions, intuition, or an idea—the way we confront and reach our decisions is now more consequential than ever before.

Here, we understand these lapses as *trivialization,* defined as an inclination to conflate ideas with substance, treat them as qualitatively the same, or dismiss the need to go beyond ideas and engage with their grounding altogether. Trivialization is a style of discourse dominated by ideas, slogans, intuitions, and other more or less familiar shortcuts, instead of evidence, logic, or coherent reasoning. As a result, we have answers to moral, cultural, social, and other matters before the questions are even posed. There is thus not much use for a dialogue, or a search for truth which the actors can easily find in their trivialized phraseology. And reality gradually takes on a very different character than one assumed since the Enlightenment. Trivialization, as we have seen, permeates our communication and, with it, opinions of both the ordinary people and, by habit or necessity, the elite. An embrace of a different worldview, the complexity paradigm, supported by the expansion of our capacity to develop higher-order cognitive styles more broadly, are seen as key steps toward a new way of dealing with the increasingly complex world, steps equally important to political or academic discourse and our own individual undertakings.

Recent years have seen a growing number of works identifying and critiquing the cultural, political, or social constraints on our ability to cope with the fallout of the fast-moving social and technological change, and calling for our collective reckoning. In parallel, we have been witnessing a sharp turn in political messaging and, with it, an increasing number of references to trivialization, among other characterizations of the flaws in the contemporary discourse. These issues, we believe, are manifestations of deeper, intrinsically connected limitations beckoning further engagement at multiple levels. With several goals in mind, we worked across disciplines, assembling an expository mosaic while drawing on arguments and findings from domains ranging from anthropology to statistical physics. In this concluding chapter, we retrace the path of our journey and close with a discussion of a proposal for a new approach to learning, one promising to help advance more effectively our predominant style of thought, our discourse and culture more broadly, changing with it the prospects for our future.

Given the assortment of interpretations of *trivialization*, limiting our capacity to jointly engage and effectively tackle it, we offered our conception of the term in Chapter 2. Aiming to reduce the subjectivity in calling out trivialization and to provide a reasonable common denominator in its engagement, our definition focuses on the parameters rather than the subject(s) of discourse. We recognize the same reality may be captured using multiple, correct descriptions (Mitchell 2012) and that our understanding of social and natural world is subject to perpetual revision. Our value systems are also evolving, whether driven by the shifts in our philosophies, the deepening awareness of the broader public, the changing availability and distribution of resources, or their combination. Our progress thus depends on the desire and the ability to evaluate and compare arguments, which is not possible without reason, coherence, and clarity. However, disconnected from these parameters, most of our discourses occur in the realm of ideas, slogans, and myths, as trivialization reigns, closing avenues to a productive conversation.

To illustrate trivialization in action, we have provided two salient examples. The first was the familiar discourse on free trade, presented to the public by its proponents or opponents in the form of a binary—either as key to economic growth and prosperity, or a cause of massive job losses and depressed wages. Yet, as we have discussed, it is inappropriate to approach the question of free trade in this manner. The outcomes of free trade depend on a range of conditions and may carry positive economic or social consequences for some, negative for others. We thus made a point that unless the economic assumptions and the logic behind the recommendations on free trade are brought forward, we will continue to trivialize this matter and will not get far in a discussion of sound policy.

The latter part of the chapter is a case study of the US health care system and the contested and complex legislation enacted to help address the costs, coverage, and quality issues plaguing the system. Our discussion of key characteristics, outcomes, and solutions hoped to illustrate that the fundamentals needed to engage in a reasoned conversation cannot be condensed into a few sentences. Anyone privy to the information we presented, easily accessible in multiple formats and sources, would appreciate the ACA was not at all the "government takeover of health care" as its opponents chose to frame it. Instead, one would recognize that, with its continued reliance on the markets as the prime vehicles for delivery of coverage and services, the enacted legislation was far from addressing the fundamental problems with the US health care system.[1] What is more, the discourse surrounding the ACA was permeated by myths and talking points stripped of evidence and logic, preventing a reasoned debate on options and effective solutions. We concluded that ideology or polarization are insufficient in explaining these outcomes, and alluded to other, more intrinsic factors making such discourses possible.

In Chapter 3, we thus identified and discussed a trifecta of "isms," a set of persistent, broadly embraced assumptions and philosophies, in our view the key enablers of trivialization. The first was essentialism, an intuitive drive to map elements of our environment into discrete categories which help us explain outcomes. Such reasoning, however, neglects the continuous, mutually evolving nature of social, biological, or environmental systems, thus misinforming our views of causes and effects, and leading us astray in science, policy making, and public discourse.

Essentializing also fuels stereotyping and groupism, damaging further our social and political fabric.

Inspired by physical sciences and their successes in splitting our world into its basic constituents and formulating elegant laws describing their interactions is the next idea, reductionism. The assumption that all phenomena can be reduced to and explained in terms their elements has fast spread across sciences. While many have long appreciated the systemic nature of much of the world around us and understood some of its properties to be irreducible, reductionism in its various guises has not only maintained its following in the social sciences but also altered significantly the way we view and solve problems. It is therefore possible to have a discourse in which complex problems and their causes can be reduced to easily manipulable tales[2] with correspondingly "sophisticated" solutions.

The final enabler, which could be seen partially as the consequence of the failings of the first two perspectives, is relativism, an increasingly popular reconception of truth and knowledge as fluid, dependent on context and situation. Truth then becomes wholly subjective, a reality of one's choosing, gradually moving the society into a world in which fact and myth are undistinguishable and substance irrelevant. These alarming trends contribute to the culture of mistrust, built not only on the failings of the elites in policy and governance but also their inconsistent, relativistic treatment of cultural values. We closed the chapter with a look back in history, a broad cognitive shift in an advanced civilization. The result of this return to irrationality—which some are beginning to discern in the contemporary developments—was a step backward in Western progress, thrusting its intellectual (and social) development into a millennium-long hibernation.

OPINIONS AND THEIR PUBLIC

The assumptions and philosophies we described along with the discourses and orientations they shape are reflected in both the opinions of the public and the prevalent methods and styles in determining them. There is much to be learned from public polling, which has become an indispensable part of democratic politics. The core of the volume thus concentrated on what people think and why, and, importantly, on how people come to their opinions, helping us understand their reasoning. While it is surely important to have an informed public—the focus of important studies and critiques, after all—decisive in the age of trivialization becomes *how* we think, as this determines how we view and approach problems, seek and evaluate information, and speak to each other.

In Chapter 4, we thus began with a brief review of select opinion surveys, which, over the recent decades indicate steady increases in the levels of mistrust of the media, the skepticism of the government's capacity to address problems, and their antipathy toward politics. Many have noted that while citizens have been historically mistrustful of governing institutions and the people populating them, they always respected the legitimacy of their system of government, liberal democracy. In the contemporary context, they point to the rise of "critical citizens" (Dalton 2017), a politically active and an increasingly vociferous part of society, who successfully pursue electoral reforms (in New Zealand and Japan), constitutional change (the UK), or engage in civic journalism, among other efforts.

It might thus be tempting, and perhaps expected, to argue for more democracy, opening the political process further and enhancing its responsiveness to the voices of the voters, for improvements in civic education, and for e-democracy, an Internet-facilitated civic engagement. However, this would mean to neglect the overall declines in the citizens' interest and participation in politics, in spite of the realized reforms (Foa and Mounk 2016). Indeed, speaking of some of the recent institutional changes around the world, Warren and Pearse noted "it is less certain whether electoral reform has helped to revive citizen participation in politics or challenge negative views of the political system," adding that in New Zealand voter turnout is still declining and in Japan the dissatisfaction continues (2008, 4). Further, it would mean to disregard surveys indicating a decreasing support for the principles of liberal democracy and an increasing affinity toward authoritarianism (Foa and Mounk 2016). And it would mean to discount the outcomes of the recent referenda and elections, defying most predictions and often the voters' own intentions. Hence, we set out to discuss the theoretical views and empirical realities behind the outcomes of the contemporary governance as well as the views of the public. As we explored what happens in a democracy and discussed the modern-day sociopolitical shifts borne of the rapidly integrating environment, we recognized the need for a fundamental rethinking of the present systems of governance. We reached to Berggruen and Gardels's (2013) blueprint for one such a solution, smart governance for the new age. It is a combination of participatory democracy, involving citizens locally, where they are the most knowledgeable, and accountable meritocracy at the top of the system, insulating the decision-making process from the flailing demands of special interests and protecting the long-term interests of the public.

To be sure, the expectations for the elites as well as the public would change in such a system, built on competition, deliberation, and multi-channel engagement. Informed by theory or survey results, some may see ordinary citizens as incapable of or disinterested in (Brennan 2017) taking on new roles in a representative democracy. In Chapter 5, we thus considered the challenges and opportunities in "bringing the public" into governance. First, through Hibbing and Theiss-Morse's (2004) research, we learned what matters to people the most in government, how they view politics, and how they prefer their democracy to work. From our perspective perhaps unsurprisingly, these preferences derive from the same assumption: the existence of a general agreement on the main policy questions. Misjudging consensus, the citizens view political conflict as suspect, a product of special interests. Since, in most people's views, the key social and economic policy questions have been settled, governance becomes mostly a technical matter, without much need for political consensus building. As the pesky nuance of policy recedes into the background, the people focus on the political process and its subjugation to the corrupt political class and special interests. Assuming this system of entrenched interests cannot be changed, the people's mission becomes simple: They can protect themselves from being exploited with their castigating vote (hence the electoral surprises of the recent years). The scholars' findings can explain the citizens' ongoing discontent with government performance, their overall disinterest in policy, their openness to giving more power to less accountable business people or technocrats, and the success of political messaging focused on process rather than substance (e.g., "government takeover of health care"). We thus witness trivialization and its consequences. Some of these ideas may be closer to reality (e.g., regulatory capture), while others are far from it (e.g., political consensus), but without a substantive engagement there is not much hope in leaving this vicious circle of reasoning.

In light of their conclusions, Hibbing and Theiss-Morse suggest implementing policies preventing corruption and capture and educating the public about political disagreement. This research, however, did not consider citizens who have had a chance to speak together—that is to participate in a managed deliberation—which we believe holds much potential for both civic renewal and learning. We thus discussed mini-publics, representative bodies of citizens brought together to augment the democratic process. We noted that, if given the opportunity and resources, ordinary people can make informed policy decisions, learn, and enhance their sense of civic efficacy. We also emphasized that in such venues the citizens begin to recognize the complexity of problems and the diversity of views, particularly when faced with moral questions, and thus begin to appreciate the nature of and the place for politics. Indeed, for scholars such as Gutmann and Thompson (1998), deliberation in the "middle democracy" is best in dealing with the persistent moral conflict, which today is inadequately settled by invoking the "single-valued principles" of existing moral theories. These decisions, in our view, are thus at peril of trivialization, if reduced merely to libertarian, egalitarian, or utilitarian claims. Yet, contrary to the traditional conceptions of American political culture, as we discussed in the ensuing chapter, most people are not constrained in their views by an ideology, a quality promising a more open and effective deliberation.

Having surveyed the bigger picture, the political and institutional environment twisting and shaping the views of the public, and some promising ways of improving that environment, we were ready to discuss the reasoning at the individual level in Chapter 6. There have been recurring doubts about the capacity of most people—assumed to be limited by their knowledge, interest, or cognitive capacity—to make good decisions. This, of course, has implications to democratic governance and individual well-being. Frequently used to question the public's competence, for example, are surveys showing often contradictory and ambivalent preferences. As some scholars have argued, this is because most people do not have one unambiguous stance, but rather several opinions, and the opinion chosen at the survey time is the one made most salient to them, whether by a recent media presentation, the interviewer, or the question itself (Zaller 2005). Some thus see these contradictions as a challenge to the credibility of the public and to the reliability of public opinion in informing government choices. Strauss (2012), however, finds a more complex picture opening new questions on the sociocultural and cognitive dimensions of public discourse. Strauss's analysis reveals that elements of people's responses on common issues are remarkably similar and, in many cases, identical. The reason, the author argues, is that public opinions are constructed from sets of *conventional discourses,*

ready-made points borne within opinion communities and gaining purchase outside of them. While these may appear contradictory or inconsistent when understood through the traditional ideological spectrum,
they are entirely acceptable to the public. Hence, we have shown both
trivialization *of* public opinion, in the elite's collection, interpretation,
and discounting of surveys based on narrow assumptions, and trivialization *in* public opinion, as most people assemble their opinions from
broadly shared ideas, rather than taking distinct positions requiring a
level of justification.

Why do conventional discourses exist, and what factors influence
their dynamics? Answers to these questions would surely help further
our understanding of trivialization and public discourse more generally.
Nevertheless, we argued, the key to understanding the formation of our
opinions is our cognitive engagement with information flows. As constituents of these flows, discourses are a reflection of what we can manage
within the limits of our cognition and the intervening cultural and political circumstances. We have made the case for the precedence of thinking over knowing, the former subject to our cognitive limits, the latter
strained by the knowledge demands of the modern age in which the reliability of information is challenged by its diversity and volume. Critical
then becomes the ability to appreciate the importance of an engagement
with and evaluation of information in discerning reality from myth, with
aims of making better decisions. We thus discussed some of our key cognitive and behavioral limitations and asked whether we can do better.
Through examples, we made a case these obstacles can be overcome with
individual and collective efforts. We have highlighted Dörner's (1997)
work providing evidence that a number of capacities—essential to elite
decision makers and increasingly important to all of us making difficult civic and personal choices in a complex world—can be developed
through learning and practice. Currently, however, such training is lacking from the public skills development systems at all levels. This surely
invites the question on why it might be and what may be needed to
tackle this, the answer to which we are working toward.

Approaching Complexity

At multiple points, we have mentioned the skepticism expressed by some
scholars and critics of the ability of most people to make reasoned civic
decisions (Brennan 2017), not the least due to their lack of knowledge

and proclivity to manipulation, all with implications to a functioning democracy. At the same time, we discussed skepticism on part of the citizens, evident in the reported doubts about the credibility of the media and the capacity and legitimacy of their governments, and ultimately in their rebuke of the status quo at the ballot boxes. We also provided a set of perspectives on the issues inherent to democratic systems, suggesting that any account placing the blame squarely on the capacities and choices of ordinary people is far from complete. We continued to engage such issues in Chapter 7, where we focused on the supply and demand for a particular form of trivialization, relating directly to social trust and the integrity of governance.

Arguably, there are no more consequential choices to be made than in regulation and policy, particularly in the systems areas such as the economy, health, and environment. Such decisions are difficult as they are made under uncertainty, demand inherently problematic analyses of risks and benefits, may carry implications for future populations, and their effects may become evident only after extended periods of time, among other challenges. Partaking in these decision processes are the public, who may express their will by voting, wallet, or otherwise; the media, who often determine the salience and weight of the matters as they notify the public; the decision makers, who weigh options under various constraints and pressures; and the scientists and advisors, who provide research informing these decisions. Needless to say, essential here is not only to strive to have as much substantive information as possible, but also to recognize its limits. Yet, as we have argued, much of our public discourse lacks in substance. And Manski (2011, 2013), speaking from his area of expertise, observed that even official recommendations on public policy often lack the recognition of the limits and exhibit *incredible certitude*. Specifically, the author showed conclusions presented to policy makers or taken up by the media have the appearance of confidence, yet are frequently based on tenuous assumptions, flawed reasoning, or their combination. Unfortunately, these lapses are reinforced by various incentives, conventions, pressures, and certainly the lack of scientific understanding (and not only by the public). For illustration, we have provided a vivid example from dietary science, where a closer scrutiny reveals that the conclusions promoted by many scientists and recommendations given by public agencies are far from credible. Yet, they are presented as settled, without an admission of their unreliability, at best-providing reasons for skepticism and, at worst, eroding the legitimacy of those in the position of authority.

"Once you accept incredible certitude and take numbers at face value when they shouldn't be, there may be a slippery slope from incredible certitude to utter disregard for the truth. I do not think this is a second-order issue," noted Manski of the gravity of these conditions and added "it may be even more important to face up to uncertainty today than in the past" (in Olson 2018, 63). Indeed, it becomes necessary if we, as a society, are to deal with risks our technologies pose to social, biological, or environmental systems, among other contemporary challenges. We thus concluded with the discussion of the precautionary principle holding a promise to refocus our attention to *uncertainty* (and action in the face of it), to help us appreciate the role and character of science, and to begin to alter the way we approach problems. Moreover, its systematic adoption could facilitate the embrace of a new frame of reference—providing an ontological and epistemological foundation in tackling the complexities of the modern world—we engaged in the next two chapters of the volume.

Recall in Chapter 3, we discussed essentialism, reductionism, and relativism, three pervasive assumptions and perspectives facilitating trivialization. The first two have deep roots, seeded by Plato and his followers and firmly implanted by Descartes and those building on his meta-theories. The third can be partly seen as a postmodern product of the failures of these philosophies, assumed by convenience or intuition to be applicable in domains which demand very different frames of reference. Among these failures is our misplaced sense of confidence about the properties and behaviors of complex systems, such as environmental, economic, or social systems. This is not only reflected in our discourse, including the certitudes described earlier, but, more tangibly, in lapses leading to recurrent social, health, environmental, or financial calamities. The latter is the starting point of Chapter 8, which uses the global financial system and its recent crisis to highlight the issues with the traditional reductionist perspectives in the understanding and regulation of such systems. While many scholars have long appreciated social and other complex systems had special qualities, it is only recently that elements of a new view, the complexity paradigm, started to find their way into scholarship and practice. It is now increasingly common to observe students of social systems to assume path dependence, emergence, nonlinearity, or feedback and cascade effects, and with these a new view on risk, uncertainty, or stability and change.

This trend toward complexity, we argued, could be part of a larger meta-theoretical shift with a promise to bring manifold changes from the way we think of, study, and describe much of world around us, to the style of our discourse. To illustrate the diversity of its application and the extent of change, we have discussed select research within the new paradigm. And technology, we noted, is enabling previously impracticable research into the dynamics of social systems, challenging the long-standing assumptions on the relationship between individuals and higher-level phenomena such as movements, markets, or institutions. For example, when considering the before ignored "effects of spatial interactions and heterogeneities in the preferences of market participants...the conclusions can be completely different, sometimes even opposite (e.g. there may be an outbreak rather than a breakdown of cooperative behavior)" (Helbing 2015, 47). These, among other findings departing significantly from our intuition or the established models of social and economic behavior, suggest a new era of progress, this time driven by transdisciplinary inquiry. This is incumbent however on success in our transition to a new paradigm. In Chapter 9, we thus explored the various dimensions of the new paradigm and its implications across domains, including ultimately to public discourse. Our discussion highlighted the complexities of a paradigm change, taking place gradually often with practitioners leading the way through pragmatic decisions within the new framework.

SHIFTING CULTURES

Throughout the preceding chapters, we alluded to the importance of thinking, especially acute in the information age as we take on new roles of digital citizens, media consumers, content creators and publishers, or our own retirement planners, counselors, insurance agents, or dieticians. Rather than to possess information—fast obsolete with changing science, technology, economy, or laws and policies, among others—we require the ability to locate, assess, question, and use it well. We have also discussed our individual and collective limitations, evidenced both in our discourses and decisions, holding us back from doing this well. There is little doubt the way we understand the world around us, its properties, causes and effects, and the nature of knowledge and reality—our predominant cognitive styles—have evolved over time. It is uncommon to find people who believe in magic, fairies, or take ancient stories literally. On the other hand, it is rather evident that by far we do not think alike, with much of our society gravitating toward myth, evaluating ideas on all but their merit, or avoiding reflection, all thinking common to our past. This is quite apparent, for example, in the elite's deep preoccupation that the views of the voters can be manipulated by online campaigns filled with bizarre inventions and fantastic claims, particularly problematic when directed by foreign adversaries (curiously paying less attention to the pervasive and much more consequential domestic manipulation).

The goal of Chapter 10 was thus to take a look into our social, cultural, and cognitive development throughout history in order to understand the present condition of our thought as well as the potentials for the future. We have begun with the work of Jean Piaget and his stage theory, which, despite being superseded by more nuanced understandings of individual cognitive development, continues to be influential both in and outside of the psychology domain. In his seminal research, Piaget described how one's cognitive ability advances with her or his development and suggested a relationship between the developments at the individual level and the cognitive evolution in human societies at large. In time, many scholars interested in the evolution of human thought have used Piaget's or similar schemas[3] in the study of our cultural cognitive condition.

Barnes (2000), for example, made a compelling use of Piaget's stages to understand our cultural evolution, namely the developments in religion and science and thus our relationship with myth and reality. In reading Barnes, we have brought forward some important points pertinent to our understanding of the contemporary discourse—deficient in reason and with tenuous connection to reality—which serves as a mirror of our cognitive culture. First, we can differentiate among a number of cognitive styles distinguished by their level of difficulty, and, in turn, their capacity for "reality discrimination" (Barnes 2000, 58). These styles are present both at the individual and cultural levels, or broadly shared attitudes toward what is valuable, right, meaningful, as well as how we collect and evaluate knowledge. Further, we can observe a historical process, unfolding within greater social, political, and economic contexts, moving societies toward more difficult styles of thought. This process is nonlinear, with possible protracted periods of cognitive stagnation or even retreats. Finally, while individuals or parts of society may be cognitively ahead or behind of their time, it is the cognitive elite, the influential stratum, whose embrace of particular cognitive techniques may facilitate or hinder progress. Despite the growing number of people in positions of influence who have mastered advanced cognitive techniques, today's culture is nevertheless dominated by less difficult styles of thought. Most people still lack the tools of logic and systematic analysis and do not appreciate the evolving nature of knowledge—which we must at once rely on and question—deeply affecting their sense of security, trust, and attitudes. Since there is little reason to believe individuals cannot acquire advanced cognitive styles, we argued, it must be culture, and more specifically the lack of the shared meaning around the importance of developing capacities different from those which sufficed in the past. These, as we have discussed (Chapter 6), have been enumerated and proven to be attainable.

Out of the many themes we have brought forward throughout the volume, at the fore stands the style of our predominant discourses, taking place in the age of information, yet thin on information, reason, and logic. This condition reflects a range of our limitations at both individual and collective levels. Many critiques as well as much hope in overcoming society's ills have focused on education. Consider, for example, Cummings, formerly a special advisor on policy to the UK education secretary,[4] who lamented

> [t]he education of the majority even in rich countries is between awful and mediocre. In England, few are well-trained in the basics of extended writing or mathematical and scientific modelling and problem-solving. Less than 10 percent per year leave school with formal training in basics [of math and statistics] … Less than one percent are well educated in the basics [of scientific reasoning]…Only a small subset of that <1% then study trans-disciplinary issues concerning complex systems. This number has approximately zero overlap with powerful decision-makers. … Most politicians, officials, and advisers operate with fragments of philosophy, little knowledge of maths or science …The skills, and approach to problems, of our best mathematicians, scientists, and entrepreneurs are almost totally shut out of vital decisions. We do not have a problem with 'too much cynicism'—we have a problem with *too much trust in people and institutions that are not fit to control so much.* (Cummings 2013, emphasis original)

Notably, these comments were made about a country whose education system had, between 1997 and 2001, underwent what has been considered a model reform (Fullan 2010). This is as the literacy and numeracy levels across England's 20,000 primary schools have climbed from 65 to 75%[5] throughout this period (Fullan 2010). Nevertheless, Cummings makes a strong set of points often less salient in the discussions of education systems: We fail in preparing our decision makers to understand and cope with the challenges of the post-industrial age. Indeed, since we appreciate it is possible to "do better" in the way we approach problems, make decisions, and think, and possess the institutional capacities to do so, we fail in advancing the rest of the people and thus the society as a whole.

The goal of Cummings's long manuscript was to make the case for an updated curriculum, one reflecting the importance of the complexity paradigm (Chapters 8 and 9) and transdisciplinary engagement. Notwithstanding their appeal, the recommendations become yet another addition to the tired debate on *what* we must teach students, which, along with other familiar prescriptions such as testing and accountability schemes, have not delivered the desired outcomes. This is, Egan (1997) argued, because the mainstream curricula are informed by three individually lacking and mutually conflicting views on the purpose of education and on its realization. First, the aim of education is to instill into pupils the prevalent values, beliefs, and mores, and develop them into productive and compliant members of society. Here, the expectation for the teacher is to be a role model, channeling the qualities preferred in an individual, a member of the community, and a citizen. The second goal is based on the Platonic conception of education as "a process of learning those forms of knowledge that would give students a privileged, rational view of reality" (13). To do this, one needs to free oneself from cultural preconceptions or filters and, through a diligent study, seek deeper understandings. In this view, the teacher, a tutor, trains the student by sharing her or his expert knowledge in one of more areas of inquiry. Finally, following Rousseau, the third aim of education is to bring out the best in all students by enabling them to pursue their interests and talents. Teacher then becomes the facilitator of this endeavor (Egan 1997). The incoherence among these goals thus suggests a more fundamental analysis is needed in transforming the education to meet the present and future demands.

Recurrent throughout this volume was our emphasis on *thinking*, outstanding not just in analyses of personal choices and behaviors but also in understanding of our scientific and cultural development. Thus, if we can draw a parallel between our individual and cultural cognitive evolution (Chapter 6)—a process of advancing styles of thought and understandings—then perhaps our education schemes should be based on the development of each of these styles. Indeed, this is at the core of a new approach to education advanced by Egan (1997), who also sees it as a way to resolve the conflicting aims of the modern curricula. To begin, Egan appreciates our innate challenges to learning, noting that

> [e]volution has not equipped us ideally for the educational tasks required by advanced literate societies. We are equipped intellectually for the condition of small nonliterate social groups sharing unquestioned ideologies and images of the cosmos....We have to adapt our undifferentiated learning capacity to deal with much more complex and flexible learning than it has been evolutionarily shaped to handle. We cannot tinker with the "hardware" supplied to us by evolution, so we have to adapt the "software" of educational programs in order to subvert the natural constraints on our intellectual flexibility. (Egan 1997, 278)

The learning processes are thus considerate of both evolutionary as well as cultural factors, with the latter playing a progressively greater role in the development of more advanced capacities. Egan distinguishes between multiple levels of understandings, reflecting "degrees of culturally accumulated complexity in language, beginning with oral language, then moving to literacy, then to the development of systematic, abstract, theoretic, linguistic forms, and finally to habitual highly reflexive uses of language" (1997, 30). The recapitulation of the acquisition of language, a product of human physiology as well as millennia-long cultural evolution, and the accompanying intellectual tools then define the reconceived education process.

Specifically, Egan's schema has five types of understandings of increasing sophistication and learning intensity, Somatic, Mythic, Romantic, Philosophic, and Ironic. Predominating until about 2.5 and 8 years of age, Somatic and Mythic understandings are tied to the body and its senses and the development of oral language and thus highly influenced by our evolutionary history. The remaining types of understanding echo three major advents of cultural evolution: the development and the spread of the written word, the rise of abstract, theoretical thought, and the emergence of a kind of "reflexivity that brings with it pervasive doubts about the representations of the world that can be articulated in language" (171), respectively. The author identifies the main characteristics of each understanding, providing bases for the development of curricula. For Egan, the goal of the education process is to advance pupils through this series of understandings while continuously probing areas beyond their horizons. The teacher then becomes a developer of understandings, one who appreciates the key cognitive tools associated with each kind and engages the students in their use.

To be sure, there is much to learn about learning, not the least on the social, psychological, or communicative aspects of educational processes. Perhaps this might be a good starting point for a conversation on education, but this was not the main intention here. Rather, we wanted to highlight once more that there, beyond the customary ideas lie realistic solutions deserving of our attention. Note some of these ideas guiding our approaches to education date back to times when education was an option for the few, not a necessity of the many. Without a doubt, Egan's schema, focused on cognitive tools and the development of understandings, takes on additional relevance in today's age of complexity and (mis) information, both of global scale.

How Do You Know?

In conclusion of his prominent treatise, Keynes lamented that the "world is ruled by little else" than ideas (2018, 340). Consciously or not, the scholar observed, people become captured or heavily influenced by ideas, especially problematic as ideas become outdated with our changing understanding. Yet, had Keynes continued and asked about the reason for this condition, the answers would likely convince him to change his famous quote (perhaps to "the world is ruled by outdated thinking"). Cognizant of the demands and the potentials of the information age, we focused in this volume on discourse, apparently anachronistic. Imprinted in political communication, public opinion, or even policy recommendations, much of our discourse exhibits a lapse—trivialization. Lacking in evidence and reason, our discourses are replete with more or less familiar ideas, frames, and tales, accepted by some, rejected by others. These often confident reductions leave little room for nuance, and thus for debate.

We hence exercised our imagination, our Mythic understanding, and envisioned a different world, an environment where these issues and their enablers have long been tackled. It is a world that prizes reason and coherence and appreciates the importance of a bigger picture. It is one in which there is less fear of manipulation, a key political and strategic concern in our age. Can we do better? we thus asked. Surely we can, and not only as we study the trajectory of our cultural evolution and its uneven, nevertheless positive trend in expanding our capacity for reflection and questioning. It is also as we learn that, with some effort, we can cope with our natural cognitive and behavioral limitations. Not to forget, there is much promise in the increasingly visible complexity research and its defining paradigm whose implications go much beyond our epistemic ambitions. These could thus be transformative times, where, with our new understandings, we begin to treat systems around us differently.

On the other hand, we also appreciate that the path of our progress has been all but linear. Some have made comparisons between the current cultural developments, possibly exacerbated by the information network, and the turn away from rationality, which had lead to a decline of the Greek civilization. Today, however, we have an advantage as we can recognize the signs and understand the implications. And so those with the capacity to act must lead the way. Our hope is to hear more questions in our everyday discourse, challenging answers without substance. Let us start with: "How do you know?"

NOTES

1. Although, as some authors argued, the ACA may "position Medicare to become a single-payer system should the coverage expansions in the ACA fail or Congress and policy makers decide to establish a single-payer system" (Kinney 2015, 2).
2. A process well-described by Stone (1989).
3. Recently, for instance, Brennan (2017) differentiated citizens based on their cognitive engagement (reflected in turn in their attitudes toward politics) and used this classification in his argument against democratic systems of government.
4. Ironically, Cummings is also considered the chief architect of the Vote Leave campaign, thought to be integral to the outcomes of the Brexit referendum (Payne 2016).
5. Gauged by the level of proficiency in pupils 11 years of age (Fullan 2010).

REFERENCES

Barnes, Michael Horace. 2000. *Stages of thought: The co-evolution of religious thought and science.* New York: Oxford University Press.

Bauerlein, Mark. 2008. *The dumbest generation: How the digital age stupefies young Americans and jeopardizes our future*. New York: Penguin Books.

Berggruen, Nicolas, and Nathan Gardels. 2013. *Intelligent governance for the 21st century: A middle way between west and east*. Cambridge, UK: Polity Press.

Bohm, David. 2013. *On dialogue*. London and New York: Routledge.

Brennan, Jason. 2017. *Against democracy: New preface*. Princeton and Oxford: Princeton University Press.

Cummings, Dominic. 2013. "Some thoughts on education and political priorities." *The Guardian*, October 11. https://www.theguardian.com/politics/interactive/2013/oct/11/dominic-cummings-michael-gove-thoughts-education-pdf.

Dalton, Russell J. 2017. "Political trust in North America." In *Handbook on political trust*, edited by Sonja Zmerli and Tom W. G. Van der Meer. Cheltenham: Edward Elgar.

Delli Carpini, Michael X. 2000. "In search of the informed citizen: What Americans know about politics and why it matters." *The Communication Review* 4 (1): 129–164.

Dörner, Dietrich. 1997. *The logic of failure: Recognizing and avoiding error in complex situations*. Cambridge, MA: Perseus.

Egan, Kieran. 1997. *The educated mind: How cognitive tools shape our understanding*. Chicago: University of Chicago Press.

Foa, Roberto Stefan, and Yascha Mounk. 2016. "The democratic disconnect." *Journal of Democracy* 27 (3): 5–17.

Fullan, Michael. 2010. *All systems go: The change imperative for whole system reform*. Thousand Oaks, CA: Corwin Press.

Gutmann, Amy, and Dennis F. Thompson. 1998. *Democracy and disagreement*. Cambridge, MA: Harvard University Press.

Helbing, Dirk. 2015. *Thinking ahead—Essays on big data, digital revolution, and participatory market society*. Cham: Springer.

Hibbing, John R., and Elizabeth Theiss-Morse. 2004. *Stealth democracy: Americans' beliefs about how government should work*. Cambridge, UK: Cambridge University Press.

Keynes, John Maynard. 2018 (1936). *The general theory of employment, interest, and money*. London: Palgrave Macmillan.

Kinney, Eleanor D. 2015. *The affordable care act and medicare in comparative context*. New York: Cambridge University Press.

Manski, Charles F. 2011. "Policy analysis with incredible certitude." *The Economic Journal* 121 (554): F261–F289.

Manski, Charles F. 2013. *Public policy in an uncertain world: Analysis and decisions*. Cambridge, MA: Harvard University Press.

Mitchell, Sandra D. 2012. *Unsimple truths: Science, complexity, and policy.* Chicago: University of Chicago Press.

Olson, Steve, ed. 2018. *The science of science communication III: Inspiring novel collaborations and building capacity: Proceedings of a colloquium,* 63. Washington, DC: National Academies Press.

Payne, Sebastian. 2016. "How vote leave won the EU referendum." *Financial Times,* June 24. https://www.ft.com/content/90c054fe-3953-11e6-9a05-82a9b15a8ee7.

Stone, Deborah. 1989. "Causal stories and the formation of policy agendas." *Political Science Quarterly* 104 (2): 281–300.

Strauss, Claudia. 2012. *Making sense of public opinion: American discourses about immigration and social programs.* New York: Cambridge University Press.

Warren, Mark E., and Hilary Pearse, eds. 2008. *Designing deliberative democracy: The British Columbia citizens' assembly.* New York: Cambridge University Press.

Zaller, John R. 2005 (1992). *The nature and origins of mass opinion.* New York: Cambridge University Press.

GLOSSARY

adaptive complexity—a view that individuals and their behavior must be understood in context of a larger system and the environment, given the existence of global properties analytically irreducible to individuals or social subsystems. Adaptive complexity thus forms the opposite pole to reductionism in social sciences.

artificial societies—computer models of interactions of a large number of autonomous agents. These have enabled the study of macro-structural phenomena arising from these interactions.

bias—in cognitive psychology, a systematic (mis)application of a heuristic, often resulting in irrational judgments.

certitude—understood here as a posture of confidence glossing over assumptions, evidentiary limits, and balance.

chaos—among its many uses, chaos may be understood from the perspective of chaos theory as a deterministic behavior in dynamical systems. Alternatively, from complex adaptive systems, said to exist at the "edge of chaos," chaos may mean a phase of disorder, irregularity, or disorganization.

cognitive style—a shared set of cognitive abilities influencing the way reality and its constituents are perceived and understood.

complex adaptive systems (CAS)—a line of research attuned to the special properties of complex natural and social systems. It views emergent phenomena as irreducible to the behaviors and properties of the elements; recognizes dynamics of social systems are nonlinear

© The Editor(s) (if applicable) and The Author(s) 2019
O. Bubak and H. Jacek, *Trivialization and Public Opinion*,
https://doi.org/10.1007/978-3-030-17925-0

and hence unpredictable; and understands there is no clear distinction between the system and its boundaries. CAS is also a concept defining the complexity paradigm.

complexity frame—per Colander and Kupers (2014), a new view on economics and on public policy more generally. Reacting to the deficiencies of the standard policy frame—thinking it is either the government or the market that holds the solution to economic issues—the authors advance the complexity frame treating the markets and states as inseparable and coevolving.

complexity paradigm—a meta-theory informed by complex adaptive systems.

conventional discourses—a term used by Strauss (2012) to describe a set of ready-made, easy to remember, and communicate statements which become the building blocks of people's opinions.

conversation analysis—a research method employed across disciplines that considers various types of human interactions to study the less salient or understood aspects of social relations.

cost–benefit analysis—a quantitative way of assessing whether the benefits of an (in)action outweigh its costs, or of selecting among various options for (in)action. The calculations are built on assumptions on probabilities, valuations, and future costs, often yielding broad ranges without much decision-making value.

crowd turbulence—a cascade effect resulting from an involuntary body contact in a mass of people generating forces capable of jolting the crowd around.

dualism—an idea that elements of the world, including the human mind, cannot be explained solely by the reference to their physical properties.

ecostructure—a term employed by Colander and Kupers (2014) in context of public policy describing the broader politico-cultural environment influencing people's views, behaviors, and choices. An appropriate ecostructure is important not only to making policies effective but also in determining the best policies.

ecosystem—or ecological system, describes a community of interacting organisms and their environment as one coevolving system.

emergence—in social systems, understood as the formation of macro-social phenomena irreducible to the properties or behaviors of the individuals. These may include the rise of new shared meanings, elements of language, social structures, political movements, or various effects such as herding.

emergence paradigm—a meta-theory proposed by Sawyer (2005) addressing the existing paradigms' deficiencies to capture the dynamics of emergence. It thus introduces intermediate levels of social reality between an individual and social structure.

emergent phenomena—system properties arising from the interactions of its elements.

epistemology—an understanding of what constitutes knowledge and how to acquire it.

equation-based modeling (EBM)—an approach to modeling system behavior with systems-level equations rather than modeling the interactions of individual entities as in MAS.

essentialism—a propensity to organize and map the elements of our environment into natural categories considering the elements' intrinsic properties, and trace causes to these categories.

ethnomethodology—the study of practices employed by social groups to establish and maintain their social order.

feedback loop—a systems process where an output from a (sub)system in time becomes an input, either reinforcing or balancing the (sub)system's behavior.

Fragestellung—an empirical orientation, or a worldview, providing a meaning and inspiration for posing particular sets of research questions which would otherwise not make sense.

Gödel-Turing-Post—a trio of mathematicians whose discoveries, coupled with key advancements in computer simulations, paved the way for the establishment of complexity science.

heuristic—in cognitive psychology, a term for a mental shortcut, a rule applied in the interpretation and solving of a cognitive task.

historical comparativist—a social scientist skilled in comparative historical research. Such research involves a methodical comparison of processes unfolding over time or geographies in order to explain a particular social or political outcome.

Holland-Bak-Arthur—a trio of scientists whose work in computational simulation was integral to the rise of a new field of inquiry, the complexity science.

ideas—cognitively manageable statements found at various levels of abstraction, from those capturing specific problems, causes, or solutions to broadly shared subjectivities including philosophies and worldviews.

incredible certitude—a term used by Manski (2011, 2013) in context of policy analysis to describe the inclination of experts to supply strong conclusions by making assumptions which, upon a closer examination, are far from credible.

information—generally understood as processed, organized, and contextualized data.

intertemporal decision making—choices that demand the weighing of costs and benefits over time.

knowledge—an understanding or interpretation of contextualized information. Knowledge can be both transferred, for example by digital means, and developed individually through learning and discovery.

meritocracy—a system of selection into education and employment based on skills and competence rather than status or inheritance.

meritocratic class—following various changes to college admissions as well as hiring procedures in the 1960s emerged a highly competitive and driven stratum of society, which, in one view, has in time become a class of its own.

meta-theory—a worldview encompassing a set of rules and principles delimiting theory building. Unlike theory, it does not make predictions.

multi-agent systems (MAS)—a major innovation to simulation of social systems, which are modeled from the bottom-up. The virtual entities, or agents, can interact and posses a degree of autonomy and control, making possible a range of experiments such as artificial societies.

multicausality—in systems science, a view that effects are products of interactions of a mix of causal factors, rather than resulting from one or more dominant causes.

nonadditivity—from complex adaptive systems, the notion that system is not merely an aggregation of its elements, but has (emergent) properties that cannot be understood by summing its parts.

nonlinearity—a property of a system in which the interrelationships between elements and various feedback loops result in system outputs being disproportionate to its inputs.

Occam's razor—a non-scientific heuristic used either to simplify the object of study or to decide among competing explanations. Given its guiding precept "entities must not be multiplied beyond necessity," the most parsimonious theory is to be preferred.

ontology—a mapping of reality, its elements, their relationships, and causal structures.

paradigm—a scientific tradition encompassing laws, practices, theories, and tools broadly accepted by the research community.

path dependence—rooted in evolutionary economics and used in explanations of stability and change across social sciences, the notion underscores the role of history in social outcomes, more specifically the constraining role past choices have on present options.

pathophysiology—the study of the impacts of a disease or other anomaly on physiology, or physical and biochemical functions, of an organism. Its findings are important to both treatment and prevention.

postmaterialist values—an expression used by Inglehart (1997) who, through a study of party platforms, noted a shift away from consumerism and social conservatism toward inclusiveness, equality, and environmental consciousness. This shift was explained by high levels of existential security broadly experienced in the 1960s and 1970s.

precautionary principle—a contested doctrine recognizing that uncertainty, inherent to complex health, environmental, or sociotechnical systems, should not be a reason to avoid regulatory action.

reductionism—a notion that all phenomena, regardless of domain, can be understood through their more basic or fundamental parts.

relativism—a view that truth, knowledge, or even an idea may be assessed only with respect to a particular situation.

robustness—the capacity of a system to resist regime shifts. More specifically, the capacity of a system to retain certain properties when subjected to particular perturbations.

S curve—a nonlinear growth model, which has gained popularity as a forecasting tool, particularly in describing the patterns of technological development.

self-organization—the capacity of some systems (complex adaptive systems) to spontaneously (without a central controller) create new structures or behaviors based on the interactions of its elements with each other and the environment.

symbolic interactionism—one of several theories of communication concerned with interpersonal interactions and their relationship to social structures.

transdisciplinary—transcending the confines of disciplinary boundaries in the search of or guided by a more fundamental, unifying worldview.

trivialization—defined here as a style of discourse conflating ideas with substance, treating them as qualitatively the same, or dismissing the need to go beyond ideas and engage with their grounding altogether.

universalism—a product of logical inquiry and its drive to find natural laws and universal order, such thinking has also lead the promotion of the universal ideas of justice, equality, or morality.

INDEX

CPSIA information can be obtained
at www.ICGtesting.com
Printed in the USA
LVHW071610130619
621129LV00003B/5/P